Forgiveness and Power in the Age of Atrocity

Forgiveness and Power in the Age of Atrocity

Servant Leadership as a Way of Life

Shann Ray Ferch

LEXINGTON BOOKS
Lanham • Boulder • New York • Toronto • Plymouth, UK

Published by Lexington Books
A wholly owned subsidary of The Rowman & Littlefield Publishing Group, Inc.
4501 Forbes Boulevard, Suite 200, Lanham, Maryland 20706
www.lexingtonbooks.com

Estover Road, Plymouth PL6 7PY, United Kingdom

British Library Cataloguing in Publication Information Available

Library of Congress Cataloging-in-Publication Data

Ferch, Shann R. (Shann Ray), 1967–
    Forgiveness and power in the age of atrocity : servant leadership as a way of life /
Shann Ray Ferch ; foreword by Larry C. Spears ; afterword by Margaret J. Wheatley.
        p. cm.
    Includes bibliographical references.
    ISBN 978-0-7391-6948-3 (cloth : alk. paper)—ISBN 978-0-7391-6949-0 (pbk. : alk.
paper)—ISBN 978-0-7391-6950-6 (electronic)
    1. Forgiveness.   2. Power (Social sciences)   3. Servant leadership.   I. Title.
    BF637.F67F47 2011
    205'.699—dc23   2011031210

♾️ ™ The paper used in this publication meets the minimum requirements of American
National Standard for Information Sciences—Permanence of Paper for Printed Library
Materials, ANSI/NISO Z39.48-1992.

Printed in the United States of America

Contents

v

PART III.   A NARRATIVE OF HOPE AND RESPONSIBLE ACTION

Publications Acknowledgments

Portions of this book appeared in slightly different form in the following publications or at the following websites: *American Masculine* (Graywolf Press, 2011), *Beatrice* (June 2011), *Big Sky Journal* (Winter 2005), *NPR: National Public Radio* (July 2011), *The Nervous Breakdown* (April 2011), and *The Quivering Pen* (June 2011).

What Is Servant Leadership?

Robert K. Greenleaf coined the term *servant leadership* in his seminal 1970 essay, "The Servant as Leader." From its inception the servant leader concept has had a rich and lasting influence on leadership thought and practice. Greenleaf spent his first career of forty years at AT&T, retiring as director of management research in 1964. That same year Greenleaf founded the Center for Applied Ethics (later renamed the Greenleaf Center for Servant Leadership). He went on to have an illustrious twenty-five-year second career as an author and thought-leader before he died in 1990. A contemporary of Robert Frost and E. B. White, Greenleaf taught at MIT, Harvard, and Dartmouth and was the author of numerous books and essays on the theme of the servant as leader. His available published books now include *Servant Leadership: A Journey into the Nature of Legitimate Power and Greatness* (2002), *The Servant Leader Within* (2003), *The Power of Servant Leadership* (1998), *On Becoming a Servant Leader* (1996), and *Seeker and Servant* (1996), along with many other separately published essays that are available through the Greenleaf Center (www.greenleaf.org). In Greenleaf's original essay, "The Servant as Leader," he said:

> The servant-leader *is* servant first. . . . It begins with the natural feeling that one wants to serve, to serve *first*. Then conscious choice brings one to aspire to lead. That person is sharply different from one who is *leader* first, perhaps because of the need to assuage an unusual power drive or to acquire material possessions. . . . The leader-first and the servant-first are two extreme types. Between them there are shadings and blends that are part of the infinite variety of human nature.

The difference manifests itself in the care taken by the servant-first to make sure that other people's highest priority needs are being served. The best test, and difficult to administer, is: Do those served grow as persons? Do they, *while being served*, become healthier, wiser, freer, more autonomous, more likely themselves to become servants? *And*, what is the effect on the least privileged in society? Will they benefit, or, at least, not be further deprived?

Robert K. Greenleaf also wrote a groundbreaking essay entitled "The Institution as Servant," in which he expressed a creed of social responsibility in which care is posited as an ultimate human endeavor:

> Caring for persons, the more able and the less able serving each other, is the rock upon which a good society is built. Whereas, until recently, caring was largely person to person, now most of it is mediated through institutions—often large, complex, powerful, impersonal; not always competent; sometimes corrupt. If a better society is to be built, one that is more just and more loving, one that provides greater creative opportunity for its people, then the most open course is to raise both the capacity to serve and the very performance as servant of existing major institutions by new regenerative forces operating within them.[2]

I first came into contact with the concept of servant leadership nearly twenty years ago. As a young professor at Gonzaga University, I was commissioned to teach a course on leadership and psychology. In the university library I pulled Greenleaf's book *Servant Leadership: A Journey into the Nature of Legitimate Power and Greatness* from the stacks and began to read. By the end of that first sitting, Greenleaf's thoughts had completely won me over. From that day on, servant leadership has made an irreversible claim on my life.

Robert Greenleaf put forth a leadership ethos in total opposition to the traditional command-and-control model. Rather, he proposed the revolutionary idea that people, organizations, and nations are designed to be servants first and that their servanthood, if fully formed, succeeds in generating personal, communal, and global responsibility. Greater health, wisdom, freedom, and autonomy, as well as greater individual and collective servant leadership, are the natural result.

Larry Spears, one of the foremost scholars in servant leadership, helped name the ten characteristics of servant leadership through an in-depth and systematic content analysis of Greenleaf's work. Spears's and Greenleaf's work continues to influence leaders worldwide. The ten characteristics of servant leadership are listening, empathy, healing, awareness, persuasion, conceptualization, foresight, stewardship, commitment to the growth of people, and building community.[3]

As former CEO of the Greenleaf Center for Servant Leadership, Spears was given access to Greenleaf's writings and devoted himself to a precise and discerning look at Greenleaf's vision of servant leadership. In the early 1990s, in what became truly a labor of love, Spears named the ten characteristics of servant leadership by meticulously going through manuscript after manuscript and placing check marks next to Greenleaf's most often mentioned and most significant ideas. Of more than forty characteristics, Spears narrowed the list to ten, which resulted in a profound contribution to leadership literature and practice. Today, the ten characteristics provide the most well-known, widely used, and profoundly accessible definition of the essence of servant leadership.

A closer look at each of the ten characteristics is warranted. *Listening*, a contemplative and active attitude toward serving the highest-priority needs of others, was Greenleaf's ultimate and most dearly held conception. For Greenleaf, the other nine characteristics, each one crucial and far-reaching, required deep listening in order to influence the heart of the world with the healing and legitimate power he envisioned.

Empathy is the heartfelt expression of leaders who identify with the humanity of others. Servant leaders laud the victories of others, but they also share in their sufferings and the immensity of their losses. *Healing*, the most rare and perhaps the most needed characteristic of leaders today, requires self-healing, great wisdom, and modesty. Few leaders in this or any age have had a true understanding of what it takes to be a healer. Healing provides the cure for injustice, oppression, wounding, and fear, and it remains for leaders an element of tremendous import and gravity. People and organizations and nations are infinitely plagued by the mediocrity and atrocity so often perpetrated by leaders who are blind to their responsibility to be healers. *Awareness* is directly linked to healing and involves an opening of one's eyes to a greater sense of the world. Greenleaf saw awareness not as something that gives peace, but as a powerful entity that disturbs and awakens.

Poor leaders coerce others. Great leaders persuade, through a way of being that involves humility, grace, common sense, and good direction. *Persuasion* engages others in dialogue that leads to the greater good of humanity. *Conceptualization* is the ability to build the most effective and meaningful response to the complexities of personal, family, and work life in a global world. *Foresight* then is the ability to see, with clarity and acuity, what needs to be seen before undesired elements of small or great impact come to pass. Though both conceptualization and foresight may be somewhat bound to the intuitive mind, Greenleaf posits it as the servant leader's responsibility to purposefully develop these in order to help people, organizations, and nations avoid undue entrapment in poor thinking, mental enslavement, lack of wisdom, or lack of autonomy.

To hold something in trust for others is to be a steward. To hold in trust for others transcendent values such as humane treatment, justice, mercy, forgiveness, and love, *stewardship* is required. A good steward is an effective guardian of the well-being of others and is often experienced as a beloved member of the community. Stewardship has close kinship to *commitment to the growth of people*. People, even under conditions of defensiveness, self-fortification, and denial, are well served by the servant leader's robust and durable commitment to the growth of others. Under conditions of transparency and authenticity, the result is high-quality critical mass and exponential individual and community potential. *Building community* requires staying power and emotional, mental, and spiritual capacities that match community challenges with creatively imagined and morally persuasive resolutions. Servant leaders build community that is responsible, loving, sustainable, and just.

Servant Leadership in the Present Day

Today a number of authors and recognized thought-leaders affirm the value of servant leadership and Greenleaf's work:[1]

> "Servant leadership is now part of the vocabulary of enlightened leadership. Bob Greenleaf, along with other notables such as McGregor, Drucker, and Follett, has created a new thought-world of leadership that contains such virtues as growth, responsibility and love."
>
> Warren Bennis, Distinguished Professor,
> Marshall School of Business,
> University of Southern California, author of *On Leadership*

> "I believe that Greenleaf knew so much when he said the criterion of successful servant leadership is that those we serve are healthier and wiser and freer and more autonomous, and perhaps they even loved our leadership so much that they also want to serve others."
>
> Margaret Wheatley, President Emerita,
> The Berkana Institute,
> author of *Leadership and the New Science*

> "I truly believe that servant leadership has never been more applicable to the world of leadership than it is today."
>
> Ken Blanchard, Chief Spiritual Officer,
> The Ken Blanchard Companies,
> author of *The Heart of Leadership*

xiii

"We are each indebted to Greenleaf for bringing spirit and values into the workplace. His ideas will have enduring value for every generation of leaders."

Peter Block, Partner, Designed Learning,
author of *Stewardship*

"Anyone can be a servant leader. Any one of us can take initiative; it doesn't require that we be appointed a leader; but it does require that we operate from moral authority. The spirit of servant leadership is the spirit of moral authority. . . . I congratulate the Greenleaf Center for its invaluable service to society, and for carrying the torch of servant leadership over the years."

Stephen R. Covey, recognized as one of
Time magazine's Top 25 Most Influential Americans,
author of *The 7 Habits of Highly Effective People*

"The servant leader is servant first. Becoming a servant leader begins with the natural feeling that one wants to serve, to serve first."

Robert K. Greenleaf, author of
"The Servant as Leader"

"With its deeper resonances in our spiritual traditions, Greenleaf reminds us that the essence of leadership is service, and therefore the welfare of people. Anchored in this way, we can distinguish between the tools of influence, persuasion, and power from the orienting values defining leadership to which these tools are applied."

Ronald Heifetz, Founder,
The Center for Public Leadership,
Harvard University, author of *Leadership without Easy Answers*

"The most difficult step, Greenleaf has written, that any developing servant leader must take, is to begin the personal journey toward wholeness and self-discovery."

Joseph Jaworski, Cofounder,
The Global Leadership Initiative
author of *Synchronicity*

"After thirty years Robert K. Greenleaf's work has struck a resonant chord in the minds and hearts of scholars and practitioners alike. His message lives through others, the true legacy of a servant leader."

Jim Kouzes, Executive Professor of Leadership,
Santa Clara University,
author of *The Leadership Challenge*

"Robert Greenleaf takes us beyond cynicism and cheap tricks and simplified techniques into the heart of the matter, into the spiritual lives of those who lead."

Parker Palmer, Founder,
The Center for Courage and Renewal,
author of *The Courage to Teach*

"Servant leadership is more than a concept. As far as I'm concerned, it is a fact. I would simply define it by saying that any great leader, by which I also mean an ethical leader of any group, will see herself or himself primarily as a servant of that group and will act accordingly."

M. Scott Peck, Cofounder,
The Foundation for Community Encouragement,
author of *The Road Less Traveled*

"No one in the past 30 years has had a more profound impact on thinking about leadership than Robert Greenleaf. If we sought an objective measure of the quality of leadership available to society, there would be none better than the number of people reading and studying his writings."

Peter M. Senge, Director,
The Center for Organizational Learning, MIT,
author of *The Fifth Discipline*

"Servant leadership offers hope and wisdom for a new era in human development, and for the creation of better, more caring institutions."

Larry C. Spears, President,
The Spears Center for Servant Leadership,
author of *Insights on Leadership*

"Despite all the buzz about modern leadership techniques, no one knows better than Greenleaf what really matters."

From *Working Woman Magazine*

The Power of Servant Leadership

Foreword by Larry C. Spears

Martin Luther King Jr. stated, "I believe that unarmed truth and unconditional love will have the final word in reality."[1] His sense of the enduring fortitude of truth and love defines the heart of the servant leader. Over the past twenty years, I have edited and coauthored a dozen books on servant leadership. Since 1990, I have also read most of what others have written on servant leadership. It is from that context I share with you the following thought: I believe *Forgiveness and Power in the Age of Atrocity: Servant Leadership as a Way of Life* is the most extraordinary book on servant leadership to be published since *Servant Leadership*, Robert Greenleaf's original classic.[2]

Why such high praise? There are so many amazing aspects of this book that move me to that judgment. Let me mention just three of them here.

First, Shann Ray Ferch's book offers the most penetrating view yet on servant leadership in relation to power, aggression, violence, and forgiveness. Dr. Ferch is one of the pioneers in the burgeoning field of forgiveness studies, as well as one of the deepest thinkers on servant leadership. In this book, Shann uniquely combines his understanding of servant leadership and forgiveness into a kind of new synthesis of thought.

Second, in this book, Shann gets to the heart and soul of what it means to embrace and practice servant leadership. As he reminds us:

> Greenleaf echoes history's hope for a justice that restores us to one another through acceptance, forgiveness and love. "We have known this for a long time in the family. For a family to be a family, no one can ever be rejected."[3] Such love takes personal and collective responsibility, not only for our wrongs but also for the greatness of our dreams. "Love is an indefinable term, and its manifestations are both subtle and infinite."[4]

Third, in this book Shann brings together the unique strands of his knowledge of servant leadership through scholarly research; his own personal experiences, which serve to make him one of the most empathetic of human beings; and his enormous skills as a writer. Shann brings all of these riches together in *Forgiveness and Power in the Age of Atrocity: Servant Leadership as a Way of Life,* where he succeeds in creating one of the most beautiful, inspiring, and lyrical books that I have read on servant leadership, or any subject.

Shann Ray Ferch first came to my attention nearly a decade ago when I received in the mail an essay from him that he had recently written entitled "Servant Leadership, Forgiveness, and Social Justice." While I did not know him at the time, Shann had sent me that essay and invited my comments. I was leaving to catch a plane, and I stuck the envelope containing his essay into my briefcase. While waiting in an airport for a connecting flight, I read his first essay on servant leadership. I was amazed by the powerful insights it contained, and by his authentic voice. As I finished reading it, I was prompted to do something that I had not done before: I walked over to a pay phone and called the phone number included on the cover sheet.

Shann answered the phone, and I told him that I thought his essay was truly groundbreaking and important to our understanding of servant leadership. That first essay was eventually published both as a separate publication and later as a chapter in a book that I edited (*Practicing Servant Leadership: Succeeding through Trust, Bravery, and Forgiveness,* Jossey-Bass, 2003).

If that first essay was the seed, *Forgiveness and Power* represents the more fully realized expression of what it means to live in an age of atrocities—large and small—and to see how servant leadership and forgiveness can help to heal the deep wounds that come from the uncaring use of power.

In the years since I first called Shann from that airport, we have become collaborators, partners, and friends. Since 2005, he and I have worked together on the annual *International Journal of Servant-Leadership,* a joint publication of Gonzaga University and the Spears Center for Servant Leadership. We have cotaught a doctoral course in servant leadership for Gonzaga University and have coedited a book of essays on servant leadership.[5] I have also had the distinct privilege of spending time with Shann and his beautiful family and to see how the spirit of servant leadership has taken root within his family. Through it all, I have come to appreciate the unusual combination of heart, mind, and spirit that Shann brings to his work in servant leadership.

Forgiveness and Power in the Age of Atrocity: Servant Leadership as a Way of Life represents a great leap forward in our collective understanding of servant leadership. Shann has done the world a great favor in writing this work. In these, the most cynical of times that our world has ever known, his book points the way toward a more hopeful and compassionate world—a world where misplaced power and aggression are countered by Martin Luther King's unarmed truth and unconditional love—through the power of servant leadership.

Balefire: The World of Violence and Forgiveness

Preface by Shann Ray Ferch

—balefire: a great fire; a beacon fire; a funeral pyre[1]

When the phone call from my mother came, it made everything seem far away. She told me that my cousin, Jacine, a beautiful and intelligent young woman, had been killed in a drug shootout in the streets of Billings, Montana. Jacie's life had been marred for some time by the hardened culture that haunts drug use everywhere, but of late she had emerged, married, and begun a new purchase on the kind of life she wanted. We all hoped so much for her, and the shock of her death came like a cold, dark undertow. But in the days ahead there would be little time to grieve or even gather to collectively remember her life. The man who murdered her had not been found, and the event took the imagination of the city by storm, appearing in the local news for more than a year. It was not until after a long, arduous passage that life seemed to return to a semblance of normalcy and the family began to come together again, though with a heavy underline of sorrow. We all tried to move on from an experience that had shattered us, but at the heart of it was something we stepped delicately around: our grief, our vulnerability . . . our brokenness.

When death comes to a family, a kind of fierce grip on that which transcends all of us can sometimes be a potent and unifying force below everything. From the dawn of time, spiritual understanding has influenced people toward meaning in the midst of tragedy; yet nothing can truly prepare a group of people for the life-altering dismay of a loved one's murder. Our family embraced a long-standing devotion to the contemplative and healing qualities of faith, but now we were severely shaken. In the life of the heart and spirit, we were at a standstill. Yet looking back, even in the dark of that time, very small, very fine aspects of grace came to us as if to whisper be still. Grow quiet. Draw near to each other. Listen. I have found that in the great spiritual plurality of the contemporary world, many Christians, like members of other faiths, seek to live honestly and with hope. In my own personal encounter with losing Jacie, some of the sacred words I had learned as a boy began to come alive in my daily experience and attend me in my dreams: light shines in the darkness, and the darkness cannot overcome the light.

I wondered how? How does light shine in the darkness? I wondered at the work of people and relationships, thought, emotion, and spirit, in warding off darkness. No answers came, but undeniably I felt a resolute sense of love and kindness in the company of family and friends. There would be no easy emergence from loss. There would be no replacing what had been taken away. Yet something of Jacie remained, like a healing presence in the family, an essence beyond words and irrevocable, even after death. Our journey together into the nature of shadow and light had begun—a journey into the great fires of loss—and here a premonition came: if we draw the loss near, if we let it break us open, it will lead us back to each other, deeper into love, and closer to our collective understanding of life together and life with God.

Some time later, after years of FBI involvement and detailed detective work, Jacie's killer was apprehended. By then her death and the remembrance of her life had quietly taken its place in our midst. So much time had passed, and the desire to move on had been so tangible, that I'm not sure we would even have heard of the events of the case if a friend had not called my aunt on a given morning and told her the man's arraignment was set for that very day. My aunt is a tiny woman, five feet tall, vibrant and powerfully caring, with a delightful personality. She went to the arraignment with the same bravery with which she approaches all of life. Later, when I had the opportunity to ask her what it was like, her countenance softened. She spoke of how the man who killed her daughter was not angry or hard at the arraignment, but broken—perhaps as broken as the family had been broken. In my aunt's face I saw tenderness, and forgiveness . . . and despite all she had been through there was love, like light, luminous in her eyes.

To be alive is to know an ever-present cycle of recovery and loss. At times we are consumed by unfathomable grief, and yet as life progresses we also detect in the ashes a phoenix of possibility and the long-awaited affirmation of life in its most effervescent forms. Across the religious traditions the reach for the divine has been colored by our collective inhumanity. Neither have traditions of nihilism, antifaith, or atheism escaped the most horrifying expressions of human atrocity. Humanity, however, has also experienced the uncommonly beautiful feeling of being fully restored and clothed in the vivid garment of forgiveness. Let it be known, faith that denigrates others denigrates itself, just as the person who denigrates others, denigrates self. On the other hand, as the true person strengthens others, faith that enlivens others fulfills itself. In my experience of the Christian tradition, forgiveness is the breath of life. Yet the work of forgiveness is long-suffering. Across time and place and religious belief, history declares that the movements of forgiveness often require more patience than we can bear, at times remaining dormant for generations, or even centuries.

In the title of this book a very important concept is raised: servant leadership. As indicated in the introductory notes, former American corporate executive Robert K. Greenleaf coined the term in contemporary times in an essay published in 1970 called "The Servant as Leader."[2] Greenleaf believed that people and institutions are responsible for overcoming self-indulgence in order to deeply serve humanity. Rather than classical leadership models in which leaders tend to dominate or control others in order to subdue resistance, wield greater power, increase efficiency, or better the bottom line, Greenleaf proposed servant leadership, a way of life in which devotion to the good of others takes priority and evokes greater integrity in individuals and in society as a whole. Healthy results follow. He believed the ultimate responsibility of the true leader is to serve, and his thoughts on servant leadership were profoundly influenced both by the image of Christ washing the feet of the disciples and by the integral character of Leo in *The Journey to the East*, Herman Hesse's penetrating novel of ideas. For Greenleaf, a Quaker, faith or action that demeans others is dishonest and in need of change in order to restore integrity. Servant leadership requires a servant-first ethos in which the impact or legacy of one's own relationships evokes self-worth, responsibility, and liberty in others. Perhaps the most ineffable aspect of servant leadership is the subtle but very challenging mandate present in Greenleaf's work: that servant leaders must also be healers.

In light of such a call, I like to think of this book as a form of elegy to Jacine, a song for her family, and for all families who suffer the violent loss of one they cherish. There is a barren land we encounter in life, and when we cry out I believe we find yearnings, experiences, and people who lead us from this barren land to a place of rest. Love and forgiveness are in that place, and as a good Kenyan friend of mine once said of seeking the center of life: "I was thirsty and I wanted to go to the deep well. I wanted to go to the source." This book is about forgiveness, love, and power—elements elusive and hard to hold, but firmly positioned in the center of life and worthy of sincere pursuit.

The book is also a journey into the extreme conditions of human conflict and human evil. Conceptually, the narrative is divided into three legs of the journey. The first section speaks of servant leadership, forgiveness, and power by giving examples that range from the personal to the global. The second section is organized around developing the personal consciousness and interior fortitude required to address hatred and bitterness with wholeness, healing, and love. The final section creates a narrative of hope through responsible action on behalf of humanity.

Forgiveness and Power in the Age of Atrocity is designed to be a unique reading experience devoted not only to how we are influenced by research and scholarly thought, but also to how we learn through the beauty and grace of compelling stories. As a professor, I have been blessed to teach poetry and fiction as well as leadership and psychology. As a poet and prose writer as well as a social scientist, I've encountered a hunger for the interrelated nature of art and science. Similarly, on a national level as a research psychologist for the Centers for Disease Control and a panelist for the National Endowment for the Humanities, I have witnessed a community of artists and scientists devoted to seeking greater human understanding. *Forgiveness and Power* engages readers in a narrative that is both artistic and dedicated to the empirical advances of systematic research across the disciplines. As people we are imbued with the mystery of creativity and the intentional pursuit of knowledge. *Forgiveness and Power* strikes a critical balance between the two, giving value to the artistic and the scientific together, honoring both the circular and the linear. The narrative progresses by showing how diverse fields of study interweave and inform one another—from poetry and prose to leadership; from psychology to philosophy; and from theology to the large-scale political forces at work around the globe.

In sincerely facing some of the shadows of our personal and collective history, we are given the opportunity to embark on a path of discovery, self-responsibility, and commitment to one another. Along the way I've placed certain touchstones of historical fact, narrative fiction, classic literature, scientific research, personal story, and poetry. I hope the juxtaposition of these will serve as a way of dis-orienting and re-orienting the mind, heart, and spirit, so we can see afresh the centuries-old problem of human violence. The reading is meant to be a personal journey in which the chapters read more like meditations or contemplations than intellectual exercises. Having undertaken a pathway to find the deep well, I know I am being called to change in profound and sometimes very daunting ways. I hope you will join me in this journey and help us travel even farther, so that together we may find the source and return with water for all who are thirsty.

—Shann Ray Ferch
Gonzaga University

Part I

Servant Leadership, Forgiveness, and Power

What is to give light must endure burning.

—Anton Wildgans[1]

Chapter 1

A Fine Grace

In the high mountains at dawn you encounter things you might never encounter elsewhere. The Beartooth Range runs through southern Montana and boasts some of the finest peaks of the Rocky Mountain front. My father and I have walked that great wide country. When we arrive and start out in the predawn blackness, the darkness attends us and stays close, shrouded by forest and granite. In late autumn the air is sharp and cold, and when the sun begins to light the world, vision opens and all around us on the high plateau we see Timothy grass encased in small intricate robes of frost. Above and to the west the sky is still largely obscured, but light seeps over the high plain on which we walk, and when the sun finally breaks the horizon, the moments that follow are breathtaking. In every direction the frost melts, the sun refracts through tiny spheres of water on each stalk of grass. Suddenly the land appears like an upside-down sky of stars.

My mother grew up in Cohagen, Montana, a town of eight people. My father grew up in Circle, Montana, a town of three hundred. My father is of mixed immigrant heritage, some German, some Irish, the rest spread throughout Europe. My mother's line is less dispersed. In fact, her parents were married in New York in the 1940s during World War II, her father of German lineage, her mother Czechoslovakian. Amazingly, her parents' marriage, filled with square dancing and ranching, card playing and good conversation, began during the very time period in Europe when Germany invaded Czechoslovakia.

My parents remain in Montana, in Bozeman now, having moved first from Billings (where Dad coached the Crow basketball players at Plenty Coups) to the Northern Cheyenne reservation at St. Labre, and from there to Livingston during my high school years, then on to Bozeman when my brother and I attended college. Some time back, on a visit to see them in Bozeman, I was seated on the couch with my mother. Arched ceilings and oak beams lead to high, wide windows that look out on the Bridger Mountains and the Spanish Peaks, the view itself a reminder of the vast wilderness that is Montana and how thankful I am to have a good mother, a good father. We had grown up in trailers, three of them, in three different towns. My parents had struggled with each other and through some weighty decisions reconciled with one another after time apart, and from there they went on to make deep sacrifices toward my brother's and my college education. I was happy for them, the life they had given us, and the life they had built for themselves.

My mom was asking me about some of my research on forgiveness and touch, and I was telling her the stories of people—how they had hurt one another deeply, how they were seeking forgiveness, and trying to return to a loving connection. South Africa, Colombia, the Philippines, Northern Ireland, the Native American reservations in Montana and throughout the United States, so many places of human atrocity, and how even in the face of such desolation, forgiveness would rise, and sometimes move to heal the human heart. I was thanking my mother for the forgiveness she had given my father some twenty or so years earlier, for how graceful she had been. Even my choice of vocation was in large part due to the integrity she and my father brought to our family. Not surprisingly, that day as we sat on the couch, the natural, true way she carried herself shone through.

After a pause in our conversation she looked at me and said, "You know, I'd like to get together with you and ask your forgiveness for the harms I caused you growing up." She said the words openly, with a pleasant look in her eyes, a look of confidence and assurance. I have always loved that look, the way she carries herself with such strength even when dealing with things that are daunting, or cumbersome. Her power as a person is gracious and subtle.

"That would be good," I said, "but I've harmed you too, Mom. I'd also like to ask forgiveness."

On my next visit to Montana we ate dinner together and had an evening of forgiveness-asking.

I work at a university where the opportunities for meaningful experience of the world abound. I'm grateful to be in a place where learning gives so many gifts to humanity through a restless sense of intellectual curiosity, a rich understanding of love, and the unique and lasting notion of educating people to become "people for others." I have the joy of serving students at a Jesuit university, teaching classes on ways of pursuing and honoring truth, as well as classes on forgiveness, justice, and reconciliation. The students gather at a campus on the Spokane River, in Spokane, Washington, a city set on the westward lie of the Rocky Mountain front along a heavily forested northern plateau that features seventy lakes in a fifty-mile radius. The city's namesake, the Spokane Tribe, a respected source of wisdom in the community, lived and thrived here long before first white contact. Spokane means Children of the Sun.

The evening with my mother, asking forgiveness of one another, reminded me of the gratitude I feel for life, and especially for the work of reconciliation around the world. Recently I was given the opportunity to chair the research of Marleen Ramsey, one of our fine doctoral scholars at Gonzaga. A woman of unique intellectual and emotional depth, Marleen traveled to South Africa to conduct her research. In apartheid-torn South Africa, human atrocity in the form of civil rights abuses had created an inferno of violence that was only quenched by the loving and forgiving ethos of leaders such as Nelson Mandela and Desmond Tutu. Apartheid, a form of legalized racism, had set in play an increasing cycle of murder, disgrace, and degradation. In a fitting tribute to making meaning of suffering, many of the people of South Africa have not only forgiven their offenders, but have invited the offenders back to the center of the community, calling each other brother and loved one, sister and friend. Marleen Ramsey's groundbreaking research on South African perpetrators of violence and their experience of being forgiven and reconciled with the victim's family revealed a solemn insight: perhaps it is not justice that brings us closer to the better angels of our nature, but mercy. Her foremost finding on reconciliation was that it was not the repentance of the perpetrator that built the necessary bridge, but the unconditional forgiveness given by those who were harmed.[2]

Amy Biehl's life ended when she was stabbed multiple times by a militant black mob during apartheid. The mob did not know she was a young Fulbright scholar at the time, working to topple apartheid. Ramsey interviewed her mother, Linda Biehl, who established the Amy Biehl Foundation in South Africa and who offered forgiveness to the violent offenders. Ramsey also interviewed two of the men who killed Amy Biehl. Ramsey's work revealed that in each case of forgiveness it was an unrelenting love that overcame the stolid denial and even haughtiness shown by the offenders. Today, the men who killed Amy Biehl call Amy's mother their mother, and she calls them her sons—a complete reversal and unraveling of hatred, and the weaving of a new tapestry of love.

In another of Ramsey's cases Brian Mitchell, a white member of the apartheid security police, ordered a night attack on what he believed to be a black arms house. He was mistaken and eleven innocent people were killed, among them women and children. After the Truth and Reconciliation Commission hearings, he went to the village to admit to his wrong and seek forgiveness. The people said no and banished him. Remarkably, in an indelible act of good will two years later, the people brought him back for a day of reconciliation in which family members of the victims offered him forgiveness and invited him to live in the village. Now he works raising funds to construct a community center, hand in hand with those whose family members he killed.

Another white woman whose daughter was killed in a black militant action offered forgiveness and reconciliation to the man who commanded her daughter's death. In a cultural ceremony in the man's home village, special names were given to her and to him. The names symbolize a unique greeting so that each time the two meet they greet one another in this way.

One asks of the other, "Where are you?"

The other responds, "I am with you."

Today they speak together internationally in honor of forgiveness.

Such immutable stories of courage give credence to one of the most intriguing hopes of humanity, that in the depths of our interior not only do we find the capacity for violence, but more importantly, we find the steadfast presence of overwhelming grace. Grace. A complex, often elusive way of being, given by God, I believe, and capable of moving us from a position of the need for justice to a position that doesn't silence or forget about or forgo justice, but rather holds faithfully to justice but with a heart of peace toward humanity—all of humanity, including the most evil among us; and in fact identifies evil not as individual and separate from ourselves, but as a part of our own personal and collective humanity in need of healing, dignity, restoration, reconciliation. This book is a book about the transcendent nature of humanity: our will to love, our will to heal, and our will to give meaning to our children so they may overcome the evil that walks the earth, making itself known.

In the context of love, even the great losses of life take on new meaning. An essential leadership idea that espouses this notion is servant leadership, a concept made accessible in the modern day by Robert Greenleaf in his book *Servant Leadership: A Journey into the Nature of Legitimate Power and Greatness*. He named the true leader as one in whose presence others become wiser, freer, healthier, more autonomous, and better able to serve, especially with regard to the least privileged of society. In essence, servant leadership helps us navigate dark canyons of individual and collective defeat, and find our way to vistas of understanding from which we can give ourselves in wholehearted love and service to others. Greenleaf's view of the devastations of life—his view of what life asks of us—is both challenging and worthy. Listen to his insight:

> To be on with the journey one must have an attitude toward loss and being lost, a view of oneself in which powerful symbols like *burned, dissolved, broken*

off—however painful their impact is seen to be—do not appear as senseless or destructive. Rather, the losses they suggest are seen as opening the way for new creative acts, for the receiving of priceless gifts. Loss, *every loss one's mind can conceive of*, creates a vacuum into which will come (if allowed) something new and fresh and beautiful, something unforeseen—the greatest of these is *love*.[3]

The fine grace represented in Greenleaf's insight is that in a world fraught with atrocity, love endures. Love heals. Power, in the context of love, is not power over others, or the power to enforce, but power *with* others and power *for* others. In this sense, forgiveness and power go hand in hand with a servant-led way of life. Power then is not only the power to forgive, but the power to evoke in others the tenacity to respond to darkness with light, to respond to evil with good, and to respond to hatred with love. These words from Martin Luther King Jr. affirm Greenleaf's insight:

We must develop and maintain the capacity to forgive. [The one] who is devoid of the power to forgive is devoid of the power to love.[4]

Chapter 2

When We Rise

Recently, my wife Jennifer and I took the time to survey death tolls due to slavery, war, and genocide. The numbers are shocking, especially when one considers for a moment the reach of the inhumanity in the past and present world. Immanently apparent is the great complexity involved in all large-scale human endeavors, the almost tactile layers of wanton power, nuance, and chaos with regard to time and place and perspective. I believe in the principle judge not, lest ye be judged. I also believe in what might be called the principle of light, something common to our experience and beautiful to behold, the simple truth that informed my life for the years after my cousin Jacine's death: that light shines in darkness, and as the sacred text foretold— the darkness cannot overcome the light. Night falls. Yet from the dark of night the sun rises. Like the sun, we too rise from darkness, and there are those whose lives, influential, crucial to the vitality of the world, help us rise. Even so, this robust notion, a notion one might call illumination, often appears nearly entirely obscured by the deadliness of our collective history. Some decisive questions, then, present themselves.

When thinking of humanity as a whole, how do we rise?

How do we rise, as Lincoln proposed, to the better angels of our nature?

The following numbers reflect conservative estimates from the readily available literature on human atrocity.[5] In facing ourselves we must admit humanity falls, and often keeps falling.

Total deaths from two atomic bombs dropped on Japan: 400,000.

Total deaths from conventional firebombing of Japan before the atomic bombs: 500,000.

In Japan alone, the United States destroyed sixty cities during World War II.

A couple of decades later, U.S. bombing of the largely peasant and non-military population of Cambodia reportedly produced more deaths than our bombing of Japan.

In light of the loss of life, and the devastation of families, industry, and culture, a deep responsibility for servant leaders everywhere presents itself. Specifically, consider the United States. From the beginning of our nation, the need for what second president John Adams referred to as a military with "wooden walls" (meaning a strong navy) became necessary if we were not to suffer greatly at the hands of those willing to assume power over America.[6] Yet as time commenced and the country played a crucial international role in ushering in an unprecedented surge of democracy and human freedoms, it is important to acknowledge that we have also been responsible for grave harms.

Arguably one of the most relentless shadows of the human psyche is our inability to honestly name our own faults, to ask forgiveness of those upon whom we've inflicted harm, to work toward meaningful reparations, and to hope for the grace to make amends. The fact that we have been a country of great promise and extraordinary accomplishment, and at the same time a country of systematic and even heinous oppression, is a difficult paradox to face. Especially stubborn and obstinate is our denial of the fatal flaws we possess. This lack of will to take responsibility for how we harm others seems to run across all demographic lines and reach into the heart of nearly every family and workplace in the United States.

In studies of leadership and forgiveness I can say that much has been accomplished toward this end, as well as toward a more full expression of the wholeness of terms such as *forgiveness* and *grace,* and their siblings, *integrity* and *justice.* And much is yet to be fulfilled. Yet before entering a deeper conversation on forgiveness and justice, a purposeful look at the contemporary reality of evil is not only warranted, but necessary. Both within U.S. borders and beyond, the death toll due to human evil is staggering and spans history, each number representing an individual human being.

Consider what many designate as the Native American Holocaust. Though scholars agree it is hard to make accurate approximations, conservative estimates place the total death count in excess of 20 million in the Americas due to the inception of Euro-American disease, slavery, famine, and conquest (some accounts range as high as 90 million deaths).[7] The shadow is an old and powerful shadow, and it reveals how the dominant culture's disregard for Native America throughout the centuries fits, precisely in fact, the United Nations definition of genocide. The legal definition is found in the 1948 United Nations Convention on the Prevention and Punishment of the Crime of Genocide (CPPCG). Article 2 of the convention defines genocide as "any of the following acts committed with intent to destroy, in whole or in part, a national, ethnical, racial or religious group, as such:

1. Killing members of the group;
2. Causing serious bodily or mental harm to members of the group;
3. Deliberately inflicting on the group conditions of life, calculated to bring about its physical destruction in whole or in part;
4. Imposing measures intended to prevent births within the group; [and] Forcibly transferring children of the group to another group.[8]

Admittedly, when exploring the subject of human atrocity, often for many Americans the history of U.S. responsibility does not readily come to mind. Yet in every nation, the dark shadow of harming others is best seen in the light of day.

The history of the world is replete with annihilation.

Total deaths attributed to the Turkish government's genocide of Armenian Christians during World War I: 1 million.

Total deaths throughout Asia attributed to the totalitarian regimes in Japan under Hideki Tojo and others for the fifteen years prior to atomic warfare: 15 million.

Total deaths attributed to Hitler: 23 million.

Total deaths attributed to Stalin: 27 million.

Total deaths attributed to Mao Zedong: 50 million.

Total deaths attributed to Pol Pot: 1.5 million.

Total deaths attributed to the Pakistani genocide of the Bangladeshis: 3 million.

Total deaths attributed to the Crusades: 9 million.

Total deaths attributed to the North African Arab (Middle East and surrounding area) slave trade over ten centuries: 14 million.

Total deaths attributed to the African/Atlantic American and English slave trade over four centuries: 10 million.

The notion of personal and collective responsibility persists and begs the question: From a world perspective, what would it mean to genuinely ask forgiveness of those who have been victimized; and what would it mean to be granted the grace to make amends?

The astounding quality of human evil makes it increasingly difficult but also increasingly more imperative to approach the past, present, and future of our violence and seek forgiveness and change.[9] Significantly, though the dominant culture often tries to conceal it, the dominant culture dominates. Gendered, economic, religious, sexual, and racial suppression that is age-old continues to be a stronghold throughout Western and American society.

An₁ ₁he violence goes on worldwide.
K₁ ₁ovo, Tibet, the Sudan.
F ₁r million war-related deaths in the Congo.
₁ ne million deaths due to genocide in Rwanda.
₁onsider Liberia, Nigeria, Zimbabwe.
Undoubtedly, the twentieth century was not only the most educated, but
₁lso the most homicidal century in human history.[10] The eighteenth century
accumulated about 5 million war-related deaths, and the nineteenth century
totaled nearly 20 million, but the twentieth century completely and grue-
somely eclipsed our former capacity for inhumanity: some 250 wars produced 110 million deaths and made the twentieth century the bloodiest one
hundred years the world has ever known—a span of history with enough killing to populate a virtual "nation of the dead" with numbers greater than the
combined living populations of France, Belgium, the Netherlands, Denmark,
Finland, Norway, and Sweden.[11] If genocides and human-inflicted famines
are added in, the number of human-imposed deaths in the twentieth century
reaches a staggering 182 million.[12]

With the dawning of the twenty-first century, certainly the current complexity of human life does not seem to carry the promise that we will fare
better. Yet against such a dark-colored canvas of inhumanity, the power of
those who have chosen a servant-led way of life is vibrantly present. Servant
leaders exist in the midst of slavery, war, and genocide, leading the way
toward healing, wholeness, and the pathway that finds its fulfillment in personal fortitude, collective safety, and peace . . . even *love*, among those who
formerly encountered one another only as hated enemies.

When we fall, we fall like night falls. Deep and dark the descent.

But when we rise, we rise like the dawn.

Today the Nez Perce, notorious servant leaders of their own nation as well
as in the context of U.S. history, hold a reconciliation ceremony each year at
the site of the Big Hole Massacre. There, little more than a century ago, Nez
Perce men, women, and children were massacred by U.S. forces. Today, the
descendants of those who were massacred meet with the descendants of the
cavalry who committed the massacre. Despite having every right to be hateful
or violent, the Nez Perce forgive.[13] They invite reconciliation. They engender
unwavering commitment by drawing the human race into the heart of truth.
They touch our brokenness and make us whole again.

They help us rise.

When we fall, we sometimes fall to our deepest expressions of
inhumanity.

But when we rise, we often rise to our noblest aspirations.

Consider Martin Luther King Jr.'s timeless message of profound social action.[14] Born the son of a preacher in 1929 in Atlanta, Georgia, he rose to become the youngest recipient of the Nobel Peace Prize for his work in attaining greater civil rights for the dispossessed. Mahatma Gandhi's victories through nonviolent action greatly inspired King, and in 1959 with assistance from the Quaker group called the American Friends Service Committee he visited the Gandhi family in India and grew more devoted to what King termed the *moral structure of the universe* and the *universal principles of the struggle for justice and human dignity*. King was cursed, beaten, shot at, stabbed, and threatened, and when the inevitable happened and a bullet broke his jaw, passed through his spine, and lodged in his shoulder, his death shocked the nation and riots broke out in more than one hundred cities. Universally accepted as one of the greatest orators in U.S. history, King forwarded a clear, sharp vision: *the oppressor will never willingly give up power*. And he placed human capacity in relation to the Divine, in direct relation to what he called *soul force*, by proposing the following: *when we love the oppressor, we bring about not only our own salvation, but the salvation of the oppressor*. Dr. King's servant leadership provided a unity that spanned the globe, a unity that he and his wife Corretta Scott King called The Beloved Community. In the face of brutal inhumanity, he and Coretta rose speaking humanity, and they helped us rise.

Consider Corazon Aquino, the woman who became president of the Philippines after her husband Ninoy was martyred. She rose with People Power, ousted a dictator, and restored the strength and excellence of her people. Corazon Aquino's husband Ninoy made the ultimate sacrifice, and Corazon's government went on to withstand seven coup attempts and return freedom and democracy to the Philippines. With her recent passing after decades of devoted service, the world mourned the death of a gentle, humble, and decisive world leader. In a final act of love before she died, she dedicated her suffering to the Filipino people and asked God to be with them and help them heal the country. In the spirit of Corazon and Ninoy, humanity is again given the grace to rise.[15]

Consider the Czech people, enduring decades of Nazi and communist suppression before they rose as a nation and gave the world the Velvet Revolution, a revolution without bloodshed. In so doing they elected Václav Havel, the poet, the playwright, as president. Consciousness precedes being, Havel declared, and led us to greater comprehension of the necessary will to engage our consciousness toward more mature ways of being.

In this spirit, in all our shadow and light, in all our humanity, we rise.

Havel stated:

The axis of this newly emerging consciousness, and at the same time, the thing to be cultivated, encouraged and expanded, is a new type of human responsibility for the world. Along with all its natural responsibilities—by which I mean responsibility for family, community, national or cultural society, for company or country—humanity, which is to say every individual, should become increasingly aware that it bears a responsibility for the whole world. All the other responsibilities, which are naturally closer to us as individuals, yet only partial responsibilities all the same, must be reflected against this wider background.[16]

Consider South Africa and the Truth and Reconciliation Commission. Consider those who work for peace in the Middle East, the Americas, Europe, Asia, and Africa, and throughout the world. A movement both of personal surrender and collective will comes to the fore and a muscular understanding starts to emerge: that within the horrific violence of the human endeavor it is at least as much the nature of humanity to rise as it is the nature of humanity to fall. So let us rise toward that which heals us, restores us, and presents us to one another full of dignity and able to reconcile even after grave human atrocity. There exist immutable movements in the history of the world in which we rise toward ultimate forgiveness and fearless responsibility in making amends for the wrongs we've committed.

When we rise, we find the light we seek.

When we rise, love attends us.

We return to beloved relationship as we surrender to that which helps us heal. Kahlil Gibran, the great Lebanese poet, said, "The strong of soul forgive."[17] What then does it mean to have strength of soul? The measure of the soul is a way of life essential and vibrant, necessary from the beginning of time to the present day. It is a way of life envisioned by the servant leader . . . not slave, not dominator, but the person willing to serve and willing to lead so that others might be free. On an intimate level, severe losses can drop us into an abyss of hunger and loneliness from which we feel we may never return. Yet interwoven in the mystery of existence is that way of life in which we fathom the depths of the sacredness found in individual and collective healing. The enduring phrase *love is stronger than death*[18] speaks to such healing, and the strong of soul are imbued then with characteristics Spears revealed as the essence of servant leaders: listening, empathy, healing, awareness, persuasion, conceptualization, foresight, stewardship, commitment to the growth of others, and building community.[19] In this light, servant leaders form the backbone of human imagination in both informal and formal positions of power, within our families and communities, within our workplaces, and in our governments. Servant leaders gift the world with action, integrity, and authentic love.

Servant leaders bring healing.

They give us hope.

They help us rise.

This rising, this ascent toward a more real, concrete, and healed sense of ourselves, is the embodiment of forgiveness and power. Power is one of the most studied, misunderstood, "essentially contested,"[20] and "privileged"[21] concepts in the world today.[22] Servant leadership opens a new paradigm of power, taking the leadership environment from being charged with coercion, manipulation, dominance, command, and control to being at peace with persuasion and example. Leadership by persuasion and example starts with listening and reveals itself in the legitimate power defined by the characteristics of servant leadership. For Greenleaf, legitimate power is a human imperative, and in servant leadership legitimate power is established by people with "servant stature" who live in caring relationship with others. Greenleaf's notions of power raze the traditionally top-heavy structures of leadership to the ground. From the rubble we rise to a more true sense of ourselves:

> In a complex . . . society . . . there will be large and small concentrations of power. Sometimes it will be a servant's power of persuasion and example. Sometimes it will be coercive power used to dominate and manipulate people. The difference is that, in the former, power is used to create opportunity and alternatives so that individuals may choose and build autonomy. In the latter, individuals are coerced into a predetermined path. Even if it is good for them, if they experience nothing else, ultimately their autonomy will be diminished.[23]

Drawing people, organizations, and nations toward healing requires boldness, and the understanding that when faced with the dominance and doom that come of bad leadership, a "countervailing power" is not only warranted but is a "necessary condition of all human arrangements." In response to the vast diminishments the modern world places on people, Greenleaf declares, "No one should be powerless!"

Servant leadership helps us see the way ahead, and in the wake of atrocity we rise and build a bridge that takes us from power that destroys to power that heals.[24]

Chapter 3

The Dignity of Life

One of the defining characteristics of human nature is the ability to discern one's own faults, to be broken as the result of such faults, and in response, to seek a meaningful change. Socially, both forgiveness and the disciplined process of reconciliation draw us into a crucible from which we can emerge more refined, more willing to see the heart of another, and more able to create just and lasting relationships. Such relationships—durable, enjoyable, courageous, form what is best in people, in families, and in the workplace. Yet moving toward forgiveness is fraught with tension. Forgiveness requires embracing both the shadow of our humanity and the light. There is a difficult paradox involved in being both leader and servant, just as there is a difficult paradox involved in acknowledging the relationship between darkness and light. Embracing the complexity and chaotic appearance of basic paradoxes, we find that "in paradox, opposites do not negate each other—they cohere in mysterious unity at the heart of reality. Deeper still, they need each other for health . . . if we allow the paradox of darkness and light to be, the two will conspire to bring wholeness and health to every living thing."[25]

Forgiveness asks us to love our way through a little bit of messiness, and in fact, often a great deal of messiness. For people who hold tight to an intense need to declare right and wrong, forgiveness is an empty vessel, but for those willing to live in the paradoxical tension of forgiving on one hand while not depleting personal power on the other, the center of life calls forth the best of our humanity. The will to seek forgiveness, the will to forgive, and the will to pursue reconciliation are a significant part of developing the kind of wisdom, health, autonomy, and freedom espoused by Robert Greenleaf in his idea of the servant leader, an idea whose time has arrived, an idea destined to remain in the vanguard of leadership thought and action. The dignity of life

17

is a nexus where forgiveness and legitimate power merge to engage human atrocity with the healing. In the aftermath of desolation, servant leadership beckons us deeper into life.

In reflecting on the uncommon vigor of Greenleaf's notion, I am reminded of the hollow existence experienced by so many, a thought captured by Thoreau's societal indictment: "The mass of [people] lead lives of quiet desperation. What is called resignation is confirmed desperation."[26] It is a difficult truth, one that runs subtly beneath the surface of our lives, our organizations, our communities, our nations. More specifically, I am reminded of my grandfather. Upon his death from alcoholism some years ago, I remembered feeling disappointed in the lack of time I had with him, a lack of good time spent in conversation, of good experiences shared. He died having lost the basic respect of others, a man without an honored leadership position in his own family, a person no one went to for wisdom or sanctuary. In his later years, filled with despondency and self-pity, he was largely alone. Though he had once been strong and vital, few family members were close to him when he died. At one time he had been a true Montanan, of unique joy and individual strength, a man who loved to walk the hills after the spring runoff in search of arrowheads with his family. But in his condition before death his joy for life was eclipsed. He had become morose and often very depressed—a depression that hailed from the sanctions the family had placed on him disallowing him to obtain alcohol for the last years of his life. In the end, it seemed he had given up.

"What happened to him?" I asked my father.

"He stopped dreaming his dreams," my dad replied.

In making this statement my father echoed a truth forwarded by Greenleaf in 1977: "For something great to happen, there must be a great dream. Behind every great achievement is a dreamer of great dreams."[27]

The idea of the leader as servant is rooted in the far-reaching ideal that people have inherent worth, a dignity not only to be strived for, but beneath this striving a dignity irrevocably connected to the reality of being human. Philosophically, if one believes in the dignity of the person, the ideas of servant leadership and the experiences of leading or being led from a servant perspective not only make sense but also contain the elegance, precision, and willpower necessary for human development.

Many people struggle mightily with the term *servant. Leadership*, yes. *Servant*, never. But in listening to Greenleaf's reclaiming of these words, a new reality begins to assert itself. Greenleaf's view opens and restores the words, reminding us of the human responsibility to serve not only those we love, but even those we do not know. In serving others in a real sense the servant leader gives others legitimate power . . . power that does not coerce or dominate, power that gives discernment and meets the highest-priority needs of those around us, and by extension all of humanity. The servant leader envisions humanity as beloved, and serves humanity; to serve the beloved other, a directive recognized in each encounter with another human being, demands our most engaged and creative sense of living, not just in common life but also in the difficulties and complexities of our experiences with others, and perhaps especially in the midst of human despair. Leadership is a necessary and an indispensable source of growth, but servanthood calls us to listen more closely to what life asks, what life requires:

> The servant leader *is* servant first . . . It begins with the natural feeling that one wants to serve, to serve *first*. Then conscious choice brings one to aspire to lead. That person is sharply different from one who is *leader* first, perhaps because of the need to assuage an unusual power drive or to acquire material possessions.[28]

Greenleaf upheld the idea that the essence of servant leadership flows beneath the inherent potential of the human community and can be genuinely approached by people of all faiths and by leaders of all creeds. Earlier in this book Larry Spears continued Greenleaf's thought on the servant-first ethos by expressing that the true leader is experienced first as a servant of others, and that it is precisely this fact that is the centerpiece of the leader's greatness. Spears points to a concept that resonates with all great spiritual traditions and is found not only in the largest of nations, but in the family itself and in the central meaning of the individual life.

The disposition of change in the contemporary climate is both complex and swift. Notably, the intensity of such complexity has brought with it the exposure of major character flaws in local, national, and international leadership personas, thus increasing the urgency for a more patient, purposeful, and lasting response in society. At the present time, leaders who are able to build community without sacrificing productivity, and who are able to embrace diverse potential rather than adhering to traditional, more hierarchical approaches, are inspiring a growing movement in business, the social services, education, and religion.[29] The more traditional model of leadership, often based heavily on hierarchical structure and a designated chain of command geared toward increased efficiency, has resulted not only in the moral decline of the relational environment, but also a pervasive malaise common to the psyche of the contemporary working person. On a larger, more invasive scale, the command-and-control leadership of nation states has resulted in the stunted and often malignant personality of dominant cultures. And on a smaller, equally invasive but more personal scale, the command-and-control fiber of the family and the individual person, framed by coercive power as a cover for fragile ego, results in people who use, degrade, and diminish others.

Do we have inherent worth? I like to believe we do, even though our own individual and collective shadow often reveals a much darker reality—the reality that we tend to use people, see others as inferior, view people as commodities, and demonize our enemies. Change is needed, but change that brings about meaningful results is elusive. Organizational scholar Margaret Wheatley provides the requisite lens:

> In our organizations, communities, and personal lives, we struggle to discover how to create change. The irony is that our struggle takes place in a world that changes constantly, that is quite adept at change. I believe that our greatest hope for moving past the ineffective change processes that plague us is to ally ourselves with life. If we can understand how life changes, we will dance more gracefully in this dynamic universe. . . .
> The work is not to introduce a few new ideas, but to change a world view. . . .
> There are different things required of us, not just some new implementation techniques. If, in fact, we are all voyaging to discover a new world, then we need to be together in this work differently, with greater patience, compassion, and courage.
> I believe the fundamental work of this time—work that requires the participation of us all—is to discover new ways of being together. Our old ways of relating to each other don't support us any longer, whether it's at home, in community, at work, or as nation states.[30]

The practices of servant leadership foster a deeper, more personal sense of vision and inclusiveness, helping us generate answers to the failures of leadership found in traditional models. On the rise in scholarly literature, studies in forgiveness and restorative justice form one expression of the present need for answers.[31] Such studies validate the capacity for moral fortitude, point to greater relational strength, and help us maintain a healthy sense of hope and meaning as people.

A common experience of being led from the traditional model is one of dominance or control, while the experience of being servant led is one of freedom. Again, in the words of Greenleaf, those who are servant led become "healthier, wiser, freer, more autonomous" and "more likely themselves to become servants."[32] A true sense of forgiveness, not a false forgiveness that overlooks the harm caused by others, but a true forgiveness inherently bound to the ideas of integrity and justice, can move us toward the kind of robust and resilient relationships that build the foundation of legitimate power, personally, nationally, and internationally. It is in legitimate power, a form of power

Greenleaf expressed from a servant-first mentality, that we experience the human capacity for love and greatness.

Throughout society, in the culture of families, groups, communities, corporations, and nations, the call for effective leadership is increasing.[33] The old leadership model in which leaders directed others toward increased output at the expense of personal meaning often concentrated on correcting problems and maintaining the status quo.[34] Change itself is at such a rapid pace that people often find themselves caught in a storm of stress.[35] Moving forward, taking the wisdom of past models, moving beyond the industrial mindset to the relational, we face the increasing need for leaders who inspire through integrity to a higher vision of what it means to be human.[36] In response to this, Greenleaf proposed we need leaders who understand the nature of humanity and who can foster an authentic sense of community. Such leaders embrace diversity, rather than insisting on uniformity. They understand what it means to develop others. They understand forgiveness and how to realize just restoration, rather than push for legality or retribution.[37] The ideas of servant leadership, uniquely positioned in contemporary leadership, can be seen in endeavors that have brought dead organizations to life and reconciliation and healing to nations gravely wounded by human atrocities.[38]

In my own life, my first recollections of trying to understand servant leadership have to do with people who gave me a vision of the dignity of life. Often these people stepped out of their world into mine, and drew me into the larger concept of living to which they had attuned their lives. This concept, something central to their own identity, inevitably had to do with internal, relational, and societal commitments that have noticeably transformed humanity—commitments to such virtues as quietness, discernment, courage, forgiveness, and love. Even without intentional knowledge of Greenleaf's ideas, each of the people who influenced me, women and men, was a servant leader. Each person had a sense of fearlessness regarding self-discovery, accompanied by a disciplined, creative approach to relational meaning that became an antidote to the "terrifying emptiness"[39] that is too often our collective experience of one another.

Before being influenced toward a greater understanding of what it might mean to be a servant and a leader, early on I was almost entirely given to images of bravery or ambition. I lived consumed by hopes of advancement and adulation. Much of my early professional development was spent envisioning others adoring me, me as the sports champion, me on top of the world, the big money maker, the professional man, the leader of large corporations. And before this, as a high school and collegiate student athlete, I lived needy for the praise of others, often carrying about a vague wish that by some chance others would suddenly devote themselves to telling stories of my talents.

Conveniently, in the world I conceived, my faults were protected. I didn't want anyone to notice my faults or point them out, and I spent most of my energy trying to please people so they would have nothing to be disappointed about concerning me, even as I lived a life that was largely unaware and unconcerned with the personal well-being of others. If someone poked a hole in my façade, as did happen on occasion, my deflation was immediate and complete, and people discovered that inside I was defensive and rigid, a fragile person. I had little idea what it might mean to be true to myself or someone else.

I grew up in Montana, a state where high school basketball was a thing as strong as family or work, and Jonathan Takes Enemy, a member of the Crow (Apsáalooke) Nation, was the best basketball player in the state. He led Hardin High, a school with years of losing tradition, into the state spotlight, carrying the team and the community on his shoulders all the way to the state tournament, where he averaged forty-one points per game. He created legends that decades later are still spoken of in state basketball circles, and he did so with a fierceness that made me both fear and respect him. On the court, nothing was outside the realm of his skill: the jumpshot, the drive, the sweeping left-handed finger roll, the deep fade-away jumper. He could deliver what we all dreamed of, and with a venom that said *don't get in my way.*

I was a year younger than Jonathan, playing for an all-white school in Livingston, when our teams met in the divisional tournament and he and the Hardin Bulldogs delivered us a crushing seventeen-point defeat. At the close of the third quarter, with the clock winding down and his team with a comfortable lead, Takes Enemy pulled up from one step in front of the half-court line and shot a straight, clean jumpshot. Though the range of it was more than twenty feet beyond the three-point line, his form remained pure. The audacity and power of it, the exquisite beauty, hushed the crowd. A common knowledge came to everyone: few people can even throw a basketball that far with any accuracy, let alone take a real shot with good form. Takes Enemy landed, and as the ball was in flight he turned, no longer watching the flight of the ball, and began to walk back toward his team bench. The buzzer sounded, he put his fist in the air, the shot swished into the net. The crowd erupted.

In his will even to take such a shot, let alone make it, I was reminded of the surety and brilliance of so many Native American heroes in Montana who had painted the basketball landscape of my boyhood. My father's good friend Cleveland Highwalker of Lame Deer. Marty Round Face and Tim Falls Down and Max Spotted Bear of Plenty Coups. Elvis Old Bull of Lodge Grass. Joe Pretty Paint and Takes Enemy himself of Hardin. Many of these young men died from the violence that surrounded the alcohol and drug traffic on the reservations, but their natural flow on the court inspired me toward the kind of boldness that gives artistry and freedom to any endeavor. Such boldness is akin to passion. For these young men, and for myself at that time, our passion was basketball.

But rather than creating in me my own intrepid response, seeing Takes Enemy only emphasized how little I knew of bravery, not just on the basketball court, but also in life. Takes Enemy breathed a confidence I lacked, a leadership potential that lived and moved. Greenleaf said, "A mark of leaders, an attribute that puts them in a position to show the way for others, is that they are better than most at pointing the direction."[40] Takes Enemy embodied this idea. He and his team seemed to work as one as they played with fluidity and joy and abandon. I began to look for this leadership style as an athlete and as a person. The search brought me to people who led not through dominance but through freedom of movement, and such people led me toward the experience of humility, forgiveness, and relational justice. One of the most potent experiences of this came with the mentoring I received from my future wife's father.

My wife Jennifer and I were in our twenties, not yet married. I was at the dinner table with her and her family when Jennifer's father said something short, a sharp-edged comment, to her mother. At the time her father was the president of a large multinational sports-oriented corporation based in Washington State. Thinking back, I hardly noticed the comment, probably because of the chaos and uncontrolled nature of the ways I had previously experienced conflict. For me most conflicts revealed a simmering anger or a resentment that went underground, plaguing the relationship, taking a long time to disperse. I did not give her father's comment a second thought until sometime after dinner when he approached me as I relaxed on the couch. He had just finished speaking with his wife over to one side of the kitchen when he came to me.

"I want to ask your forgiveness for being rude to my wife," he said.

I could not imagine what he was talking about. I felt uncomfortable, and I tried to get him and me out of this awkward conversation as soon as I could.

"You don't have to ask me," I said.

But from there, the tension only increased for me. I had not often been in such situations in which things were handled in an equitable way. My work experience had been that the person in power (typically, but not always, the male) dominated the conflict so that the external power remained in the dominant one's hands, while internally everyone else (those not in power) suffered bitterness, disappointment, and a despairing, nearly hopeless feeling regarding the good of the relationship. Later in my family and work relationships

I found that when I lived from my own inordinate sense of power, I too, like those I had overpowered, would have a sick feeling internally for having won my position through coercion or force rather than through the work of a just and mutual resolution. In any case, in the situation with Jennifer's father, I felt tense and wanted to quickly end the moment by saving face for both of us. "You don't have to ask me," I said.

"I don't ask forgiveness for your benefit," he answered. "I ask in order to honor the relationship I share with my wife. In our family, if one person hurts another, we not only ask forgiveness of the person who has been hurt, but also of anyone else who was present in order to restore the dignity of the one we've hurt." Later I found the same practice was common in the culture he had created in the corporation he led.

From a relatively brief experience, I gained respect for myself and began to see the possibilities of a family and work culture free of perpetual binds and rifts, and free of the entrenched criticalness that usually accompanies such relationships. My own life was like a fortress compared to the open lifestyle Jennifer's father espoused. I began to understand that much of my protectedness, defensiveness, and lack of will to reveal myself might continue to serve as a fortification in future conflicts but would not lead me to more whole ways of experiencing the world. I also began to see that the work of a servant leader requires the ability to humble oneself and a desire to honor relationships with others as sacred. In Greenleaf's work, this takes the form of listening and understanding, and only the one who is a servant is able to approach people first by listening and trying to understand, rather than by trying to problem-solve or "lead." Just as "true listening builds strength in other people," it follows that a lack of listening weakens people.[41]

In the present day, and in fact throughout history, humility has often been taken for weakness. Our collective understanding is strengthened when we reconcile the fact that the power of servant leaders emerges from their devotion to being transparent with regard to their own faults and humble in their approach to self, others, and leadership. Because our culture values strength in the guise of force-based power, we often engender leaders who negate, degrade, and dominate. In servant leadership, the opposite is true: humbleness of spirit leads to strength of relationship, whether the relationship be personal, familial, organizational, or global.

Finally, despite the intent of true servant leadership, to listen well and to serve can give rise in some to the feeling of slavery. But let it be recognized: servant is not slave. The servant leader is reflected in the father whose tender embrace blesses his child, the mother whose song brings peace. Servanthood is a conscious choice to listen, to discern, and to respond, whereas slavery is a state of being locked in the oppressor/oppressed dynamic, a dynamic that is incapable of transformative responsiveness. Etymologically to listen is to obey, to give heed to the beloved other, while not listening is linked to being absurd.[42] For the servant leader, to listen and obey is to surrender one's own desires to more ultimate desires, while not listening is to disregard the needs of others and place one's needs above theirs. Fear of loss, pain, and rejection can make us cling to self-protection, which is the absence of trust. Without a sense of trust, our lives become increasingly absurd. The servant leader builds trust by seeing the Divine in the other, and by serving the Divine. Philosopher Hans-Georg Gadamer said it well in what he called the hermeneutical (interpretive or discerning) experience of the Thou:

> Anyone who listens is fundamentally open. Without such openness to one another there is no genuine human bond. . . . When two people understand each other, this does not mean that one person "understands" the other. . . . Similarly, "to hear and obey someone" does not mean simply that we do blindly what the other desires. We call such a person slavish. Openness to the other, then, involves recognizing that I myself must accept some things that are against me, even though no one else forces me to do so.[43]

My father's sorrow is the sorrow of watching his own father decline into a highly fortified and fundamentally closed posture. For my grandfather, the openness of the true life—the life characterized by love and beauty—eventually turned into the slow march toward self-annihilation. Life's inherent dignity is found when we open ourselves to the mysterious relationship that exists at the center of forgiveness and power. Here servant leadership becomes a way of being. Openness, then, is the gift of a father or a mother to a child, the gift of a brother or sister to one another, the gift of a mentor to the one who seeks; when this gift is welcomed with wonder and joy and we receive it fully, we inspire the concrete reality of dignity and openness in others.

Chapter 4

The Eloquent Question

Traditional leadership models can create environments in which leaders take action without accountability to the emotional or spiritual well-being of themselves or those they lead. We encounter in such leaders a wasteland of deafness, a place where habitual lack of listening accompanies inappropriate ambition or abuse of power, be the pursuit of such ambition and power conscious or unconscious. Even in well-meaning leaders, the result can be an elitist mentality in which the leader carries a false sense of direction. In the following paraphrase of the Tolstoy story entitled "The Three Hermits," the bishop is just such a leader, a person with good intentions, but blind to the value latent in those he seeks to lead. In this way, even considerate and thoughtful leaders who do not make themselves accountable to the issues of the interior end up diminishing self and others by approaching the work environment as leader first rather than servant first.[44]

The arts, in seeking to understand the world transparently and with increased acuity, lend resonance to our knowledge of one another, and Tolstoy's revelations in his well-crafted works of fiction create insistent echoes for those ready to hear.

A bishop was traveling on a merchant ship when he overheard a man speaking of three hermits who had lived for years on a nearby island, devoting themselves to prayer. Crew members did not believe the man, saying it was just a legend, an old wives' tale. But the man persisted. He related how some years before he had been shipwrecked off the island in question, taken in by the hermits, and sheltered and fed by them while they rebuilt his boat. He told the crew the hermits were devout men of prayer, the most saintly men he had ever met. Overhearing this, the bishop demanded that the captain take

27

him to the isle. It was out of the way, and the captain was reluctant, but the bishop was determined and offered to pay the captain for his troubles. The captain relented, and in the early morning, while the ship anchored off shore, the bishop was let off on the hermits' island. The hermits emerged, walking slowly toward the visitor. They were old and of grizzled appearance, with long beards. Having been so long from civilization, they spoke little and appeared meek or afraid. The bishop asked them how they'd been praying. The tallest one seemed to be the spokesman.

"Very simply, my lord," he said. "Three are we. Three are Thee. Have mercy on us."

"I must teach you how to pray then," said the bishop.

"Thank you, my lord," the three hermits replied, and the bishop proceeded to require them to memorize the Lord's Prayer. It was long, hard work; the hermits were out of practice. Throughout the day they fretted at how difficult it was for them to memorize it, and they feared they were disappointing the bishop. In fact, night had nearly fallen before the three could recite back to the bishop the prayer he'd taught them, but finally the last of them had it and the bishop flagged the small boat to take him back to the ship. He felt he had served his purpose that day, served God, and enlightened the three men.

When the ship set sail he was on deck, high up in the fore part of the ship near the captain, looking back at the ship's wake and the path of the moon. They had been moving for some time now, but he did not feel like sleeping. He felt satisfied. The work had been hard work, but good work, and neces-sary. Just then he saw a silver sphere far back on the dark of the water moving toward the ship at a tremendous pace. The bishop was afraid. The entire crew was on deck now watching it, trying to make out what it might be. At last the sphere seemed to split off into three. Then he saw clearly three lights, three men, long beards flowing in the wind—it was the hermits, moving over the water with great speed. They approached the ship and floated up to where the bishop was seated, stopping in front of him just beyond the railing. They had pained looks on their faces.

"What is it?" cried the bishop.

"Father, Father," pleaded the taller one, "forgive us. We've forgotten the prayer you taught us. Please teach us again."

Hearing this, the bishop immediately fell on his face. "Go your way," he said. "Pray as you have prayed. God is with you. Have mercy on me."

By falling to his face, Tolstoy's priest is finally ready to be of real service. He is able, in the end, to approach others with listening, humility, and sur-render—and in this place of self-shattering realization, his ego and pride fall away and the sense of awe and mystery about life and connectedness to others and God is reawakened.

In listening, and being willing to be transformed by our encounters with others, we come into a dialogue that can liberate us, restore our sense of peace, and create healing. We ask questions in order to gather greater understanding.

Gadamer in philosophy, and Freire in education, speak of the importance of dialogue in knowing the world and initiating change across broad human science, societal, and interpersonal levels.[45] Gadamer's notion of the eloquent or elegant question forms a philosophical bridge into the kind of assured personhood that opens real dialogue, develops authenticity in self and others, and forwards a view of human relationships that helps us transcend our own hidden or overt will for self- and other-annihilation. He proposed the shining idea that the eloquent question is one to which we do not already know the answer. By doing so he freed us from the fortified sense of ourselves that disallows the truths of another to change us. In transparent receptiveness we can truly encounter the beloved other, of all races, all creeds, and be changed. In overcoming conflict, dialogue is essential. Dialogue, in this context, is the will to enter into a conversation in which we put on hold our own preconceived ideas and seek to understand and be transformed by the ideas of the one with whom we dialogue. At the same time, dialogue holds firmly to the idea that two identities can be healed by each other and that a third, higher perspective—alluding to the Divine or the transcendent—is necessary for us to be as giving as we are strong and to forgo our own will to defend our territory. Different from discussion, dialogue seeks restoration with others and resolves conflicts through sacrificial giving as well as attention to fairness. Listening is the cornerstone of dialogue. Reconciliation is dialogue's end result.

Greenleaf speaks of the absolute necessity of trust, a form of love in which people are free of rejection. He states, "The servant always accepts and empathizes, never rejects. The servant as leader always empathizes, always accepts the person, but sometimes refuses to accept some of the person's effort or performance as good enough."[46] In meaningful dialogue the servant as leader submits to a higher perspective, one that can be pivotal to the development of the self in relation to others. Greenleaf addresses this when he states that the real motive for healing is for one's own healing, not in order to change others, implying that the true motive to serve is for one's own service, one's own betterment. In this light one seeks to heal or seeks to serve not only for others, but for the greater good of oneself, which inevitably results in the greater good of the community. Greenleaf's progression is common sense: when one pursues one's own healing, the will to serve and heal others becomes authentic. Such healing takes place best in a community that initiates and sustains meaningful dialogue.

Meaningful dialogue gives rise to the forces that unhinge the way we harm each other, opening us toward a more accepting and empathic awareness of one another. Greenleaf, in forwarding an ideal of love in community, places servant leadership firmly in the contemporary ground of the family, the workplace, and the global realization of social justice. In this ground, the retributive justice represented by the legal system in mediating conflicts is joined by the idea of a community of forgivers, people with the foresight to build a just and lasting reconciliation, people interested in the restoration that results from a disciplined and unflinching look at the wrongs we do to one another.

Servant leadership is the kind of literary image that is sown into the fabric of life, and when applied to personal responsibility in relationships, reconciliation and forgiveness replace retribution and blame. Gadamer's eloquent questions emerge from the heart of the leader to enliven the world: What is to be done with our own *individual* ego, pride, and even evil? And what is to be done with our *collective* ego, pride, and evil?

Hallowell refers to forgiveness not as a sweet old lady, but as a veteran of many wars.[47] The work of forgiveness is a work of tenacity, often against logic, that results in the opportunity to see our own impact on others, our own faults, and take responsibility for our faults, ask forgiveness, and become more true. From self-responsible living, grace draws near, and from grace rises the ability to forgive others, to face the atrocities done to us or our loved ones, and not only embrace the violent heart of humanity, but also see the heart of humanity whole, healed, and strong again. Here, we return to integrity, and find again the goodness we had lost.

Forgiveness studies in the social sciences have gathered an ever-increasing following through research that is beginning to connect the will to forgive with lowered anxiety, lowered depression, lowered anger, less heart disease, and stronger immune systems.[48] New bridges are being formed from the social sciences to the study of leadership, pointing organizations and nations toward the acceptance, empathy, and healing Greenleaf envisioned. This involves the development of leaders who are able to understand the way people diminish one another, leaders who are able to invigorate a culture of acceptance, empathy, and relational justice. From this perspective the servant leader creates an environment in which forgiveness can be asked and granted, and the servant leader creates this by example. Two people who come together to reconcile, who choose to forgive and be forgiven, can experience a cleansing in which embittered rigidity becomes transformative openness.[49] The leader exemplifies this process, and in settings of strong relational trust, the process defines and enhances the life of the organization and the deeper development of nation states.

Globally, in the contemporary landscape, the traditional route of retributive justice is shown in the response to World War I and World War II, reaching its apex in the international spectacle of the Nuremberg trials. Here, the world outcry for justice was nearly all-encompassing. Such an outcry carries with it the essence of our collective desire to right wrongs and bring about a just result, through legal trial, in response to the horrific inhumanities perpetrated by Nazi warlords. Though retributive justice seeks a just answer to wrongs committed, it usually does so through punitive or violent means (e.g., imprisonment, death, and so on). Retributive justice, especially in its most undisciplined or wanton forms, tends to beget greater alienation between people, continued oppression, greater atrocities, and greater spiritual poverty.

Restorative justice, promoted by leaders such as Martin Luther King Jr. during the civil rights movement, and Nelson Mandela and Archbishop Desmond Tutu in response to the atrocities of apartheid in South Africa, presents a different answer to the harms of humanity. Undeniably, the comparison between the Nuremberg trials of World War II and the American civil rights movement or the Truth and Reconciliation Commission of South Africa is riddled with complexity. Yet there are momentous insights to be recognized. My colleague from the United Kingdom, Stephen Prosser, provides guidance, beginning by remembering and honoring those who spent their lives to give the world new life: "We can all look at aspects of our country's international track record and be ashamed—there are things we ought not to have done. However, that should not lead us to ignore other noble achievements that have benefited humankind, and we should try and avoid judging our forebears through our 21st century moral lens."[50] World War II and Nuremberg represent not only the height of retributive justice, but also a collective Allied sacrifice of monumental proportions that resulted in a vital, almost inexpressible triumph of good over evil. With good reason, many in America name the World War II generation "The Greatest Generation."[51]

Whenever we approach forgiveness, an age-old responsibility asserts itself: retribution as a necessity for maintaining the social order. Who can deny the real and tangible role of retribution throughout the course of history and especially with the advent of large-scale systems of justice and law enforcement aimed at preventing crime and confronting those who enact categorical human transgressions? It is not for nothing that members of our law enforcement are called peace officers. In democracies retribution is designed to undergird peace, and common retributive deterrents such as community service, jail time, and prison are a reminder of the responsibility of society to erect appropriate boundaries.

On an even larger level, what is humanity to do when the shadow falls and we are confronted with the velocity and vastness of absolute evil? Is not military engagement necessary to deter it, and are there not times when in fact war is required, in essence, to free humanity when evil aligns itself to wreck the world? The question that follows must also be asked: In the middle of the bloodiest century humanity has ever known, where would we have been without the indispensible military victories of the Allies of World War I and World War II? Without the bedrock character of those who fought and gave their lives so that the world could be free, in all truth, humanity would have suffered far greater losses and the devastation might well have been incalculable.

Ellis Cose spoke of the bald fact of evil with clarity and force in the introduction to his book *Bone to Pick: Of Forgiveness, Reconciliation, Reparation, and Revenge*:

> This is not to say that forgiveness and reconciliation are always possible. Brutes, bullies, and people beyond redemption will always have a place in the world. Rogue states are, by definition, beyond civilized constraints. And at times they must be met with something significantly more compelling than an understanding heart. The need for justice, the call for war, the hunger for revenge: all are as old as mankind, and no less enduring.[52]

There is a sacred sense of memory and respect that attends us in our finest hours and is associated with the dignity of having paid the ultimate price in order to prevent human destruction and defend human freedoms. Consider the Tomb of the Unknowns, a symbol, solemn and weighty, of such dignity—the dignity of those who have given their lives for the good of their country, and often for the good of the entire world. Housed in Arlington National Cemetery, the U.S. military cemetery in Arlington, Virginia, the tomb consists of seven rectangular slaps of marble that together weigh seventy-nine tons. Initially the tomb site contained the unidentified remains of an individual soldier from World War I. Later the remains of an unidentified soldier from World War II were added, and eventually those from later military engagements. In the cemetery at large more than 300,000 soldiers are buried in an area of 624 acres. Veterans and military casualties from every one of the nation's wars are interred in Arlington, from the American Civil War to the present. The Tomb of the Unknowns is located on a hill overlooking Washington, D.C. Soldiers have stood perpetual watch over the tomb, every minute of every day, from its opening on April 9, 1932, to the present.

Carved on the front of the tomb are three figures in remembrance of the spirit of the Allies of World War I. In the center panel stands the female figure,

Victory. On her left, a male figure represents Valor, and on her right is the Figure of Peace, a female holding a palm branch in honor of the devotion and bold sacrifice of those who pursue a righteous cause and emerge triumphant. On the rear panel of the tomb, the following statement is inscribed in block letters:

HERE RESTS IN
HONORED GLORY
AN AMERICAN
SOLDIER
KNOWN BUT TO GOD

To serve as a sentinel at the Tomb of the Unknowns is no small task. The official language regarding service states, "A soldier seeking the honor of serving as a sentinel at the Tomb must possess exemplary qualities, to include American citizenship, a spotless record, and impeccable military bearing."[53] The sentinels go through a grueling selection process, and very few are chosen. Sentinels wear no military rank on their uniforms so they will not outrank the Unknowns. As the sentinel on guard walks from side to side across the tomb, the sentinel carries a rifle on the outside shoulder and takes twenty-one steps, symbolizing the twenty-one-gun salute, the highest honor granted to military or foreign dignitaries. On the twenty-first step the sentinel pauses, makes a ninety-degree turn, and faces the tomb for twenty-one seconds. The sentinel then makes another ninety-degree turn to face back down the walk and changes the weapon to the outside shoulder again. The sentinel again pauses for twenty-one seconds before beginning the return walk. The sentinel repeats this process until being relieved of duty at the Changing of the Guards. The sentinel's gloves are moistened to ensure a grip on the rifle, which is always carried on the shoulder away from the tomb, as a "gesture against intrusion."[54]

The Changing of the Guards occurs in an elaborate ritual either every half hour or every hour on the hour, except when the cemetery is closed, during which time the guard is changed every two hours. The guard's shoes have soles and heels of equal height so that the back remains straight and perpendicular to the ground during marching and at attention. The shoes have a steel tip and a steel plate on the heel to make the loud click as the sentinels come to a halt. Guards dress for duty before a full-length mirror, and all aspects of dress are kept precise with no wrinkles, folds, or lint on the uniform. Every guard spends time each day preparing uniforms for guard duty.

To apply for guard duty at the tomb, the sentinel must be between five feet ten inches and six feet two inches tall and the waist size cannot exceed thirty inches. The first six months of duty a guard cannot talk to anyone, or watch TV. Off-duty time is spent studying the lives of the175 notable people laid to rest in Arlington National Cemetery. A guard must memorize who they are and where they are interred. Among the notables are President Taft, boxer Joe E. Lewis, and Medal of Honor winner Audie Murphy, the most decorated soldier of World War II. Guards must commit two years of life to guard the tomb, must live in a barracks under the tomb, and cannot drink any alcohol on or off duty for the rest of their lives. They cannot swear in public for the rest of their lives and cannot disgrace the uniform or the tomb in any way. After nine months, the guard can earn a wreath pin that is worn on the lapel signifying that he or she served as a guard of the tomb. There are only four hundred currently worn. If unable to keep from disgracing the tomb or the uniform during his or her lifetime, the guard must give up the wreath pin.

In 2003, as Hurricane Isabelle pushed into Washington D.C., the U.S. Congress elected to take two days off in anticipation of the storm. On the ABC evening news it was reported that because of the dangers from the hurricane, the military members assigned the duty of guarding the Tomb of the Unknowns were given permission to suspend the assignment. They respectfully declined the offer. Soaked to the skin, marching in the pelting rain of the hurricane, they reminded the media that guarding the tomb was not simply an assignment, but the highest honor afforded to a service person.[55]

Understanding that military engagement is sometimes warranted is a reminder of the cost of peace. Be it necessary military action or strategic and purposeful nonviolence, the essence of humanity reveals itself in the permutations of justice and mercy, actions and inactions that are not unassailable, but worthy, rather, of deep introspection. Retributive justice is justice that exacts retribution from the offender, and the consequences and punishments associated with retributive justice are a central part of the instrumental function of developing societies. Imprisonment and other forms of retributive movement sometimes create the ground for interior change, thus opening the door for a more restorative effort at social justice. Restorative justice is justice that restores offender and offended to a relationship of mutual reconciliation and common humanity. In this context, seeking an answer to human atrocities is one of the most serious responsibilities of human life. Again, the eloquent question can lead us to a greater understanding of one another.

Yet the answer remains elusive. Retribution may sustain social order, and yet love itself points to restoration as a more ultimate form of existence. Ultimate healing, in the life and action of the servant leader, is often found in the inexplicable and far-reaching realities present in the human experience of forgiveness. Forgiveness directs a subtle light on the fortitude involved in standing in for another, sacrificing the will to blame or seek revenge and voluntarily taking on the wounding meant for those who have wounded us. In this light, the one who forgives absorbs pain, and in the end mercy leads to regeneration. Van Gogh, an artist who believed in love as the foundation of all art, beckons us, saying:

[We] must grasp life at its depths.[56]

Grasping life at its depths requires vigor—the decisions inherent to national and international interest are infused with import and the latent capacity to heal or harm. Most often no clear pathway is present. Justice itself cannot be diminished or passed over, even if peace and mercy are the desired end states. Notably, Mandela himself was not opposed to the use of military action to confront human evil.[57] Even so, Mandela's patience and capacity for forgiveness brought about unimaginable change. The buoyant mysteries of restoration after an agonizing breach in relationship are manifold and often infused with hues of light not generally perceived with the naked eye. Leaders such as King, Mandela, and Tutu represent the appeal to a richly layered restorative justice as a response to the perpetrators of inhumanity. From this restoration, an exterior justice comes to the fore, represented by legitimate and mutual power in the economic, educational, social, and spiritual realms of life.

Consider again the words of Martin Luther King Jr., the exquisite servant leader on an international scale, who stated that the oppressor will never willingly give up power—a statement of clarity that often ignites violence in an attempt to overthrow the oppressor or silence in an attempt to escape the oppression: the fight or flight response. King, a pupil of Gandhi (and Gandhi, notably, was influenced by Tolstoy's writings when he studied in Great Britain), advocated neither violence nor silence.[58] King furthered his discernment regarding the unwillingness of the oppressor with the following revolutionary idea, an idea akin to Greenleaf's idea of the servant leader's response to injustice: King proposed that rather than hate or distance ourselves from the oppressor, we should love the oppressor. He believed that when we love the oppressor we bring about not only our own salvation, but the salvation of the oppressor. With this love, a revolutionary form of transcending oneself and engaging solemn personal and communal responsibility, King revealed the unbroken nature of justice itself. His approach to the atrocities of humanity was not condemnation and shame, nor was it retributive in the purely punitive sense. With a form of perfect or unconditional forgiveness, in effect unconditional love, King reminded us that there are powers beyond us and their workings are not only subtle and mysterious, but natural and compelling.

Into the void in which we ask the most eloquent questions of life—about the nature of evil, legitimate power, and human dignity—comes the fragrance of love. Love, not so much sweet and kindly as wild and revolutionary, evokes its own deeper justice that cannot be legislated or controlled. Rather, this love heals every harm, restores every rift, gives sight to the blind and hearing to the deaf, and breathes life into that which was dead. We see it in individuals who forgive those who have so gravely wronged them, just as we see it in nations who reconcile. Love then, and its closest kin, forgiveness, combine to form the hidden lodestone beneath one of the most notable truths Dr. King gave to America and the world. On March 25, 1965, after his third march to Montgomery, the birth-city of the American civil rights movement, Dr. King spoke the following words on the steps of the Alabama State Capitol:

The arc of the moral universe is long, but it bends toward justice.[59]

Chapter 5

Of Love and Human Violence

Still, the question presents itself: What of human violence?

A closer look at Nelson Mandela and the Truth and Reconciliation Commission in South Africa is warranted. After the fall of apartheid, Mandela became the first democratically elected president of South Africa, and his example as an extraordinary statesman and the embodiment of a humble and powerful contemporary servant leader became apparent the world over. From a country of bloodshed and hate, he and those around him effectively built a country of hope. He held to a vision of South Africa involving complete restoration, where black and white Africans could live and rule together without retribution or violence over the past. He spent more than twenty-seven years as a political prisoner, eighteen imprisoned at Robben Island, yet Mandela refused to be vengeful either personally or politically. Upon his release from prison he refused to gain power through suppression of dissent. Finally, his refusal to deny the humanity of those who imprisoned him or those who confessed to the most heinous abuses drew the people of his country toward the colossal task of forgiving in the face of grave human rights violations, forgiving even with regard to atrocities that had demonstrated the brutality of the human condition at its worst levels.[60]

Mandela, Tutu, and other democratically elected officials designed the Truth and Reconciliation Commission in response to the atrocities committed during the apartheid years. Tutu became the chairman of the commission.

His father a teacher, his mother a cleaner and a cook at a school for the blind, Desmond Mpilo Tutu was born in 1931 in Klerksdorp, Transvaal, South Africa, and took a life path of education and integrity to the good of humanity that led through the catastrophic landscape of apartheid all the way to the Nobel Peace Prize. He became the first black archbishop of

Cape Town, supported the economic boycott of his own country in order to break apartheid by convincing two of the world's superpowers (the United Kingdom and the United States) to disinvest or halt investments in South Africa, and eventually organized peace marches that brought thirty thousand people to the streets of Cape Town and finally set the stage for the release of Mandela and the repair of the nation. As the country emerged from apartheid into the new future, Mandela and Tutu felt that retribution, either legal or punitive, would only result in widespread violence, a violence that had plagued many African countries in their emergence from colonization. The commission Mandela and Tutu envisioned set a specific and drastic vision, and because of the deep loyalty and respect the majority of South Africans felt for these leaders, the country implemented a plan of forgiveness and reconciliation, of restorative justice, unlike any the global political community had ever known. Rather than seek out those who committed crimes against humanity, bring them to justice and punish them, the commission asked for honesty. The commission asked people to honestly admit what they had done, where and when and how they had harmed, abducted, tortured, and killed others. The result of telling the truth was that the perpetrators would receive amnesty; they would go free. At the same time, the commission asked the people of South Africa to engage a forgiveness response. The commission even made truth and reconciliation an act of law, writing forgiveness directly into the new South African constitution, hoping it would give people a chance to hear word of lost and dead family members, friends, and loved ones, and a chance to truly grieve the harms the nation had experienced.

Tutu, in chairing the Truth and Reconciliation Commission, stated it clearly:

> The Act says that the thing you're striving after should be "ubuntu" rather than revenge. It comes from the root (of a Zulu-Xhosa word), which means "a person." So it is the essence of being a person. And in our experience, in our understanding, a person is a person through other persons. You can't be a solitary human being. We're all linked. We have this communal sense, and because of this deep sense of community, the harmony of the group is a prime attribute.[61]

The act forwarded six main objectives:

1. To generate a detailed record of the nature, extent, and causes of human rights violations in South Africa during the period 1960–1994.
2. To name the people, organizations, and political parties responsible for gross violation of human rights.

3. To provide victims of gross human rights violations a public forum to express themselves in order to regain their human dignity.
4. To make recommendations to the government on how to prevent the future occurrences of human rights violations.
5. To make recommendations to the government regarding reparations and the rehabilitation of victims of human rights violations.
6. To facilitate the granting of amnesty for individual perpetrators of human rights violations.[62]

South Africa, now some years after the commission hearings, though not without complex systemic problems, remains largely free of bloodshed. The country's legacy, unique to the political, governmental, and military communities of the world, has begun to be defined by forgiveness and reconciliation rather than by force, retribution, or violence.

Now consider one of the specific moments of the South African truth and reconciliation process. Brian Mitchell, the white apartheid police officer referred to earlier, underwent a grueling personal journey in which the black community he had so severely harmed eventually received him into their midst and helped him find hope and life again. Listen to his story.

A police station commander in a remote corner of the Kwa-Zulu Natal Midlands, Brian Mitchell stood watch over Trust Feed, a village of seven thousand black people. Generally the violence against the apartheid government had been contained in the townships, but when it spread to the rural areas and all the way to Trust Feed, Commander Mitchell was charged with controlling the region and thwarting the activities of the black African National Congress forces and United Democratic Front forces who had grown angry, hungry to overthrow the atrocities and unfair practices associated with the bastion of white power, apartheid.

In fulfilling what he saw as his duty at the time, on December 3, 1988, Mitchell ordered an attack on a terrorist cell located in a house in Trust Feed. The house was reported to be an ammunition holding house and a location where petrol bombs were being manufactured. In the early morning Mitchell dropped four special constables off a few streets from the targeted house, ordering them to attack the house and subdue any combatants. The four constables entered what they thought was the house of the terrorist cell and killed eleven people, mostly women and children.

When Commander Mitchell entered the house the next morning he realized the wrong house had been targeted. He said, "I walked in . . . and all these people were lying on the floor, because someone had moved all the people against the side of the wall as though they were sleeping. It wasn't what I foresaw . . . nothing I could ever imagine in my entire life." Blood covered the room and the bodies of women and children lay completely still.

Brian Mitchell had witnessed much in his years as a police officer. He was involved in stopping the riots in Soweto during the 1976 uprising. The fighting and death he saw in Soweto both horrified and desensitized him, and in 1988 in Trust Feed he was still not consciously aware of the level of his own participation in the vast machine of indifference and human rights transgressions that was apartheid. Years after the accidental killing of innocents in Trust Feed he stated, "As a policeman . . . you only see the bad side of life. You are involved in that evil side of life."

Immediately after the discovery of the mistaken hit at Trust Feed, he continued to walk in the cloak of evil that surrounded much of white South Africa's police work. There was concern that a leak of the event would damage the image of apartheid's South African State Security Force, so he and his superiors commenced a planned cover-up of the atrocity by blaming the black United Democratic Front forces for the attack. Fearing international exposure through the press and deep damage to the image of South Africa, they lied, a tactic that succeeded initially, and the atrocity remained a mystery.

Yet the event haunted Mitchell, and his encounter with his own interior intensified when a reinvestigation was opened three years later and Mitchell and his four special constables were arrested and tried for the massacre of the people at Trust Feed. Mitchell was convicted and sentenced to death eleven times for the ordering of the massacre. In Westfall prison awaiting execution, for the first time he began to become aware of the life he had lived.

The four constables each received ten years and were later released on a presidential pardon that also commuted Brian's death sentence to thirty years. Brian's commuted sentence opened the door for him to apply for amnesty in 1995 through the Truth and Reconciliation Commission, something he could not have done if he were still on death row. At the commission hearings Brian spoke the truth about his involvement in the lies and violence of the apartheid system, and the massacre at Trust Feed.

"I knew that the time was right, the time had come for me to go and do what I had to do and expose the whole system, because none of the evidence I held had been released before, at trial or anything. It was all completely new documentary evidence so it was a new start. When it was finished it was such a relief."

Mitchell was given amnesty and released from prison one year later.

A few months after his release, he met with the community of Trust Feed and made a public apology. In this meeting he asked the people of Trust Feed to forgive him. Members of the community expressed anger and hatred, and they did not receive his apology.

"There was a lot of hostility, an enormous amount of hostility from the community," Brian said. "I think a bullet would have been easier for me to take than answering their questions or hearing their accusations." Brian's spirit seemed to him to die then. "It was futile," he said. "I had done my part, the only other thing I could do for the community was to assist them as I promised in establishing some sort of community center." His life was not his life. He felt held hostage to his former deeds, hostage to the hostile acts that had torn a whole community apart. "Reality sinks in," Brian said, "then fear descends like a heavy black tarp that makes you feel like you are trapped and unable to breathe. I felt as if I was being suffocated. I felt pressed with a huge weight." That weight had been on Brian since he first walked into the house of the massacre on that morning in 1988, and the dark weight had stayed with him through his years of hiding the secret, through his trial and years on death row, even through the amnesty process with the Truth and Reconciliation Commission—and all had been compounded now on the day when his request for forgiveness was rejected by the people of Trust Feed. Brian went from that day feeling extremely depressed and caught in the excruciating memory of the massacre. He wondered how he could begin a new life or go from being "murderer" to "builder" of community. He considered growing his hair and beard so others could not easily recognize him, and he thought of moving far into the hinterlands to try to lose himself.

Yet in an act of tremendous collective generosity, one year later Brian Mitchell received a call from Thabane Nyoka, son of Sara Nyoka, a woman killed in the massacre. Thabane asked Brian if he would be willing to return to Trust Feed and join the community in a ritual of forgiveness and reconciliation. Thabane said to Brian, "I had a dream and in this dream my mother spoke to me and said I must forgive you and not seek revenge." On a day in September of 1998 the people of Trust Feed welcomed Brian Mitchell into their community, a day of cultural blessing and a return to unity, a day of dancing and singing. The day ended with Brian standing with joined hands in a circle with the survivors of the Trust Feed massacre in an expression of reconciliation. The people forgave him and with open arms they extended an invitation for him to return and live in their community again.

"This was absolute genuine forgiveness," Brian said.

They openly forgave me for what had happened and that closed the chapter for me. I knew I was completely cleansed. It brought finality for me, the request for forgiveness. They had accepted me back. The process allowed me to realize I could forgive myself. . . . One can pray and ask God to forgive you for what you have done. You can understand why you did certain things, but it seems to haunt you all the time until the day when the other party comes and accepts your wish for forgiveness. If there was no acceptance from the offended party . . . for me . . . self-forgiveness wasn't a reality. The barriers were removed, which opened a way for me to work with the community in a more genuine way, without reservations. We as human beings want to be accepted, or need to be accepted deeply. This process of saying "I forgive you" is one of the principles of feeling that you are wanted, that you are needed, that you are accepted. Especially when you have requested it.

Brian Mitchell did return to Trust Feed, and in the ensuing years he raised funds throughout South Africa and abroad and succeeded in helping to build a community center, working hand in hand with the friends and family members of those whose lives he had played a significant role in taking.

Reconciliation became a rebirth, a communal offering of grace and love strong enough to heal the hateful fractures of the past. The day of forgiveness initiated by the people of Trust Feed surfaced a miracle of endurance and redemption. "[It] was the most important day of my life," Brian Mitchell said. "I was dead until that day. After that day I lived."[63]

Mandela and Tutu and other servant leaders in South Africa foresaw the need for the richest sense of restoration. They asked offenders to tell the truth. They asked the people of South Africa to choose forgiveness in response to human evil. And this made Brian Mitchell's experience possible. Tutu and Mandela, among the great servant leaders of the twentieth century, are men who endured suffering while helping to buoy the heart and spirit of others. Most importantly, their behavior, their way of leading, was a way of healing. From a close look at the impact of their lives we see the legacy of the servant leader as healer . . . the leader with deep love who steps forward to help heal the world.

An example of such reach, from the southern tip of Africa all the way to the hearts and homes of Americans, also causes me to question the nature of my own and my country's blindness. I do not think it far afield to say that most Americans have not read the works of leaders such as Mandela and Tutu, let alone the works of Martin Luther King Jr., one of our own. Often we generate an egocentrism that insulates us, even from the kind of international servant leadership ideas that inspire today's global relations. In an unrelated but poignantly fitting statement made while attending an international symposium in 1976, Greenleaf stated, "Our African friend has said that we Americans are arrogant. It hurts—but I accept the charge."[64] In acceptance, empathy; in empathy, listening; and in listening, understanding. Such understanding may turn our self-absorption into learning from others about the nature of real care.

Even so, despite the illumined moments in which a sense of perfect forgiveness restores us to our most human capacities, the hope of forgiveness and reconciliation is not without its critics. We shed our naiveté when we realize that human evil exists despite our best efforts to forgive and reconcile. The echo of King's words remains—*the oppressor will never willingly give up power*. And in the twenty-first century these words could not be more true, considering the vast social and economic disparities and power abuses that exist today.

Yet the greater echo of King's words still rings true: *when we love the oppressor, we bring about not only our own salvation, but the salvation of the oppressor*. In these words we find solace regarding our own failures, the inequities and injustices, the character flaws, the great harms. Members of our own families can live with an ongoing sense of loving and being loved. Women and men in our communities can be true women, and true men, not displaced, not diminished. And in our workplaces we can work with joy, a sense of calling, and the personal meaning that accompanies good work. These things are possible, for it is in the servant leader, in the servant leader's journey toward healing the self, toward serving the heart of humanity, that an answer to the failures of leadership emerges. On the horizon of this landscape, a landscape that is as personal and spiritual as it is political and global, we see ourselves free of what binds us, and we walk in such a way that others are drawn forward so that they too may be free.

We walk with purpose and strength.

Love is our close companion.

Chapter 6

Emerson on Love

Mediocre people want to be loved. True people are lovely.[65]

—Ralph Waldo Emerson

When I first discovered Emerson's two-part understanding I was caught short, thinking of the implications.

Mediocre people want to be loved.

Wait a minute, I thought. *I* want to be loved . . . does that mean I'm mediocre?

Yes, I have to admit I am often mediocre. When I'm needy or reactive, defensive or self-absorbed, when I live from basic anger or anxiety or fear, in effect I place the responsibility for my own existence in the hands of others, expecting them to fulfill the needs of life for me. I lose sight of my own responsibility to the concrete as well as the less tangible realities of love. I am unable to access an interior devoted to the service of others, life, or God.

True people are lovely.

The very words invoke quality of life. They hearken us toward vulnerability, humility, surrender, and a word so often hated in the present world: submission. But the submission Emerson calls us to is not of the groveling form. Rather, it is submission to love itself—the ultimate expression of legitimate greatness and power. When Jennifer and I read Emerson, we were struck by the nuances of what it means to be lovely. Emerson gives of his own abounding loveliness and in so doing leads us to a more precise and fearless appreciation of self-responsibility and collective responsibility for life together. In self-responsibility we recognize how we harmfully impact the body, heart, mind, and spirit of others. The idea of noticing our own weaknesses and moving away from the desire to name the faults of others may be the very source of the capacity to heal disjointed and painful relational

45

systems. Unfortunately, often what we discover when we descend into our own interior is a dangerous and pernicious tendency to hold the beloved other (family members, colleagues, other people in general, our leaders, humanity itself, and of course our enemies) in a dark light. By doing so, we hide ourselves and fail to notice the reach of our own shadow in the world.

Self-responsibility is a foundation stone of servant leadership as a way of life. Forgiveness and legitimate power give servant leaders confidence and footing as they cross the chasm of personal growth to arrive at a life devoted to helping fulfill the highest-priority needs of others.

As a systems psychologist, I find that the pervasiveness of how we fortify and self-protect is readily apparent. In my experience, unless we are presented with the idea, we rarely think of forgiveness. For most, forgiveness and the world of relationships in which forgiveness exists and finds its home are like an alternate universe behind an ever-hidden door. And even on the chance that we find the door open and light sifting from the opening, our own anger, bitterness, fear, and shame often keep us from entering in. A unique progression asserts itself: (1) we don't often think of forgiveness; (2) when we do, we often resist the idea; (3) when we cease our resistance, we may think, *maybe I need to forgive someone*. Strangely, however, if the progression stops there, life remains somewhat muted. The real essence of forgiveness can take us further. When we reach beyond ourselves we come into a more revolutionary thought—(4) we affirm that *we need to ask forgiveness*. With this knowledge we go to others, humble ourselves, ask forgiveness, and change—and it is precisely this lifestyle of modesty and real change that draws others near and evokes in them their own desire to be responsible.

When we return to appropriate vulnerability and responsibility, the soulful life Robert Greenleaf envisioned opens to our awareness. After summoning the will to surrender, to *ask* forgiveness and change in ways our beloved ones find meaningful, the act of *granting* forgiveness becomes fluid and natural. We find that our own human evil is connected to the darkness of all humanity, and we forgo the desire to "set others straight." From here an earned ground develops in which we call on a way of life that reconciles relationships, ends injustice, and creates a reverberant systemic influence.

No one can doubt it is a difficult task to move from a stance of resentment, bitterness, or hatred for another, toward a stance in which we are no longer focused on how we've been wronged. Bravely, we begin a movement that engages the disciplined life of self-responsibility and generates greater collective responsibility. Desmond Tutu helps us navigate the complexities: "Forgiving and being reconciled are not about pretending that things are other than they are. . . . True reconciliation exposes the awfulness, the abuse, the pain, the degradation, the truth."[66] To truly encounter the idea that mercy triumphs over justice requires internal fortitude and the kind of human tenacity that brings the truth out in the open, not to criminalize or demonize the one who has harmed us, but to create greater ground for personal and collective integrity. In fact, as Tutu states, "In the act of forgiveness we are declaring our faith in the future of a relationship and in the capacity of the wrongdoer to make a new beginning on a course that will be different from the one that caused us the wrong."[67]

A profound movement within the scientific literature is taking place, a movement that reflects Tutu's call to transparency and real change. Research on gratitude, hope, love, and forgiveness is currently renewing the foundations of social science. As a specific example, the experimental studies of Robert Enright have begun to call people back to the virtue of forgiveness by showing the robust connection between forgiveness and greater health. In studies involving randomized experimental and control groups, Enright's findings declare that people who undergo a forgiveness process achieve significantly greater health than those who don't. Specifically, he and his research team conducted studies across a broad range of groups, including incest survivors, drug users, cardiac patients, emotionally abused women, terminally ill elderly cancer patients, grade school students, and at-risk middle school students. Data were gathered in the United States, Northern Ireland (Belfast), and Korea (Seoul). Within the groups and across nations, those who underwent a process of forgiveness experienced some astounding effects: less depression, less anxiety, less anger, fewer drug-seeking behaviors, fewer PTSD symptoms, greater hope, greater self-esteem and self-worth, greater academic achievement, greater forgiveness capacity, more efficiently functioning hearts, and greater overall emotional well-being.[68]

Researchers have discovered that the healing powers of forgiveness are not only astonishing but also long-lasting—people continue to experience greater emotional well-being at four-month and fourteen-month follow-ups and on into the lifespan. Even more central to the human endeavor is not just forgiveness, but the will to ask forgiveness, the will to take responsibility and change. Yet this reversal of human nature, this quiet embrace of a more divine will, requires great courage. Who among us wants to admit we are at fault, let alone come to terms with the fact that sometimes we are the cause of pain . . . abuse . . . degradation? "We do not usually rush to expose our vulnerability and our sinfulness," Tutu writes, "but if the process of forgiveness and healing is to succeed, ultimately acknowledgement by the culprit is indispensable."[69] Finding strength to admit our own darkness, along with the will to change our behaviors in order to honor others—this may characterize the primary gift of a generous God. With this hope we become healthy, and when we are healthy we become a healing presence in the lives of those around us. We become healers.

A good test is to note how much time we spend talking about the faults of others. An appreciative measure of health, verified in Gottman's research on mature relationships, is five to ten encounters of meaningful, sincere, and positive regard for the "other" to every one critique—and in the context of moving conflict from degenerative to life-affirming, this is done regardless of the perceived level of the "other's" fault.[70] In other words, a mature person is capable of turning relational deficit to relational potential, and this is generally done through actively choosing gratitude. Understandably, under heavy resistance the process may be realized late or never, but even so, in a circular sense, when the ground for true relationship is established, the potential for interpersonal integrity is unleashed. This is the unconditional forgiveness we see in South Africa, time after time, that eventually breaks the hard-heartedness of the offender and returns him or her whole to the human family; it is the echo of People Power from Ninoy and Corazon Aquino and the Philippines, one of the first nonviolent revolutions of the modern age; and it is the constant theme in Martin Luther King Jr.'s groundbreaking work to heal the center of American life.

In this light, though motive can be questioned, even one of the most rabid racists of the last century communicated at long last that the thought and life of Martin Luther King Jr. had gone to work on his interior and called him to do something he'd formerly set his whole life against. Near death, former governor of Alabama, George Wallace, a man infamous for vindictiveness and vicious racism, sought forgiveness for the harms he'd caused African Americans.[71] Martin Luther King Jr. effectively reached beyond death and spoke life, and such life endures and does not diminish.

When we are lovely we consider what it means to understand our own weakness or personal darkness, whether in our homes or at our jobs or between nations. We begin to embrace our own brokenness. The natural tendency of humanity is to externalize blame for a given communal conflict—but the life of love sustains the truths that heal us and we begin to internalize self-responsibility for system health rather than externalize blame; in this context, in the family as well as in work, and even in the course of nations, resilience and moral power, infused by love, breathe life into the system. We are lifted out of our own self-embeddedness and given a Martin Luther King Jr. sense of self-transcendence, a way of living that engages humanity's greatness: "Everybody can be great because everybody can serve. . . . You only need a heart full of grace, a soul generated by love, and you can be that servant."[72]

People who are lovely, as well as communities that are lovely, have their own inherent fortitude. They form a pattern of servant leadership whose designs reveal the art of emotional discernment and intellectual discipline at the center of spiritual love. In so doing, they call each of us toward vital responses to human suffering. Such responses are grounded in wisdom regarding human conflict, maturity in the face of oppression, and real answers—familial, societal, and global—that rise from the crucible of potential that is our humanity.

One of the most striking people I know, intellectually, in her convictions, and in her physical way with the world, is an African American woman named Sharon Canda. For years she taught young people physical education. She is a woman of brilliance and ready engagement with the world. I've often wondered, as people of shared humanity, how do we overcome the great atrocities we've suffered? Her life speaks an answer that rings like a trumpet of justice.

Consider the horrors and terrors faced by the millions who died terrible deaths during the North American slave trade. Consider the unmitigated suffering of those who were oppressed day and night in a common fight for freedom from slavery, here on American soil. And now consider the generations of children who have arisen from a long line of former slaves to become leaders of this country, a powerful and undergirding force of wisdom, perseverance, and love in the face of a history replete with violation suffered at the hands of those who not only enslaved them, but often sought to systematically destroy them. Finally, consider Sharon Canda, a woman who speaks with such gravity and compassion that just to be in her presence is to be given the gift of life. A woman who as a child was ridiculed and shamed, given repeated beatings by her peers, and raped by a local shop owner, Sharon rose to become a healer of our society. Listen to her words:

> I was mad at God because he made me black, poor, and female—three things that our society hated and ridiculed. I grew up believing I had no worth, believing I'd never amount to anything, believing I was lower than dirt, and also believing I deserved ill treatment.
>
> But as a child I was very "aware" of things. I sensed them. I felt them. I saw them. I knew there was an ultimate good, I didn't know the good as God at that time, but I had hopes and desires of this good. The evil I sensed, the entitlement, the inferiority, the dominance, the tyrannical raping of the innocent and weak—it seeped into my pores and choked the life and creativity out of me. And yet, I just kept going forward.
>
> Forgiveness is the way out of self damnation: to ask forgiveness and to grant forgiveness . . . These things change you—and if forgiveness is the way out of self-damnation, then redemption keeps one from crawling back in. I have been

as a wanderer on the face of this earth, looking for truth and goodness. I have learned to allow others to love me and have learned to love in return; herein is the tension and the balance. My family's investment in me is priceless, for without that how could I know where I've come from or to whom I am connected?

My mother and father were born in Vicksburg, Mississippi in the mid to late 1930s. I was born in Vicksburg, Mississippi in 1957. We moved from there in 1958. Did you know that black families were frequently hung from the Mississippi bridge?

My students have been the best teachers of true worth and integrity. Their love and acceptance is simple. Their purity of heart allowed me rest, healing, and courage.

I've been counted out. I've been made fun of, beaten up, and raped. I've been thought of as a loser.

But one day, the Lord spoke these words into my heart:

"You are a thoroughbred."

William Wilberforce is an excellent example of honor. From him, I've learned the importance of standing one's ground; to never concede that which is good and right. Ironically, while Wilberforce fought to abolish the slave trade in Great Britain in the late 18th and early 19th centuries, Roger B. Taney, the United States chief justice, proclaimed that blacks were an inferior race and not worthy to be counted as citizens.

Who stood up for me? Who will stand up for the children and people everywhere who suffer? No longer do I count myself as insignificant. We all have an important role to play in this life, for oppression is the bully who hits you and dares you to get up. Within my heart is recorded every single injury and insult. Also within my heart is the audacity to get up and keep on moving. I see it more clearly now through Paulo Freire's lenses. He would say, yes you've been oppressed and it is through you that your oppressors will be taught. He would tell me that freedom is mine only if and when I take the initiative to teach, love, and lead with integrity; as I recall Freire's mandate, my heart leaps within me.

If I choose to hate and persecute others, Freire would tell me that I've ceased to be a worthy guide and have instead become an oppressor. Oppressors cannot liberate others because the sheer nature of an oppressor is to deny and destroy the rights of others. It is not difficult to hate and blame others, the more difficult thing is to humble oneself, find out what is the right thing to do and go do it with reckless abandon. I don't need permission to help; the fact that I'm breathing is my light and right upon this path.

I have embraced the mystery of forgiveness; it is something Christ has been telling me all along—it is a choice. I stand in excellent company with those who have understood ridicule, poverty, and loneliness. Their courage and sacrifice is my badge of honor. Their persistence leads me along narrow paths. I see the devastation. I hear the torment of the soul, for it once was mine. But now simplicity, forgiveness, and love guide my steps.[73]

In dialogues with people like Sharon Canda the reality of love and power shows itself not only in personal life, but also in business, politics, the arts, philosophy, theology, and all forms of human endeavor. From a true sense of love, an underlying and very potent will emerges and points toward restorative justice. Historically, economics, race, and gender, as well as sexual and religious preference, have often conferred on a select few in society an undue amount of power. We see this both in the slavery policies in early America and in the Native American genocide. Atrocities as severe and grievous as the Nazi crimes against humanity are harbored in U.S. history as well.

Consider the Ku Klux Klan, the lynch mobs, individuals and groups who hanged, tortured, and killed African Americans in the dark, yet went to church on Sunday in the light. Consider the Sand Creek Massacre, barely more than a hundred years past, in which U.S. Cavalry troops killed Cheyenne women and children, disgracing and mutilating their bodies. Consider a more present echo: the My Lai Massacre perpetrated by the U.S. military in Vietnam. Today, the shadow of atrocity extends in generally more subtle but still pernicious forms of economic, race, gender, sexual, and religious oppression. Consider the international sex slave trade, victimizing millions even now. Command-and-control leadership is another remnant of a profound ignorance latent in the culture: the idea that in conflict (or even during peace) we consciously or unconsciously establish our own view by dominating or violating the humanity of another. Peggy McIntosh's work on unveiling white privilege and bell hooks's clarity on patriarchal white supremacist societies orient us toward thought in critical theory, and Paulo Freire's critical pedagogy, education that frees others from oppression, moves us to greater perception and truer living.[74]

Servant leaders are attuned to the individual and collective paradox of liberty and responsibility. Servant leaders step forward and lead. Greenleaf, again working in a counterintuitive vein, helped show us that the enemy is "not evil people. Not stupid people. Not apathetic people. Not the 'system.' Not the protesters, the disrupters, the revolutionaries, the reactionaries. . . . *In short, the enemy is strong natural servants who have the potential to lead but do not lead, or who choose to follow a non-servant.*"[75]

Some time ago in the Philippines I was given the opportunity to do collaborative work with Filipino leaders on servant leadership and nation building. A groundswell of care was imparted to me and my family from my Filipino colleagues and their families. The tenacious resolve that shines throughout the Filipino culture won me over: from the Spanish execution of José Rizal, which led to the Philippine Revolution of 1898, to the atrocities Filipinos faced at the hands of Americans, to the brutality endured by Filipino and

American troops together in the Bataan Death March of World War II, all the way to more recent history and the assassination of Ninoy Aquino under the Marcos regime. Ninoy's death became the seed for a nonviolent revolution that was globally evocative, unseating the despot Marcos and leading to the democratic election of Ninoy's wife, Corazon Aquino, as president. Just as South African leaders would do some years later, those in positions of power in government made a bold move. Corazon Aquino and her cabinet wrote love, yes *love*, directly into their new national constitution. Corazon Aquino and her own "beloved community" preceded and heralded an inspired *zeitgeist* of nonviolent revolutions the world over: the Velvet Revolution in Czechoslovakia, the fall of communism, the forgiveness-based revolution in South Africa. Because of love, Corazon's husband made the ultimate sacrifice. He chose to live and die for his people.

Because of love, Corazon Aquino chose to lead her nation with dignity and honor.

When she died, her people remembered her legacy with an outpouring of compassion, reverence, gratitude, and song. Like Emerson's call, and like the example of Corazon Aquino, the servant leader aspires to a lovely way of life, one that inspires the dreaming of great dreams, even when such dreams are confronted by seemingly insurmountable losses. In the midst of such losses, the life of the servant as leader is true.

The life of the servant leader is lovely.

Emerson's discernment draws near to the heart of the world as if to whisper, do not be afraid: true people are lovely.

Chapter 7

Sand Creek

Now, after the reality of love, it is critical to turn and face the evil so insidious in the human heart.

As a boy living on the Northern Cheyenne reservation in Montana, I was greatly influenced by my friends—Lafe Haugen especially, as well as Russell Tall White Man and Blake Walks Nice. Being Cheyenne, and being themselves, they lived with a real strength of heart, a dignity tied to a deeper, more enduring collective dignity. Most of America forgets the kind of violence that attended westward expansion and the credo of Manifest Destiny. Such violence against the lives of others, a self-absorbed and self-insulated leadership in the name of "progress," often decries the dominant culture's frail and failing sense of humanity. When we are unaware of our own personal and collective cultural identity, we continue to perpetuate unconscious and conscious hatred for those who appear different from ourselves. Currently in the dominant culture, white privilege remains the norm. To address the inequity, Greenleaf, known for his maverick approach to social problems, called for white people to voluntarily give up their leadership positions and make room for new leadership. This idea, radical, even iconoclastic, might be considered ridiculous but for the fact that Greenleaf did the very thing he called others to do. As a leader at AT&T, after having significantly transformed AT&T's ethnic diversity, he stepped down from an executive position and left the corporation to further devote himself to community and the work of serving humanity.

For our oppression of others in the past, and now in the present, it is good to humbly seek forgiveness. It is good to make amends. To do so, we need an understanding of how we harm others and how we evoke in them the desire for violent recompense. The following historical account illustrates an attempt to more directly encounter one of the major massacres by U.S. military on the Cheyenne nation in the late 1800s. The narrative is true to known facts about the massacre, facts retrieved from governmental records of the event, from Dee Brown's classic work *Bury My Heart at Wounded Knee*, and from Cheyenne chronicler of oral tradition, John Stands in Timber.[76]

Denial is the dark side of the privileged position, a position that unconsciously or consciously seeks to annihilate the dignity of the other. In the following example, the response from the Cheyenne people, a proud nation who had been grievously harmed, was natural: revenge.

BLACK KETTLE'S DREAM

Black Kettle, chief of six hundred Cheyenne, led his people following buffalo along the Arkansas River of Kansas and Colorado. They passed through the scablands of the north, rock outcroppings and veins of sage, swells of sparse grass that led to coulees where a few scraggly cottonwoods remained even in the dry dirt. The trees looked barely alive, waiting on storms and flash rivers, roots like slender fingers seeking water in the deep underground, and Black Kettle moved from there and brought the Cheyenne to Big Sandy Creek in the Colorado territory. Though they had no signed treaty, he and his people relied on good will, camping near the white man's fort, Fort Lyon, making peace, accepting sanctuary.

In the West, John Chivington, his family having immigrated to America two generations before, raised the Third Colorado Cavalry with a rough-hewn force, a hodge podge militia mixed equally of drunkenness and the wish to kill. Chivington led a force of seven hundred men into Fort Lyon and gave notice of his battle plan against the nearby Cheyenne encampment. Although he was informed that the Cheyenne under Black Kettle had already surrendered, Chivington left the garrison, directing his men to pursue Indian extinction.

Black Kettle lay in his lodge on a bed of sagebrush covered with robes, warmth of his wife like a bird in the palm, and he remembered in former days how the band asked to be brought as blood into the white man's family; he was a young soldier chief then, and listening to the head chief he'd thought the request very wise: the chief asked the white chiefs for one thousand white women given as brides to the Cheyenne, to unite the Cheyenne with the white man.

Lying still, seeing night overhead through the tipi opening, Black Kettle remembered capturing eagles as a young warrior to gather emblem-feathers for the peace chiefs. I am an old chief myself, thought Black Kettle, and he remembered how with singular hatred the white man had said no to the Cheyenne request for white wives.

He whispered to his sleeping wife, "An eagle can take in nearly the whole world with his eyes and know it as clearly as a man looks at the ground by his feet." In this way Black Kettle saw the heart of the white man, and saw it was dark. Still he hoped in the good of all men, for an end of fighting and a beginning of new days.

Black Kettle's camp meandered along the Big Sandy, 120 lodges, people of skeletal hunger, sunken eyes, and burnished skin, near dead, he thought. For them he held tenacious hope, and great despair, because everything seemed now to be made of starvation and war. In the darkness he rose and walked among the sleeping lodges. He passed the lodges of Elk Society Headsman Standing in Water, Kit Fox Headsman Two Thighs, and Yellow Shield, leader of the Bowstrings. He passed the lodges of chiefs Yellow Wolf, Warbonnet, Sand Hill, Bear Tongue, Little Robe, Bear Man, Blacktail Eagle, Spotted Crow, Bear Robe, White Antelope, and One Eye. A strong village once, but now with so much hunger Black Kettle's sorrow was heavy. He had fought wars with the white man, Fremont's Orchard, and Cedar Canyon, and Buffalo Springs, where the soldiers killed Chief Starving Bear. He had made raids along the overland routes and killed the Hungates at Box Elder Creek and killed Marshall Kelly and captured his white woman Laura near Little Blue River. But the white man only increased in number and took more Cheyenne lives. Black Kettle walked the full length of the village along the north side of Sand Creek and heard the sound of the river, and no one rose to greet him and he was glad of it. He sang his chief's song, for he would do a good thing and he decided he would do this thing tomorrow: he'd take the people all the way into the white fort and make peace so they might receive food and not starve.

Today was not the same as former times. It wasn't like when Wolf Tooth and the Cheyenne made peace with the Ute. Then they just came together, and each man chose a friend on the other side and gave him gifts, clothing, and moccasins, and a horse or two. Wolf Tooth had gained a Kiowa friend the same way, who gave him a good horse and some beautiful clothes, and those different moccasins the Kiowa wore with leather soles all in one piece and fringes on the heel and on top. Wolf Tooth gave the Kiowa man all his best clothes in return, and an excellent war horse he hated to give up, but he was happy to have a friend in the tribe they used to fight. The whites were different. They gave as a group, clothing and calico and flour and sugar and coffee. One time they butchered a hundred head of cattle by a river, but the white men let the meat set too long and the Cheyenne never touched those carcasses and just let them rot. The meat tasted funny and sweet and they wouldn't eat it.

At the end of camp Black Kettle stood watching the river for a great while. In a meadow across the water he saw One Eye's black-white paint standing, a horse strong and fast, staring back at him. Black Kettle returned to his lodge and lay down and drew his wife near again, and held her as she slept and he waited for sleep.

Deep and dark the dream. Darker the waiting day.

CHIVINGTON'S TREACHERY

Black Kettle raised an American flag and a white flag of peace over his tipi.

Chivington raised a hand to quiet his men.

He sat astride a big-haunched pale horse on hardscrabble dirt under a gray predawn sky. He was a man of thick face and eyes, small ingrown beard and wide nose, overly fat and pink-skinned like his father, far son of those unknown to him. Chivington positioned his men, along with their four howitzers, around the Cheyenne village of Black Kettle.

"Remember boys, big and little, nits grow up to make lice. Kill them *all.*"

Children were child-wealth to the Cheyenne, but to Chivington, a former clergyman, the children were vermin and less than dogs, worthy only to die, and worth less than his words of dispatch, and barely worthy, he thought, of the time it took to kill them.

Scream of gunfire in the waking hour. Shouts of warriors and wails of women, children waking and running in the pale half-dark over the surface of the water, the far side of the river a small barrier between the charge of the white man on foot and horseback, bloodlust over the ill-prepared, small band of warriors putting up return fire of bow and arrow and some few guns, making time for Black Kettle to move with those he could and follow the children through the water to the other side, and take the far bank, seeking cover.

Behind Black Kettle the sleeping woke to bullet fire and white men walking like darkness painted pale, the point of knife and hatchet blade and butt of axe, bayonet and big guns in smoking towers rolled on wheels, spitting fire down on the body of the Cheyenne, herds of guns issuing malice and burning lead through flesh and bone.

Below him in the riverbed, Black Kettle's wife fell, shot multiple times in the back, and he thought her dead, and fell silent, watching. He saw the white interpreter emerge from his lodge near the southern point of camp, hands raised, waving his arms, pleading. The white men pushed him aside and walked over him and Black Kettle thought how like a windblown young tree the man looked, bent to the ground, arms white, leaning off to one side. He saw the hands of the attackers in hard circles in the air as they struck children and killed them, shot old men and kneeled in fierce strokes over women, the white men with vigorous knife-work, sawing roughly, desecrating the dead.

Black Kettle turned and faced uphill and shouted, "Fly! Keep alive! We gather after nightfall."

Chivington rode engulfed by those well-armed and drunk on liquor and blood, rushing down on those who asked for restraint but who garnered only his measure of hate, his method borne of the small heart, unfit and rabid. He wanted victory, no prisoners, and the cannons and rifles pounded the Cheyenne, and as the tribe scattered in panic most were hunted down and shot; the soldiers charging, killing all that moved. The group of Cheyenne warriors holding the river ran over the water and up the hillside, following the few who escaped. Near the far bank a single dead tree, white as bone and nearly limbless, stood in stark contrast to the dark of the water. A lantern moon, full and grainy in the early dark, filled the land with opaque light and winds sent a flock of black swifts swerving so that they banked upward along the river and fell away, reckless with speed.

Still dark. Light-burn on the edge of the world. Into dawn's light Chivington cantered, and dust rose from the ground and bullet fire banged like hard rain around him. He led the men forward with their howitzers, up the river bed to kill those who tried to escape. The remaining Cheyenne, mostly the old and the weak, the elders, the women and children, dug small trenches in the ground, sand pits in which to conceal themselves and use what meager weapons they'd taken hurriedly from camp to counter the onslaught.

Chivington pressed forward with his howitzers and laid suppressing gunfire, and blew them from their moorings. Seven hours all told and when everything grew quiet he stopped and held up his arm, and again his men halted. He dismounted and took them on a tour of the dead over which he held himself and jerked each head taut, woman, child, man, and carved away their hair and opened their deerskin clothes and set his hand on their genitals and scalped women's pubic hair and carved away breasts and took the genital skin of boy and man to use and sell, coin pouches for the privileged, fine place, he thought, to carry what economy a man might have. He'd share with those Denverites he knew would turn a gleeful smile. The men followed him, spitting epithets, gathering what they willed as they ran with curved backs and took as he took and carved as he carved, pocketing grotesque treasures and laughing aloud and choking on laughter, busy building frenzy to nightfall as they gathered and built their fires, their conflagrations licking like tongues, phosphorescent orange and red in the hovering dark.

Outside on the long night the remnant of the Cheyenne smoldered on the plain, largely alone, and still. Finally, they rose and moved and found one another, children of the day who bore silently the massacre that turned women to warriors and made every Cheyenne man pledge his life to kill the white man.

See one woman. Black Kettle's wife. Shot nine times. Left for dead, she survived and joined others, many who were also wounded, and sought refuge in the camp of the Cheyenne Dog Soldiers at Smoky Hill River. It was not for nothing she was called Woman Hereafter. The rest who survived also joined the Dog Soldiers, and Black Kettle came leading them and lay down with his wife again in the healing lodge.

See the old men of the Cheyenne over their fires whispering the old words:

A nation is not conquered
until the hearts of its women are on the ground.
Then it is finished,
no matter how brave its warriors
or how strong their weapons.

Into the dark Chief Leg-in-the-Water said, "What do we want to live for? The white man has taken our country, killed all of our game; was not satisfied with that, but killed our wives and children."

"Now no peace."

"We want to go and meet our families in the spirit land. We loved the whites until we found out they lied to us, and robbed us of what we had."

"We have raised the battle axe until death."[77]

See the women wail. See the quick speed of the Cheyenne warriors, an arrow to the heart of the white man.

THE SUICIDE WARRIORS

In an avenging wildfire the Cheyenne gathered and healed their wounds and rose with vindicated eyes to find and kill white people, and little more than a decade after Sand Creek they entered the battle of the Little Bighorn in southeast Montana territory, where they took the gold-headed leader of the white men, called Custer, and kissed the earth with his blood.

This they did in a most unassuming and subtle way; the lowest and weakest among them gave their lives for the people.

Of the Cheyenne, four men. Men of varied age—some young, some old, the poorest ones, having no guns, only bow and arrow, club and hatchet, having little and having as yet won little honor. The four made a vow to the people.

"In our next engagement with the white man, we fight until we die."

Whirlwind, son of Black Crane. Noisy Walking, son of White Bull or Ice. Cut Belly. Closed Hand. The suicide boys of the Cheyenne.

The Dying Dance was prepared, and when the men entered the circle the people cheered them, celebrating their bravery. The men danced all night, the reckless way, painted of white and dark, dancing until morning, when they emerged and went out through a camp of eight thousand Cheyenne, Sioux, and Arapaho, spread four miles along the river.

When they walked, the old men went on either side of them and the criers called out in a loud voice: "Look at these men for the last time they will be alive; they have thrown their lives away."

The four joined suicide warriors from the Sioux and together they went with the war party to the field of war. Strategically, they were last to enter the fight, diving on horseback into the enemy's final position, flying as the spearpoint, piercing the enemy, dying at gunpoint, the larger mass of warriors flowing in behind, killing Custer, routing his white soldiers, killing them all.

Sitting Bull and Crazy Horse and the combined forces of the Cheyenne, the Lakota Sioux, and the Arapaho orchestrated an advance that left Custer and his two hundred men dead in less than an hour. A battle of two fronts, one on either side of a winding ridge, the warriors ran the distance between and decimated their enemies.

Over two valleys of dead men, blue sky.

CHIVINGTON, AFTER THE SAND CREEK MASSACRE

"Hey John," shouted a man from the balcony, "where'd you get them scalps?"

Chivington mounted the stage at the Apollo Theater in Denver.

"Ladies and gentlemen," he bellowed, big-bodied, feet stamped in a wide stance. In each hand he bore flagpoles. He loved the American flag under the lights, the knot of fifty scalps tied to the tip of each pole, pubic scalps of Cheyenne women topping the mass. He pounded the poles against the stage, the bang like a gunshot, and the people jumped and hooted.

After news of the massacre had reached his superiors, John Chivington was dismissed from service to his country.

After years of mistreatment by the whites, still Black Kettle sought peace.

Back at the Apollo. "Though our government did not see fit to reward my accomplishments, I accomplished much. What you see here is the toil of a single day!" On a low table set on the floor in front of the audience he displayed the body parts he'd gathered at Sand Creek, some few hands and feet, human fetuses, adult genitalia.

"See here!" he yelled.

"Tell us, John!" cried a fat woman in the front row.

"Gladly," he said, placing the flagpoles in their dark wood bases. He could hold a crowd. "Just the facts," he said, "I call Indian children nits, you know. Now nits make lice, so I figure we better kill 'em all so as to ward off infestation."

The applause was deafening.

When the sound died a large man yelled out, "What about those men of yours, they did some clean work, didn't they?"

"Sure did," he answered. "Carved things up right."

"How'd they do it, John?"

"Just like you think," he said. "Sat right down on the bodies after we killed 'em, took out the broadknife and cut off the parts. Brought 'em to town for braggin' rights. See for yourself." He drew his own broadknife and brandished it over the table before him, turning the knife and his head slowly side to side, staring at the faces in the crowd as they whistled and cat-called. Sweat ran from his temples, his big head felt red and hot, and he shouted, "Now, listen here!" He moved the knife quick near his neck in a gesture of throat-cutting, and the people grew quiet.

He held still and when there was total silence, he said what he wanted:

"Today I declare my unequivocal desire to run for governor of Coloradah!"

Clapping wildly, the people stood and hollered their approval.

John Chivington had talked for God and led men, he'd conquered armies and death, but he'd never before felt the surge he felt as the crowd lifted its voice, shouting full-throated just for him.

Chapter 8

The House of Light

Light shines in the darkness, and the darkness cannot overcome the light.

–John 1

There exists a fork in the road of leadership, one path leading toward Chivington, the other toward Black Kettle. The intonations of that which calls in one direction or the other are subtle and require deep listening. Hatred is a continuum, as are the acts of hatred. Recognizing our own individual culpability requires awareness, as well as the personal and collective work of good will that follows raised awareness.

When night falls darkness comes, but in the morning when dawn is full light fills the world. In the literature of humanity light is vision, clarity, and hope—the long-awaited answer to the cry heard in darkness. Servant leadership is such a light, profound, noted for its dignity, and shining on the edge of a broad landscape, drawing the people of the world to a more full experience of what it means to be with one another. The human spirit, in its hope for interior depth, lasting community with others, and ascension toward the good, is the place from which significant societal change emerges. Yet understanding of the human spirit remains elusive, a pearl of great price that is often out of reach and has become increasingly difficult to find in the attitudes, behaviors, and influence that accompany the contemporary leader.

When a person is hidden, that person's leadership is also hidden, and he or she tends to use hidden measures such as dominance, manipulation, and fear. Such measures can be very effective, at times achieving concrete results, but they keep those who are led in darkness, subservient, and oppressed. Servant leaders become students of the areas of their own life they try to hide, working to bring these areas to light. They recognize the ways their leadership oppresses those they serve. They seek to replace oppression with wholeness, forgiveness, and reconciliation.

Robert Greenleaf, in his view of the interior of the person, returned the human spirit to a place of longing, an appropriate and refreshing longing that can result in a deep-seated sense of calling toward one another. From such a calling the freedom to dream great dreams comes to the fore, as well as the will to see such dreams through to their completion. Until recent times it was difficult to envision anything but violence, atrocity, and death in conflict-ridden Northern Ireland and apartheid-locked South Africa. Now, Nelson Mandela and Desmond Tutu in South Africa have led the world to new ground, a ground fertile with the soil of forgiveness and tilled with a desire for truth and restoration. In Northern Ireland the work not only of the Irish and British prime ministers, but also of people such as Catholic archbishop Cahal B. Daly and Protestant minister David Hamilton, resulted in very important inroads. On a national scale the peace process is made possible by the acts of public leaders, as well as countless relatively unknown people. In so doing, such people have pointed us to discernment hard-won in the midst of chaos and human evil. These people are the modern-day expression of a long line of visionaries, people with foresight, able to hear the voice of others, and capable of leading in such a way that others are given greater light, greater life. Gandhi and Martin Luther King Jr. in recent social history are the forerunners of today's leaders who live and work reflecting servant leadership principles. Greenleaf's own words, elegant and discerning, are a clear statement of the responsiveness that accompanies remarkable leadership:

> I am hopeful for these times, despite the tension and conflict, because more natural servants are trying to see clearly the world as it is and are listening carefully to prophetic voices that are speaking *now*. They are challenging the pervasive injustice with greater force and they are taking sharper issue with the wide disparity between the quality of society they know is reasonable and possible with available resources, and, on the other hand, the actual performance of the whole range of institutions that exist to serve society.
>
> A fresh look is being taken at the issues of power and authority, and people are beginning to learn, however haltingly, to relate to one another in less coercive and more creatively supporting ways. A new moral principle is emerging which holds that the only authority deserving one's allegiance is that which is freely and knowingly granted by the led to the leader in response to, and in proportion to, the clearly evident servant stature of the leader. Those who choose to follow this principle will not casually accept the authority of existing institutions. *Rather, they will freely respond only to individuals who are chosen as leaders because they are proven and trusted as servants.* To the extent that this

principle prevails in the future, the only truly viable institutions will be those that are predominantly servant-led.[78]

Again, in an important echo of Greenleaf's premise, the present viability of South Africa can be credited to the servant leadership of people like Mandela and Tutu. By their exquisite personhood they elicited an unremitting love in the people of South Africa. Perhaps it was due to this vast love, between Mandela, Tutu, and the people, that the people responded when these two leaders asked the country to make a forgiveness response, not a retribution response, over the atrocities committed during apartheid. Mandela himself, upon being granted freedom after nearly three decades in prison, forgave everyone, from his own jailers to the original prosecutor who had unjustly imprisoned him. Though South Africa, like any country, faces a difficult future, the response of the people, a response characterized by fullness, inimitable grace, and love, continues to revitalize the world political scene. At present, South Africa remains one of the only governments in history to escape widespread political violence in the aftermath of a former violently oppressive regime.

Servant leaders form the foundation of a free society, from the individual serving within the family community to the leaders of nations. In fact, it is especially those not in formal leadership positions who herald the coming of a more humane response to human evil. Such individuals are the bedrock of humanity, and in their presence we are given greater insight into others and ourselves. Because of their giftedness the interior of the leader is no longer cloaked in hiddenness and fear, and we walk in a different light, the light of purpose and meaning.

SERVANT LEADERSHIP AND THE INTERIOR OF THE LEADER

The discipline involved in growing the interior of the self creates a complex, often unwieldy mystery for all who aspire to lead. Greenleaf's reversal of this aspiration forms a first step for many in the pursuit of a more compassionate and appropriately powerful interior. For Greenleaf, the true leader aspires first to serve, and this simple revolutionary thought has unseated the entire historical foundation of most leadership traditions. The person who has lived and grown up under the command-and-control mentality finds it very difficult to turn the self toward servanthood. Even so, the underlying premise of servant leadership becomes readily apparent whenever and wherever it appears. The essence of servant leadership, shown in the wonderfully subtle interactions between people, often takes us unaware, heals us, and draws us to a better sense of ourselves.

When I was a young boy, my mother's own manner of living was invaluable in helping me understand the heart of the servant leader. A series of events arose that would change the course of our family indefinitely. The following passage reflects some of the uncertainties and closely held desires that accompany family life, and that become so crucial in later years when the opportunity to embrace servant leadership presents itself more fully. Despite the initial intensity of the crucible that came to our family, a graceful outcome brought about unforeseen nuances of hope.

I was nine years old. My brother, Kral, was eleven. We were in our parents' bedroom, a place we walked through quietly so as not to disturb anything. A mirror plate trimmed in silver lay flat on the dark wood bureau, holding Mom's rings and lead crystal vials of perfume. We sat on the end of the bed, our feet hanging toward the floor. The bedspread was military sharp, pillows encased and tucked with a feminine hand. I think it was the femininity of it, the absence of the masculine, that surprised and hushed us, because even then we considered the great power Dad had over her, and I think we felt palpably the façade of this room, the fear that held her here, her sanctuary in the evenings and into the night when he manned the living room watching TV, or when his presence downtown with alcohol and whatever he did when he was gone became a silence in the home that was physical. I imagine her mind ran circles while she lay off to one side in the bed under the tight curve of clean sheets; she would have heard the sound of Kral and me breathing, sleeping down the hall. At night, we had heard her weep so many times it seemed uncountable.

We sat there, me and my older brother, in the silent feel of that place, at the edge of the bed. We had never met in our mother and father's bedroom. We met here today. Our father had never cried in our presence. He would cry today.

My father is a big man, six foot four inches tall, and over two hundred pounds. I remember how he held his hands together, then pushed them against his forehead.

"Your mother and I are getting a divorce," he said.

He looked away. He pressed his hands together. He was standing above us.

"We can't seem to work it out. We're getting a divorce."

He stared at us and cried.

"Well?" he said, still looking at us.

Mom looked to us also, into our faces. She was crying too.

Kral said nothing.

I had no idea what Dad was saying.

"What does this mean?" I said finally. It was decades ago in small-town Montana, I was in fourth grade, and at the time I didn't know a single friend whose parents were divorced. I don't think I understood the word.

"I'll be seeing you guys less," Dad said. "I'll be moving out."

I didn't say anything. Kral had his head down. Mom was quiet. The meeting ended.

This was the arrangement: Dad came home every other Tuesday night for an hour or two. On one such night when he was ten minutes in the door my mom kicked him back out, cursing at him. I remember how his head and hands hung slack as he walked and how her fists pounded dents in his green down-filled jacket. She herded him over the front steps, along the front walk and down the driveway. With our knees on the couch and our bodies leaned up the back of it, Kral and I watched from the front window. My arms were folded tight over my chest. I touched my nose to the glass and I saw Mom's face was red and I heard her yelling at him.

"Stay away from my kids!" she said, and followed it with louder, sharper language. The words were hard, four-lettered words, ugly and new from her mouth, difficult to listen to.

Kral put his arm around me. He grabbed my hand and took me to the kitchen. Mom returned, gathered me and Kral in her arms in the kitchen, and sobbed. I had never heard my mother cuss, and she'd never been physical. She'd also never gotten her husband, directly, to do what she asked.

Dad continued to see us every other Tuesday night. Mom didn't attack him anymore. Dad took us to basketball games again. He was a teacher and the head coach at Plenty Coups now, thirty-five miles south of Billings on the Crow reservation. He introduced Kral and me to his girlfriend. She was much younger than he was. She worked with my father. The games were at the Shrine Gymnasium, a small hot box in the middle of Billings with the thick smell of people and popcorn and the blond lacquer of hardwood. The young athletes flew like birds, my father's boys—Marty Roundface and Max Spotted Bear, Tim Falls Down and Dana Goes Ahead—and they often won.

At home around the oval oak table in the kitchen, my mother sat with dead eyes and her hands folded in front of her.

"Is she prettier than me?" she asked.

Kral and I raced to answer first.

"No, Mom."

"Never."

"Not even close."

The darkness and the pain of this time were not the end. Significantly, it actually became an astonishing beginning. Yes, they had divorced when I was nine, but after a year of divorce and through some very bold personal choices they turned back toward each other, and toward a meaningful understanding of God, and they remarried one another. My mother had led the way, offering my father forgiveness for the deep wrongs he had done to her. Her courage opened the door for his new lifestyle, his overcoming of alcoholism and his decision to stop seeing other women and return to her, to the family. They remarried one another and formed a new marriage, over thirty years strong now, and I had always been so proud of this accomplishment, so moved by their years of hard work. They remarried when I was ten years old, and I felt my mother and father had become for me the cornerstone of a new way of being.

My mother taught me the elegance of a forgiving life.

My father, too, taught me about inner resilience, but in a different fashion. Early on, my experience of him was often one of distance and anger. When it came to issues of leadership, command and control was the typical style. In my recollection he rarely expressed love verbally or physically. He often shamed my mother, and he lived a life that was self-fortified, wary of the influence of others, and highly defended. Then he changed. The first big change was his desire to return to the family after he and my mother divorced. This was a brave and beautiful choice on his part, one that succeeded in reuniting our family and restoring much of our love for him. The second change came when my wife entered our family. She carried with her a vibrant, outgoing, and very expressive form of love. She said "I love you" often, she hugged everyone, she admitted her own faults, she was humble and open regarding the faults of others, and she drew out much of the love that was latent in my father. He gave himself to this influence, and within a few years he had become more expressive, more verbally and physically loving, less rigid, and less distant. He became loveable; he had begun to love well; and the light shined in the darkness and the darkness did not overcome the light.

The house of light is a symbol of the world as dawn rises on the horizon. The house of light is also a symbol of the human heart, as healing comes and makes all things new. On a given weekend some years into my marriage, Jennifer and I traveled to Montana so I could go deer hunting with my father. Deer hunting, in our family, has its own tension-filled history, so much so that in our teens and early adulthood my brother and I refused to go hunting with my father, though my father was an avid outdoorsman. For me, hunting with my father coincided with loud tones, being dominated or discounted, and made to go along with a relationship in which I felt demeaned.

Now, because of my father's changes and the work we've done as a family, being outdoors together, hunting or fishing, is something we cherish. When Jennifer and I come in the door after the seven-hour drive from Spokane, my father greets us and hugs us. He kisses me on the cheek. He kisses Jennifer on the cheek.

"Good to see you," he says. "Glad you're safe."

He pulls us in, one at a time, to a full embrace. He is a big man with a bright smile.

"I love you," he says.

That night he and Mom and Jennifer and I eat together and talk. In the early morning he sits at the side of my bed and wakes me. "Time to get up," he says. His voice is gentle. He is happy we will be together today. He has prepared everything: boots, wool socks, wool pants, gloves, my coat, my hat, our lunches. He prepares my breakfast, and as we eat together he reads something from the Bible, a line from Proverbs about how a friend loves at all times. He serves. We drive together in the early dark past the Bridger Range and through Livingston to a place outside Big Timber at the foot of the Crazy Mountains. He guides me as I shoulder the .243, taking aim. He puts his hands gently on my arms, and speaks softly to show me how to hold the rifle level. His voice reminds me to grow calm, to breathe. In the silence of the valley the shot rings out. He cleans and dresses the deer in an open field under a wide sky, and we work together, making things ready for the return home.

On the way back we stop to eat somewhere, a hamburger place in another small Montana town. As we enter the restaurant he puts his arm around me and says, "You are a great son. Thanks for being such a great son." When he says these words I am in my late thirties, and still I want to cry. He speaks words most men don't speak. I am grateful he speaks them.

Part II

Personal Consciousness, Interior Fortitude

There is nothing more truly artistic than to love people.

—Vincent van Gogh[1]

Chapter 9

Shame and Forgiveness

Servant leadership enters the crucible of human understanding and seeks to affirm the deep losses and suffering that attend every human life. Servant leaders help others find their way to love what can and must be loved. In this quest for love, the mystery of personal and collective power asserts itself. There exists in each of our encounters with others the true nature of that which desolates and that which consoles, and the attendant paradox of the sacred and the profane. When facing atrocity, understanding forgiveness and power is necessary for servant leadership to generate healing for individuals and for communities. In this place of human devastation, where light seems to wane, personal consciousness and interior fortitude are a bulwark against the gathering storm.

Darkness and shame often accompany each other, and in darkness, vision becomes obscured. We have all experienced the shame of having wronged either ourselves or others, and the painful rift that results. For some of us the rift is momentary, or at least short-lived, but for others it develops into a chasm of confusion and fear, a gaping span that seems uncrossable. The life that ends in work at the expense of intimacy . . . the life that ends in alcoholism, or cynicism . . . the hard despair that leads to suicide . . . the anger that creates a life of isolation and sorrow—people often live from shame and many die in it. Yet forgiveness, an element as vital as oxygen or water or fire, brings into being a more robust and absorbing experience of the world.

Every person has generated and sustained alienation in the self, the family, or the workplace. But not all people have experienced the abiding loveliness of being welcomed back to community after having gravely wronged others. The servant leader, familiar with the servanthood that develops life and mercy in others, is a person who seeks forgiveness for harming others and grants forgiveness to those who have done harm. Such forgiveness or compassion is given freely, not based on the willingness or remorse of the offender, but based on the higher image of humanity to which the servant leader is called. Forgiveness is not cheap; it requires a form of personal integrity that is hard-won. A certain lifestyle results, reflected in humble awareness of one's own faults and the integration of strength, hope, and grace with regard to the faults of others. Again we turn to forgiveness researcher Robert Enright, whose developmental stages help people build the capacity for forgiveness.[2] Enright posits that the highest developmental level of forgiveness is unconditional forgiveness. Preceding levels are often clouded by self-protection and the need for retribution, while unconditional forgiveness is an overarching regard for the humanity evident even in the center of human evil. Greenleaf's call toward servanthood that creates wisdom and freedom, Martin Luther King's call to love the oppressor, and Tutu's will to engender love through a forgiveness that heals our violence are potent expressions of the interior of the leader oriented toward healing.

In lives such as Greenleaf's, Martin Luther King's, and Tutu's, the intrepid core that is at the heart of servant leadership becomes very clear. The same relational fearlessness, the same love, is evident in people, small to great, who have transformed not only individuals, but nations, and the world. The work of the servant leader, whether as a government official, a laborer, a business executive, a spiritual director, a janitor, a mother, a father, or a child, points through the center of the human endeavor, into the interior, and from there out to humanity. Servant leaders worldwide contribute life-giving and heartfelt though usually unheralded service in expanding international good will and human understanding. A hallmark of servant leaders is that they heal others, and they do so through mature relationship to self, others, and God.

In the life of the servant leader, it is this maturity that helps form the backbone of organizational integrity. Of note is the fact that many of the organizations who top the list of Fortune's "100 Best Companies to Work For" are servant-led companies. These organizations base their direction and their resource allocation on servant leadership, usually with full-scale implementation of servant leadership training and development throughout the organizational structure. Many are familiar names, such as Southwest Airlines, Starbucks, the Vanguard Group, and Synovus Financial, and often we have personally experienced the excellence and care of their effort. Not surprisingly, the organizations on Fortune's list generally perform at twice the market rate of their competitors.[3]

Excellence is hand in hand with a lifestyle and a leadership ethic devoted to servant leadership. Organizations that serve society are beacons; they are change agents like Greenleaf, King, and Tutu, and they lead us to greater light. Excellence in many forms defines the servant leader, but the source resides in the interior, in discernment and relational capacity.

The fine arts provide a vessel for further illumination, for in honoring the interior, in honoring relationship and mystery, the arts undo the malaise that is often evident in the family, the workplace, and the national psyche. There is a glorious light that makes darkness cower, and it is often found in literary works of art. In the following section, a story by Victor Hugo reveals the legitimate power and greatness that form the heart of the servant leader.

HUGO ON INTERIOR WISDOM AND FREEDOM

Usually the leader who commands and controls has good intentions even while failing to see the impact of diminishment he or she is having on others. Attending to this impact, even giving others voice to articulate the ways they feel diminished in our presence, and then making a meaningful response to their desires, brings about relationships and organizations characterized by vitality and joy. But building the bridge from personal character that is hidden or cloaked, self-consumed or self-absorbed, to character that leads through serving is often an arduous journey requiring consistent outside accountability and immense personal vulnerability. In the following paraphrase of a small portion of *Les Misérables*, Victor Hugo's priest gives us a better grasp of the interior of the servant leader. The life and action of the priest eventually leave Valjean, one of the "least privileged of society," stronger and more able to be a servant leader to others.

In the south of France in the late 1700s there lived a condemned man, a man convicted when he was twenty-five for stealing a piece of bread to feed his starving sister. He was promptly sentenced to five years of prison. Near the end of the fourth year he escaped. He was caught after two days and he received three additional years for his attempt. In the sixth year he tried to escape again and failed, and was given five more years. The tenth year he tried and was caught again, and three more years were assigned. Finally, around the thirteenth year he escaped for four hours, was retaken, and three more years were tacked to his term, now nineteen years in all. At the end of his term he walked free, unable to find a single member of his family, determined to be bitter, resigning himself to hatred and cynicism. In those days a criminal was required to identify himself to the magistrate immediately upon entering a town. Word then flared to the entire town almost without a moment's passing.

After his release the man enters his first town hoping to drink his first real drink and sleep in his first warm bed in nearly twenty years. He reports his presence to the magistrate and then walks to the first pub, eager to spend a piece of the meager money he earned for his prison labor.

"Beer please," he says to the innkeeper. "I have money." And he places a rough coin on the bar in front of him.

The innkeeper smiles approvingly. "Beer it is then," he says and pours the prisoner a drink. Just then a man approaches the innkeeper from the side and with cupped hand whispers in his ear. The innkeeper draws back the drink he has poured. He empties the glass back into the beer vat. "We don't serve your kind here," he says. "You'll have to go now."

The condemned man argues for himself: "I have money. I can pay."

"We don't serve your kind," repeats the innkeeper.

"I can pay," says the condemned man.

"You will have to leave." The innkeeper does not change the stern face he wears.

The condemned man leaves embittered and tries the tavern across the street, but here the host has already heard and the man is refused entry.

The man wanders the street in search of food and a bed. He sees the open glow of a window, a home, a family dining inside. He knocks at the door. He asks if he might sleep in the stable, perhaps share in the leftovers of their food. They push their children behind them. They loathe him with their eyes, and with their voices they despise him. They ask him to leave; they too have heard.

In the early dark of evening he walks slowly and turns his face from all who pass him by. He finds a makeshift lean-to in the ill-used garden of a small hovel. I will sleep with the dogs, he tells himself, and he moves on hands and knees into the warm, dark crawlspace of the hut. But he has invaded another's comfort again; the sleeping dog awakens and bites his face. The man scrambles wildly back out into the street. I am even lower than a dog, he tells himself, and after walking at length he sets himself down on the cobbled pavement to shut his eyes, to sleep on the stones beneath his feet.

He leans his head against a wall and closes his grimaced face to wait for morning and to leave this place. But a woman's voice rouses him.

"Sir, can I help you?" She is a young nun and her face is kind.

"No," says the man. He looks angrily away from her.

"Will you sleep on the street tonight, friend?" she says.

"For nineteen years I've slept on a bed of wood, tonight it will be stone." He crosses his arms. He closes his eyes. "I am not welcome here."

"Have you knocked at every door?" says the woman.

"Yes."

"Have you knocked at that one?" The woman points.

"Which?" he asks.

"There," she says, "knock there."

The man ignores her, but after she has gone he stirs himself and trudges to the door she mentioned. He knocks and is met by a priest. The priest welcomes him and prepares a table for him with bread and wine and cheese. A bed is prepared as well. The man is dumbfounded. He sits and devours his food and tells the priest, "I am a prisoner of nineteen years, a convict, a condemned man."

The priest says, "This house is not mine, but Christ's. You are welcome here."

"I haven't hidden how despicable I am," says the man. "You don't even know my name. Yet you have treated me with kindness."

"Why would I have to know your name?" says the priest. "Besides, before you came, I knew it."

The man looks surprised: "You knew my name?"

"Yes," answers the priest. "Your name is my brother."[4]

FROM THE INTERIOR OF THE LEADER TO SERVANT-LEADING THE WORLD

Family systems writers such as Virginia Satir and Murray Bowen and relational experts such as John Gottman and Shirley Glass articulate the pain of families that promote a sense of emptiness rather than wholeness, and their work leads to a conception of the self not made of protectedness, privilege, or the abuse of power, but given to appropriate vulnerability, a sense of personal brokenness or humility, and the desire for unity and mutuality. King and Tutu epitomize servant leadership on a social and global scale, having drawn the people of their country and the world to greater freedom, autonomy, health, and wisdom. Fittingly, both men were also given the Nobel Prize for peace. The writings of Greenleaf, King, and Tutu provide a compelling view of relationships meant for dignity, mutual respect, truth regarding personal failure, and the hope of a lasting reconciliation that can emerge from grave wounds to the self and the human community.

Greenleaf, King, and Tutu have helped mend the human heart by bringing to light our motivations and uses of power. In light of generational and historical processes of authority and coercion, abuses of power result in the degradation of the weaker elements of any given system, and inherently the more powerful elements as well. White colonialism and male authoritarianism are significant examples of this cycle, with people of color, women, and children suffering the results such abuses have generated, and whites and males often reflecting a unified poverty of spirit. Like many modern organizational leaders, today's fathers tend to revoke their place of intimacy with beloved others, choosing a form of distance and isolation that is cloaked either in hyperambition or deep-set apathy. From the perspective of generational systems, those who grow up in an oppressive system tend to engender and live in oppressive systems throughout the lifespan and tend to evoke oppressive systems in the next generation. An amount of empathy is garnered for victim and victimizer from this perspective, as each person rises from a pattern of relationality that is continual and decidedly bound to the pain of the human condition. The abusive generational family, the depressed generational family, the emotionally distant generational family, the organization that degrades people, the nation that is either quick to war or blind in the presence of grave danger—all are examples of how difficult it is to recognize and overcome our own considerable weaknesses, how difficult we find it to recognize and remove our own substantial lust to use manipulation, force, or violence in the guise of leadership.

The great psychological thought-leader of the twentieth century, Carl Jung, believed that the most stubborn and obstinate of human weaknesses is our denial of our own shadow: the many ways we project blame away from ourselves onto others, the environment, or God, therefore denying our own capacity for evil.[5] Jung said we deny because to face our own evil is to look over the edge of the abyss into the nature of humanity, and find therein the capacity for absolute evil—and this look, Jung proposed, this coming face to face with such an ancient and abiding darkness, is self-shattering. Our denial keeps us mediocre, Jung declared, or worse, ignites the kind of ravenous appetite that has risen throughout history to devour the weak and the innocent and plague the human endeavor with shame.

There is a need for change, not only internationally with regard to the atrocities of humanity, but here in our own cities. Races who have oppressed others can ask forgiveness of those they have oppressed—for the massacres and violence of the past, most often perpetrated by whites against people of color, against Native Americans, African Americans, Asian Americans, and others, and for the sense of entitlement and privilege that is often subtle and insidious today. Jung affirmed that what we need in order to face our weaknesses and the ways we harm others is the timely embrace of two elements: insight and good will—in other words, a richer understanding of ourselves and others, followed by a more vitally expressed love. Even now, our nation is faced with vast economic, political, and power-based distortion. A balance in these areas, rising from a mutual endeavor, is one of the most pressing current avenues of servant leadership. People in concerted action, seeking peace and greater relational as well as economic parity, are leading the way.

Consider Robbie Paul, the Ni Mii Pu (Nez Perce) woman whose work has illumined in her family five generations of powerful servant leaders.[6] These leaders, though often quiet and largely unknown, have been a force for strength and healing of the national psyche. Paul's accounts of going with her father to the site of the Big Hole Massacre in Montana remind us of the necessity of creating a vessel for people to grieve, mourn, and heal. She and her father engaged openly and with dignity with the children of their enemies. A ceremony of reconciliation took place between descendants of Nez Perce who were massacred and descendants of the cavalry who committed the atrocity. Grace was extended and received; peace was given.

Other races, through open-hearted living, are leading whites (generally of European descent) to a place of wholeness and restoration where the roots of change are found in the servant-first mentality. Larry Spears, quoted Latina leader Juana Bordas of Mestiza Leadership International, who said, "Many women, minorities, and people of color have long traditions of servant leadership in their cultures. Servant leadership has very old roots in many of the indigenous cultures. Cultures that were holistic, cooperative, communal, intuitive, and spiritual. These cultures centered on being guardians of the future and respecting the ancestors who walked before."[7] Similarly, people of poverty have the capacity to lead people of privilege to an idea of mutuality that can revolutionize the world poverty cycle and unseat the spiritual poverty that often accompanies the world's elite. Such a stance of life rising from death, though unfamiliar in circles of authoritarian power, has resonance in the natural world; it is the dawn of spring that follows winter's night, and each time we experience it we are thankful.

In present-day Montana, with its cold winters and far-distant towns, the love of high school basketball is a time-honored tradition. Native American teams, Cheyenne and Crow, Blackfoot and Assiniboine-Sioux, have often dominated the basketball landscape, winning multiple state titles on the shoulders of modern-day warriors who are as highly skilled as they are intrepid. Basketball itself often comes like a fresh new wind to change the climate of the reservation from downtrodden to celebrational. Plenty Coups with Mark Spotted Bear and Dana Goes Ahead won a couple of state championships in the early eighties. After that, Lodge Grass, under Elvis Old Bull, won three straight championships. Jonathan Takes Enemy, whom I mentioned earlier, is also counted among the most talented Native American hoop legends. He shot deep finger rolls with either hand, his jump shot was a thing of beauty, and with his quick vertical leap he could 360 dunk, and with power. His senior year he averaged forty-one points per game in the state tournament. He and I had played basketball against each other numerous times in high school, his teams notorious and still revered by the old guard of hoops fans in the state. The competition was fiery and glorious, but then we went our separate ways. Recently we sat down again at a tournament in Billings. We didn't talk much about the past. He'd been off the Crow reservation for a number of years and was now living on the Yakima reservation in Washington. He said he felt he had to leave in order to stay sober. He'd found a good job; his focus was on his family. The way his eyes lit up when he spoke of his daughter was a clear reflection of the servant leader, someone willing to sacrifice to enrich others. His face was full of promise, and thinking of her he smiled. "She'll graduate from high school this year," he said, and it became apparent to me that the happiness he felt was greater than all the fame that came of the personal honors he had attained.

In a living metaphor for seeking the light, Jonathan Takes Enemy successfully navigated the personal terrain necessary to be present for his daughter in meaningful ways. By walking into and through the night instead of running from it, he eventually left the darkness of alcoholism behind and found light rising to greet him—he loved and served—he became a truer person.

Bowen considered the true person one capable of immense discipline in the center of human relationships, a person able to withstand his or her own desire to either attack or run, and instead able to discern and maintain health even in the face of power abuses.[8] Satir considered the true person a person of congruence, wise, imaginative, and spontaneous emotionally, physically, mentally, and spiritually.[9] This nexus of courageous living experienced by a person with strength of heart, mind, and spirit is the light Greenleaf shed in the workplace and King and Tutu on the world political scene.

With regard to faith, Greenleaf, King, and Tutu lived and worked within a line of reason, emotion, and spirit that rose at least in part from their own individual understandings of the Christian tradition. Significantly, it is imperative that we recognize that much of the blood-spilling the world over for the last two millennia has been done in the name of Christianity, again indicating that threat and perpetration are too often a way of life, even for those seeking something greater than themselves. While the ideas of Christ are of importance in the writings of Greenleaf, King, and Tutu, each man expressed a sense of honor for all people and found invasion of others in the name of religion, privilege, or any other source of power repugnant. They espouse respect for the human community in all its mature faith expressions. This balance of personal autonomy and connection to others is a vital aspect of their social leadership. Their approach articulates a just and lasting resolution of human conflict, a resolution that leads through suffering to a new, more whole sense of life. In their leadership they cherished the durable truths of all people, regardless of religious orientation: self-awareness, willingness to engage, and a sharp loathing for anything that degrades others.

In servant leadership, the balance of mercy and justice, and purpose and peace are elegantly aligned. In many of the world's religions, a unified ideal is present.[10] In Judaism, the Talmud forwards the notion that we are all responsible for one another. Christians heed the call of Christ, who stated he did not come to be served, but to serve, and indicated that the greatest one will be a servant, declaring that those who exalt themselves will be humbled, and those who humble themselves will be exalted. The *Shantiveda* of Buddhism echoes this paradox, pointing out that the one who employs others for his or her own purposes will experience servitude, and those who serve others will experience true lordliness. In the Tao, the pathway of heaven is found by being of benefit to others, not harm. The Hindu *Bhagavad Gita* champions selfless service, invoking the promise of the Creator as present in every moment of service. Islam promotes empathy, asking devotees to take on the pain and suffering of others, offering helping hands to soothe the suffering.

Again, the faith that violates others violates itself. Similarly, faith that subdues or suppresses itself loses its vitality. Like all people, people of faith tend toward the extremes, either by trying to dominate others with their particular faith, or by silencing themselves in the attempt to do no harm. The balance of living one's faith while honoring others is accomplished beautifully by Greenleaf, King, and Tutu. Their work is an expression of both their faith in God and their faith in people. I believe this comes from a personal, active knowledge of love *and* power, their misuse as well as their potential, and the fulfillment that is the result of taking significant risks on behalf of humanity. Love helps us recognize our shame without the need to run away. Shame then is healed by forgiveness, and forgiveness returns us to a right countenance in which we look up to find the sun shining on our faces.

Chapter 10

The Family, the World

All who have worked at marriage and parenting know that gaining the wisdom to create a good family requires a richly honed sense of personal integrity and sometimes involves factors that seem beyond our control. Consider, then, the even larger, less controllable environments of the organization, the nation, and the world. The individual responsibility to initiate, develop, and sustain a way of life self-sacrificial and life-generative is daunting. Inevitably, in response to the crisis of humanity engaged in each new age, those who seek answers enter a way of being in which the paradox of the tragic and the comedic overlap, where the sacred is touched by the profane and human evil is not a separate entity but found even in the heart of human good. The tension of the paradox asserts itself again. The complexity and the initial agony of this ambiguity make fertile ground for the pessimism and nihilistic tendencies of all societies.

Again, the need for discipline presents itself, but not discipline bound to rigidity or dominance. True discipline, in the sense of servant leadership, is oriented toward freedom, health, and healing. M. Scott Peck's great foresight in *The Road Less Traveled* becomes increasingly more poignant in the contemporary age: life is difficult, and therefore discipline is required.[11] Such discipline results in a deepened sense of personal consciousness and greater interior fortitude, which in turn enlivens people and nations toward forgiveness, healing, and true mutual power.

On the most basic level—the level of the individual person, everywhere present in cultures of privilege and increasing consumerism—an interior decadence inevitably comes to the fore, a cynicism evident in the center of the gendered struggle between men and women, neither believing the other capable of meaningful change, and each maintaining a fortified isolation with regard to intimacy with each other. Socially, the impact of this isolation, both in the family and in professional life, is a crisis of emptiness, loneliness, and in the end, despair. Even so, many people are leading the way to a more resilient experience of intimacy, and with the great potential for change that exists in the inner life, women and men have a crucial role to play in helping heal the family and the world. Men and women who are servant leaders inspire the unbroken promise of each new generation.

To engage well is to evoke in others a sense of their own best potential. Each aspect of this evocation points to human maturity based in mutuality, listening, and dialogue. Again, Gadamer the philosopher, Freire the educator, and bell hooks the activist draw us back to true dialogue, in which we not only give influence, but also listen and receive the influence of others. Paulo Freire, the radical servant of the people who transformed the face of the Americas, conceived of a dialogue-based deconstruction of all socially constructed oppressive systems. "Dehumanization," Freire stated, "which marks not only those whose humanity has been stolen, but also (though in a different way) those who have stolen it, is a *distortion* of the vocation of becoming more fully human."[12] Liberating ourselves, then, "will actually constitute an act of love opposing the lovelessness which lies at the heart of the oppressors' violence."[13]

Bell hooks envisioned a world in which we willingly attune ourselves to the deeper disciplines associated with such love. "Genuine love," she said, "is rarely an emotional space where needs are instantly gratified. To know love we have to invest time and commitment."[14] People who live well love well, they understand power and become artistic in conversation, and they live transparently and develop integrity in response to their own individual and communal faults—in other words, they know and they are known. They lead others, and their relationships are largely free of diminishment. Engagement is infused with a sense of the appreciative mystery of life.

Returning to Gadamer's concept of the eloquent or elegant question, we find a lucent manner of relating in which we seek to ask of one another questions to which we do not already know the answer. The eloquent question forms a pathway of listening in which we overcome attitudes and behaviors of dominance, negativity, reactivity, fear, anger, or apathy. When we live from darker, more self-absorbed philosophies we effectively force others to submit to our way of living, especially when their views conflict with ours. But when we live from more hope-filled philosophies, we approach those around us as sacred, as Thou or You, rather than It, and our conversations result in fulfillment and shared meaning.[15] Initiating and sustaining meaningful dialogue reflects a positive sense of self and other. The servant leader attends to, heals, and transcends the burden of his or her own emptiness and evokes similar transcendence in the lives of others.

Ornish, in his decisive work *Love and Survival*, argues (with convincing scientific evidence) that lack of intimacy or lack of emotional and spiritual closeness to others is the root of human illness, and the positive experience of love is the inner core of what makes us well. Accordingly, the great epidemic of the age is what Ornish calls "emotional and spiritual heart disease, the profound sense of loneliness, isolation, alienation, and depression that are so prevalent today as the social structures that used to provide us with a sense of community and connection break down."[16]

When we consider the children of the nations we consider the next generation, and the opportunity to forgo our self-insulation and sacrifice ourselves for the good of others seems almost to cry out to us, inviting us to listen and take action. The gift of knowing others, and closer still, knowing our own children, can completely renew us. Because of inspiration from writers like Ornish, but especially because of the influence of my wife and her dynamic life, in the morning I go now to each of my three young daughters and touch her face and look into her eyes and give her a blessing.[17] The words take me into a quietly enchanting encounter, and I go from the blessing better prepared to face the day, and more grateful. For Natalya, "God has given you the garment of praise instead of the spirit of despair." For Ariana, "I have loved you with an everlasting love. I have drawn you with loving kindness." For Isabella, "God knows the plans he has for you, plans not for calamity, but for peace. Plans for a future and a hope." Yet even in the echo of a morning ritual that heals me, my own frailty and lack of maturity sometimes stalk me throughout the day and rear up in my defensiveness, my will to dominate, my lack of patience, my apathy toward even my most valued relationships. Asserting itself in the daily routine of life is my greed to be served . . . my failure to serve.

Freire's idea of critical pedagogy, or education that liberates us or frees us from oppression, and the sumptuous wisdom of bell hooks, a wisdom that secures a generous humanity in the center of legitimate mutuality, form the foundation for the architecture of the mature identity.[18] This involves accepting the invitation to look at one's self, gifts and weaknesses, and draw self and others toward liberation from fear. In this sense what liberates us is love, an identification with the suffering that always precedes life or growth, and a resolved will to seek that which is necessary to make us whole. Greenleaf's notion that love is only love in the context of unlimited liability lends confidence. This love separates the chaff from our lives and brings us to our loved ones in a more vulnerable and more truly powerful sense. We can then come to a place of sanctuary with one another in which we find we are capable of living for one another rather than against each other. In this sanctuary joy accompanies us, and we begin to go about the necessary work to move beyond ourselves and willingly give ourselves to others.

A well-earned delight takes shape. Servant leaders delight in life, and in people. Servant leaders embrace paradox and the creative tension that accompanies every great dream. Their work is found at the crossroads of ingenuity and a keenly discerned sense of reality. Emerson referred to this crossroads as the *oversoul*, the place in our collective humanity reserved for transcendence, humility, wisdom, and generative capacity.[19]

> . . . that Over-soul, within which every [person's] particular being is contained and made one with all other; that common heart, of which all sincere conversation is the worship, to which all right action is submission; that overpowering reality which confutes our tricks and talents, and constrains every one to pass for what [he or she] is . . . and which evermore tends to pass into our thought and hand, and become wisdom, and virtue, and power, and beauty. We live in succession, in division, in parts, in particles. Meantime within [humanity] is the soul of the whole; the wise silence; the universal beauty, to which every part and particle is equally related; the eternal ONE.[20]

Servant leaders generate new horizons; they are creative and imaginative, patient, observant, and vigorous. The notorious complacency, toxicity, and entrenched vacancy of contemporary society are replaced with the life of the possible. In such possibility, be it in the family, the organization, or the global encounter, we freely follow those who serve, we serve them, and we find at the end of our work that we have contributed something worthy, and in so doing we rediscover the vivacity of life. The gift to our children is immeasurable, and we, like children ourselves, are blessed with the discovery.

People of enduring interior maturity help us seek life. After the deep-rooted shame experienced in remembering the Sand Creek Massacre in which Chivington's U.S. military massacred the Cheyennes under Black Kettle, it is graceful to return to the restorative care and tenderness that sometimes, against all odds, come again to be a healing presence in our lives. Just as present-day Cheyenne dignity and resilience give a precise picture of how people overcome atrocity and violation, another of the individual moments of clarity from the South African truth and reconciliation process is worthy of close attention. Amy Biehl's death, and the ensuing actions taken by her mother and father, Linda and Peter Biehl, astonished the world by revealing new depths of ultimate forgiveness and unconditional grace. Amy's life remains a touchstone of humanity the world over. Her story, interwoven with descriptions of the forgiveness between Amy's parents and the men who killed Amy, sheds light on the nature of the human capacity for love and wholeness. From the heart of the family, from two parents united by the death and life of their daughter, comes a form of servant leadership capable of healing the world.

Amy Biehl was born in 1967 in Newport Beach, California. She was valedictorian of Newport Harbor High School, attended Stanford University, graduated with honors, became a Fulbright Scholar, and went to serve at the University of the Western Cape Community Law Center in Cape Town, South Africa. In preparation for the country's first democratic election set for April 1994, she assisted in the development of voter registration programs for black South Africans. Having served with distinction, she was preparing to go back to the United States and begin graduate school at Rutgers University. On Wednesday, August 25, 1993, a week before her scheduled return, Amy drove three coworkers to their homes in Gugulethu Township, Cape Town. On this fateful drive she was tragically killed by a black mob shouting "One settler, one bullet!" Her black friends tried to save her by shouting she was a comrade, but Amy was dragged from the car and stoned and stabbed to death.

Four young men were convicted for Amy's death in 1994, and each was sentenced to eighteen years in prison. In 1997, the men applied for amnesty through South Africa's Truth and Reconciliation Commission. Amy's parents, Linda and Peter, wanted to honor Amy's belief in the truth and reconciliation process to bring about restoration and healing for those who confessed to politically motivated crimes that had occurred during the apartheid years. Not only did the Biehls not oppose these men in their application for amnesty, but they offered support and even asked the young men to link arms with them and together continue Amy's work.

The journey was filled with anguish and became a long disciplined walk toward healing and peace. The experience of these men in being forgiven by Amy's parents details the hardiness of those who forgive, and the new life of the forgiven. The family met the world with potent and far-reaching consequences.

Considering the words of these men, we see both how driven and how delicate our collective humanity can be:

At the rallies [for the black anti-apartheid forces] the slogan was taken up, "One settler, one bullet. We want our country right now, liberate." The point being that there wasn't much ammunition and so if one settler was targeted, it was necessary to use just one bullet to kill that person. . . .

The barrel of a gun took our country, so the Pan African Congress believed that our land must come back to the rightful owners with the barrel of a gun. Someone who is oppressing and exploiting people, someone who is being angry, killing everything, someone who calls himself the settler—make sure you use one bullet and you kill that person. . . .

The years of 1993 and 1994 were the years of the gun and barrel. These were the years of the killing of the [white] cops. . . . singing freedom songs and shouting slogans: "One settler, one bullet. Kill the whites . . . one settler, one bullet, hundred settlers, one grenade. . . ."

Remember the Pan African Congress was not fighting the buildings; it was fighting human beings that were oppressing us . . . the white people. So we were looking for a target, a white person. We find a truck; a government truck and we throw rocks at that truck. Behind that truck was Amy driving a Datsun, a yellow Datsun. There were lots of [us] and we hear "Settler! There's a settler!". . . . This was said in Xhosa. . . .

In the passenger seat there's a colored guy in orange; he got out and ran, leaving her alone. Then she came out of the car and ran away. So one of [us] just tripped her; they were throwing stones, beating and stomping her, so a lot of [us] just stop her with stones, chanting, "Settler! You're a settler, you take our land." Others try to turn her car to burn it, but unfortunately the police came. . . .

I was prepared to be arrested but the police were not sure that it was me. I built a small shack at the back of my mother's house so I was staying there and there were lots of pictures of my fellow comrades, soldiers, even my weapon was there. They came to me and ask what is my name? I tell them my name is Mzikhona, so that's my Xhosa name, so they say, "No, it's not you that we want." They went to arrest my brother, the older one. One of the police comes into my room and looks at a picture of the Sharpeville massacre—the massacre where [black] women, men and children get killed by the [white] police. I told the policeman that I hadn't given him permission to be in my room. We start to fight, arguing and fighting. My mother started calling me . . . that is when I start to give. I said, "Okay, you want me, get out of my room, I'll give." So I was arrested for killing Amy Biehl.

In 1997, some years into serving the prison sentence, the men applied for amnesty after being encouraged to do so by the Pan African Congress political party. Previous to this, they were determined to boycott the Truth and Reconciliation Commission, believing they would not get a fair hearing.

We don't go to the Truth and Reconciliation Commission because a perpetrator and an oppressor, sitting together . . . we are not believing in it. We said you are oppressor and I'm supposed to come and sit down with you and tell my life. I kill you because of that and that and that. You know why I kill you.

But when the men came to the truth hearings and told their story, they also learned about Amy, about who she was and why she had been in South Africa. One of the men said the truth hearings were pivotal, indicating there was a moment when he looked across the room at Linda and Peter and saw their daughter Amy through their eyes. Before that he had thought of Amy as just another white person. Yet in that moment of seeing them, he felt the "picture begin to open wide" and Amy became a real person to him—a real daughter with parents who loved her just like his parents loved him.

> I saw them [Linda and Peter Biehl] in trial—I know these white people just come to contribute to us getting a sentence of—to get hanged. So I was just waiting for that moment. I don't care at that time. So I go straight to the TRC just angry. But I go there and find out, oh my God, starting to think, asking myself questions, things can happen out of liberating . . . bad things. But I also tell myself that if there was no apartheid in our country. . . .
>
> It shocked me. I think she must have been adopted—these are not her real parents. But they said to me, no, it's her parents and they are telling you, if Amy was alive she would have supported this process, she would not have been opposed to amnesty, that's why they are not opposed. . . .
>
> When I saw Amy's parents holding up a big picture of Amy I started to realize who this girl was and I felt—I felt more guilty, but my attitude, I stood firmly; it happened, it had to happen. But I felt the pain, and I started to realize this person was on our side and we didn't know. Even if we knew on that day, it would have been difficult to spare her life. . . .
>
> I wanted to sit next to them. I wanted to hug them and to speak with them to explain what happened. I wanted that connection with them but I don't have the time. But they express Amy, who is Amy . . . they start to say that South Africans must learn how to forgive each other. . . . I said to myself, "Thank God these people want to speak with us."

The Biehls shook hands with the men in the back hall at the amnesty proceedings, but for a time no further contact came of the event. Amy's parents said, "Amy was drawn to South Africa as a student and she admired the vision of Nelson Mandela of a 'Rainbow Nation.' It is this vision of forgiveness and reconciliation we have honored." The men were set free, but life for them seemed to be full of dead ends. Two of the men who killed Amy Biehl eventually made contact again with Amy's parents.

> When [we] got back home we could see our former friends, former colleagues, were more involved in shebeens which are informal taverns. They were drinking liquor Monday to Monday. That . . . frustrated us because these people are former combatants, some are former good students and they are doing nothing

but drinking. Whatever the situation is, that's not the way to respond to this situation. . . .

We needed more training and we heard over the news and the papers about the Amy Beihl Trust Foundation. Linda and Peter had resources that we needed. They had developed a training center where we could be trained as workers . . . brick makers, and mechanics. That's when we knew we had to be brave and stand ourselves once again for the benefit of the people. . . .

Peter would meet us at our club house . . . We met him there and after listening to us he said, "Rest assured I will help." Late that night he phoned Linda in California and told her of our meeting together. She was very happy that there was some communication between us.

The two men who met with the Biehls later reported that the Biehls helped redeem their lives and helped them find again a meaningful purpose for living. The Biehls took them to dinner, invited them to their home, took them to sporting events, and included them in many day-to-day activities. They listened to the men's burdens, listened to their dreams of a better life, not just for them alone, but for all people in Gugulethu.

Linda and Peter gave [us] water bottles for hiking in the mountains. There was a written message in the bottles and it will stay forever with the bottle. It said that *life is a joy and we will help you.* The message simply meant that they were prepared to help us and that's when the friendship grew.

One of the men gave the following description of the role the Biehls played in his life.

I would not be here today if it was not for them, possibly I would be in prison again. I couldn't find work and I was frustrated. I told myself sometimes I will engage myself in armed robberies. . . . Without being aware they assisted us towards achieving a medium goal, which is taking us to our long-term goals. . . . I feel hope. Hope for this country and for the globe as well, and that gives me strength to believe and concentrate more. . . .

I've always wanted to be myself and . . . Linda and Peter Biehl were sort of a bridge. A bridge over the trauma that I, the militant, killed this lady, ended her life . . . but somehow has forgiven himself and has been forgiven for what he did and he can go on. But the problem for me was that whenever I tried to be myself, I would find it too difficult to accept that early in my life, I happened to be involved in murder. . . . Your soul is not militant, it is not a machine, it is human. Your soul feels, it feels things strongly, it remembers, and the memories, they never leave you.

Hearing this man's story of time with the Biehl family, hearing his pain as well as his wisdom, reminds us how crucial it is to recognize that the family is symbolic of the whole world. Ten years after the Truth and Reconciliation hearings, my friend and colleague Marleen Ramsey interviewed Linda Biehl and the men to whom the Biehls had given so much friendship and support. On the day of Linda's interview, when the interview was over Linda thanked Marleen for coming, and as they emerged from Linda's office at the Amy Biehl Foundation in Cape Town, Linda's secretary asked her if she could work in another appointment that afternoon. Linda told her secretary she could visit with that person before three o'clock, but not to make any appointments after that. She indicated she would be running a very important errand.

What was the nature of Linda's task?

She would be going with one of the men who ten years earlier had taken part in Amy's death.

Where were they going?

She was taking him to buy a car seat for his own young daughter.

To protect her. To keep her safe.[21]

Chapter 11

The Way of the Child

What is the most central expression of human life?

Perhaps it is the touch of a child, or the look of contentment in a child's face. When we witness the grace of a kind word, or encounter forgiveness, or loyalty, or the simple gift of another's presence, we witness the legacy we leave for our children. Birth and death attend us in a form of daily communion if we only draw back the veil and look with open eyes. Be it consolation or desolation, or the dynamic music of the living paradox they share, the contemporary world cries out with sacredness even as it reviles with profanity. Therefore, a form of personal and collective wisdom Robert Greenleaf referred to as foresight becomes paramount.

The way of the child leads us back to the vulnerability and immanent openness of children, and when we carry this innocent desire for good and this irrepressible desire for learning forward into adult life, true mutual power goes with us and we find ourselves capable of asking forgiveness, capable of forgiving, and capable of building relationships, communities, and nations known for a powerful and forgiving ethos.

I believe when we hear the voice of leaders such as Martin Luther King Jr., Desmond Tutu, and Nelson Mandela we recognize the servant leaders in our own life who loved us from the start, and without condition, and called us to who we were meant to be. A grandfather, a sister . . . a mother, a brother, a friend—they refined us, and as our dross fell away they helped us rise and we discovered in the encounter the timeless notion that perfect love casts out fear. The point is not how vast or worldwide our impact. What matters is how committed we are to live in reconciled relationships, to offer to our children the gifts of love and courageous living . . . the gift of naming our weaknesses, asking forgiveness, and changing in meaningful ways.

So let us consider again the life of a child. What is it about a child's voice, a child's smiling face and exuberant laughter, that reminds us of the wonder of existence? Something of freedom is found in that smile, and peace, the simple unburdened splendor of being young and alive. Yet so often this freedom is clouded in adulthood, becoming increasingly more elusive, and for some seemingly unreachable. At times our lives can be so filled with rapid motion, entanglements, pressure, and confusion that we find it difficult to breathe. Here, in the center of our humanity, the opportunity to live differently presents itself. Again, Greenleaf stated that the true leader aspires first to serve, and this simple thought can remove our personal fortifications and bring us back to a life of freshness and hope.

In the eyes of children there is something delightful to be noticed, something resilient, perhaps even invincible. I'm speaking of how they are so full of joy. It is difficult to find a depressed child, unless basic needs are not taken care of, and even then their resilience is disarming. I remember a time when my first daughter was four years old. She was sleeping in our bed. She loves to get up early in the morning. I don't love to get up early in the morning. I like to sleep in the morning. That's gone now. But she loves to get up early in the morning, and you recognize that if a child is on your bed and stands up, she might walk a little bit close to the edge of the bed. It's a sixth sense with parents; even if we are half-asleep there is a heightened awareness; we are always ready to grab her ankle if we need to, to keep her safe, to save her if we need to, to catch her, or hold her. So she's walking kind of precariously on our bed on that day, it's pitch black, dark, and she leans over to the window. There are some Venetian blinds there, and when she parts the blinds, sunlight pierces the room. She turns around and says in a loud voice, "It's a sunny day!" Just like that and I'm still thinking, *Well I'm not ready for the sunny day. I want to sleep.* She walks back to the middle of the bed and at that point, it's July, the height of summer, and very hot. December and winter are a long way off. She walks back to the middle of the bed, and she stands in the middle of the bed and I have half an eye on her. She puts both hands in the air above her head and shouts in total happiness, "Christmas presents!"

She's like that. That's joy.

Now consider the counterpart to joy: despair.

To live with the power involved in servant leadership, not a power that dominates or controls, but a power that heals, restores, and reconciles, one needs humility. The servant leader submits to the forces of life that lead away from self-embeddedness and toward the kind of transcendence that is capable of leading and healing the self and beloved others. Herman Hesse's quiet call from *The Journey to the East* gives a telling description of this process:

Children live on one side of despair, the awakened on the other.[22]

Real joy is a unique entity, a significant mover in our society, and one of the great engines of humanity. Some years ago I had the honor of going to the Philippines to interview former president of the Philippines, Corazon Aquino, a woman so filled with joy that merely her presence brought joy to others. Some decades back, only a few short years after her husband Ninoy's martyrdom, her spiritual, nonviolent, and love-imbued leadership rallied the great spirit of the Filipino people and left a lasting image of the recurring boundlessness of life. Joy is something that Ninoy and Corazon Aquino brought to the world—a great joy in the possibilities, the heightened possibilities of humanity. Some things are worth fighting for: our children, our joy, the fulfillment of a whole life . . . these are worth fighting for, which brings to mind the arresting and graceful sentence Ninoy uttered before returning to the Philippines from exile in the United States, only to be shot and killed immediately upon his arrival in Manila. The image of his body, dead on the tarmac, became a touchstone of justice and liberty for oppressed people everywhere. Before his arrival, before facing the death he imagined he might face, Ninoy said, "The Filipino is worth dying for."[23]

You see real joy in Ninoy and Corazon Aquino. You see boldness and even the willingness to die so that others may have a better life. These are great dreams. Others too have generated great dreams, and in America, a man I would call a spiritual brother of President Aquino, Martin Luther King Jr., also dreamed a great dream, and it is good to return to him, for he showed us how to begin to unseat the power abuses, privilege, and elitism that have tended to surround circles of economic, political, and religious leadership in every society. King, a man who saw all people as worthy of freedom and equality, led through service, action, and a resounding voice of strength and light. He stated:

> Hatred paralyzes life; love releases it. Hatred confuses life; love harmonizes it. Hatred darkens life; love illuminates it.[24]

Like Ninoy and Corazon Aquino, and like Martin Luther King and Tutu, Greenleaf too was unafraid to dream a great dream, and his life and thought have richly influenced leadership worldwide. One of the things we notice about America today is that Americans often consciously and unconsciously promote leadership that is egocentric, overly market- and consumer-driven, and harmful or even violent to ourselves and others. It is an area in which we need both much help and much healing in our nation. Servant leadership, from nation to nation and within nations, draws us to a better, more whole way of being.

Again I am reminded of Greenleaf's statement:

> For something great to happen there must be a great dream. Behind every great achievement is a dreamer of great dreams.[25]

Consider Vincent Van Gogh, the meditative and vibrant iconoclast. He was not known for his art in his lifetime, yet one of his paintings recently sold for more than $80 million. Though Van Gogh was a lion-hearted, sensitive, and perceptive man, full of hope for the world and delight in God, he was also very troubled at times, and in fact, he died in despair. Yet his truth lives on. He said:

> There is nothing more truly artistic than to love people.

Yes, there is nothing more truly artistic than to love people.

Johann Sebastian Bach, the musician and composer, is another who was largely unknown. His music did not gain an audience until nearly one hundred years after his death. If one of us set out right now to script Bach's music, if we took a pencil and copied each note he wrote in his lifetime, it would take more than a decade. On every piece of music, Bach wrote the letters S. D. G.—Soli Deo Gloria in Latin—meaning "to God alone the glory." Because of his fluid and prolific quality and the unique subtleties of his music, Bach is considered a genius. He could compose entire orchestras in his head, the entire musical notation for every instrument, without even going to the piano.

George Frideric Handel was alienated, alone even in the midst of the great dream he dreamed. He was at the bottom of his career, disrespected in society, dejected, living in obscurity, and at the low point of his life when an intensely focused moment of inspiration came to him, and in just over twenty days he wrote "The Messiah," the music that forms the glorious landscape of so many of our lives today.

With my wife Jennifer's reading of William Shirer's *The Rise and Fall of the Third Reich*, the scholarly and shocking book about Hitler's meteoric rise to power and then the tremendous fall, she relayed to me so many stories of people showing love and care for each other even in the face of the most atrocious conditions the Nazis had forced on them.[26] Some time back, before I flew to the Philippines, she said to me, "You know, I believe it is possible for us to get better in chaos and suffering, and in difficulty, rather than getting worse." That's a captivating sentence. That's something that heals me as a person just to hear her say it and heals our family just to have her as a part of our family saying it, living it. That we can get better in chaos, suffering, and difficulty rather than getting worse; this is what Ninoy and Corazon Aquino exemplify. This is what Martin Luther King Jr. exemplifies. This is what Robert Greenleaf and servant leadership exemplify.

In the leadership that rose from the Aquinos, Martin Luther King, and Greenleaf, we see two significant qualities: rich spirituality and abounding love. Their interior fortitude and their love for people and life reflect one of the most honored truths of sacred scripture alluded to earlier:

Many waters cannot quench love. Love is stronger than death.[27]

Robert Greenleaf devoted himself to silence and to reflective quietness from his spiritual tradition, the Quaker tradition, and out of that he started to form the idea of servant leadership. His definition remains a compass for all who desire to lead. He listened with awakened purpose. He spoke a lasting vision:

The best test is: Do those served grow as persons? Do they, while being served, become healthier, wiser, freer, more autonomous, more likely themselves to become servants? And, what is the effect on the least privileged in society; will they benefit, or, at least, not be further deprived?[28]

The servant leader proceeds from within the heart of humanity, to heal the heart of humanity. The servant leader is necessary. The servant leader is good, and with avid conviction the servant leader unknowingly becomes the antidote to the pernicious philosophies and ways of life that too often haunt the individual, the family, and the globe. The world is inlaid with devastating consequences. Servant leadership calls us together, with gratitude and confidence, to overcome.

Marilynne Robinson's elegant and entrancing novel *Gilead* won the Pulitzer Prize in 2004. In rendering a character as whole as John Ames, Marilynne Robinson imparted to her audience a much-needed sense of spiritual origin, the life of the mind, and the intrinsic force of grace as a healing undercurrent to the nihilism and darkly reductionist tendencies we so often and so unconsciously forward in the world.[29] When *Gilead* is read in tandem with Robinson's *The Death of Adam*, the result is a crystalline representation of the human tradition of respect for the Divine.[30] Her scathing rebuke of Darwin, Nietzsche, Marx, and Freud is worthy and resonant, and points out how a given palate of nihilistic thought leans the world into overobjectification and eventually the dogma of fortified antivalues that exhibits itself in the unnatural promotion of meaninglessness. She reveals the kind of robust mind, heart, and spirit that help awaken the human community.

Certainly, in the name of religion, the world has often suffered. One of the primary arguments of outspoken atheists is that religion not only does not help humanity, but it invasively and pervasively harms. Without question, all religious traditions must come to terms with the truth of this accusation. Yet what is overlooked in the accusation is that invasive and pervasive harm is not only bad religion, it mirrors the same hypocrisy found in bad nonreligion. Mao and Stalin, paragons of the atheist tradition, in addition to Hitler, a man whose bent religion mirrored more of an atheist stance than a theist one, are responsible for over 100 million deaths, by themselves far exceeding the number of deaths in all the "religious" wars of history. In reality, invasion of others is just plain bad personhood, whether it is perpetrated by an atheist or a person of faith. My wife asked me recently, what has been accomplished in the name of atheism . . . what great efforts have arisen in the name of atheism? How does atheism engage the world's violence and poverty of spirit with an answer? The case can be made that the more militant forms of atheism often apparent today, just as in the work of Nietzsche and Freud, evoke an ego of the intellect that in effect not only precludes the heart and life of the servant leader, but also demeans and degrades the servant leader, framing her or him as weak, ineffectual, and slavelike.

Further questions arise. What kinds of questions does a militant atheism permit? What are the intellectual tendencies such an atheism protects? What culture does the more aggressive forms of atheism promote?

Interestingly enough, Freud "had numerous psychosomatic disorders as well as exaggerated fears of dying and other phobias."[31] He conducted ongoing self-analysis that concluded with his realizing the hostility he felt for his father and his recollection of childhood sexual feelings for his mother.[32] Freud's theories resulted in his brazen statements framing human life as largely determined (lacking free will) and inherently bound by aggressive and sexual drives, and these theoretical positions became the basis for his psychodynamic school of thought. For the purposes of furthering scientific inquiry he became a heavy cocaine user, and this fact led Jurgen von Scheidt to conclude that most of Freud's psychoanalytical theory came of cocaine-induced states.[33] Freud denounced religion, faith, and mysticism as unscientific, and he eschewed all pursuit of the afterlife. Ironically, though Freud is considered one of the fathers of psychology—the study of the psyche—or the "soul," the "life," the "breath"—in September of 1939 Freud convinced his doctor and friend Max Schur to assist him in suicide. Schur administered doses of morphine over several hours until Freud died. Though ironically still revered, many of Freud's primary theories are commonly known to have been confabulations that do not hold water scientifically and are consistently among the most debunked in contemporary science.[34]

Nietzsche's life was equally fraught with mental discord and the ambition to assert his own greatness at the expense of others. He died a lonely man, plagued by insanity. He was born into a family in which he suffered his father's death when he was only five and his younger brother's when he was six. In early adulthood he studied theology briefly before taking on a disdain for authority characteristic of many of the philosophers of his day, and he ended his life with severe revulsion both for Christianity and democracy. His antifaith, anti-God modalities have procured for him allegiance to this day from staunch Darwinians, cynics, nihilists, and atheists throughout the world. However, similar to Freud's, much of Nietzsche's thought is infused with absurdity, narcissism, and adolescent aggrandizement. His list of ailments, from a symbolic perspective, is staggering. He was plagued by moments of shortsightedness practically to the degree of blindness, migraine headaches, and violent stomach attacks, and in the last two years of his life he suffered multiple strokes that left him unable to speak. After a psychotic break, he entered a time of intensified mental illness, and his descent into madness ended with his death in 1890.[35]

The ideas of Freud and Nietzsche—often based in ruthless disregard for opposing views, dogged rebellion against or blatant disregard for former systems of thought, and in many cases very limited scientific and critical evidence—continue to feed the intellectual machine of Western thought even after cardinal scientific and philosophical discoveries have made much of this work obsolete. Critics point to conjecture and often fabrication as inherent components of their body of thought, yet even today much of the atheistic movement continues to celebrate their work.

Darwin's shadow too has an immensity of flaws, as does the shadow of Marx.

Again, the question arises, what has atheism contributed of personal and collective responsibility to the human community? Healthy questioning perhaps, or perhaps a groundwork of skepticism toward the beliefs of humanity . . . that is, calling such beliefs into question, or demanding that an account be made. To be sure, hypocrisy accompanies people who believe in a "moral" universe, as the more vocal atheists in contemporary society are quick to point out. Yet the same hypocrisy haunts the atheist, but without a living ideal or premise of human or divine value in which to place hope and action.

The case can be made that overobjectification has been the brother of atheism, and the death-dealers of the twentieth century became the tyrannical leaders of this family of thinking: Hitler, Lenin, Stalin, Pol Pot, Mao.

Significantly, where action and hope join hands with integrity, the moral universe finds humble and spellbinding resonance, as shown in the work of people such as Paulo Freire, Mother Teresa, Martin Luther King Jr., William Wilberforce, Sojourner Truth, Frederick Douglass, Corazon Aquino, bell hooks, and Cesar Chavez. From this legacy we find evidence, defensible and sustained, of significant change in the human heart. In the wake of this change, we see lasting contributions to the common good; to social, economic, and racial justice; and to the grandeur of what it means to be true and mature . . . to love and serve others.

The pathway from life into life, and the complex and very painful passages that must be navigated, have accompanied the human project from the dawn of time. The more shortsighted the person, the less likely that a compelling and sustainable engagement will emerge to draw us to a better communal sense of one another. The more farsighted, the less capable we are to address the healing of the individual within the collective. An artistic sense of living helps us reconcile the polarities and gain a sense of concrete reality with regard to some of the most meaningful aspects of human existence: the true, the loving, the beautiful, the good, and all that is essential to being. In art as in life, the sacred can fall toward the sentimental. Through a nonrobust presentation of the world, then, the sacred becomes saccharine and loses the subtlety and force that accompany all great artistic expression. Not unlike this, the polar form in art and life is that which might be called the secular. Yet in contemporary times when the secular lacks restraint, it ramps toward a profanity that not only goes unchecked, but is often exalted. The travesty of the pendulum asserts itself: in hating values or seeking to make them meaningless, we lose the innate resonance of the sacred and unconsciously glorify the profane. The servant leader is capable of holding in tension and with compassion the great paradox of humanity: the knowledge that we have within us the capacity not only for divine love, but also for profane hatred—the capacity not only for generosity and care, but also for wanton greed and cruelty. Therefore wholehearted living, and the individual and collective action that rises from such living, is required.

When one of my three young daughters approaches me and crawls up into my lap and touches my face, I am reminded of the weight of responsibility that has laid a claim on my life . . . a responsibility to love, and develop, and give of myself so that another life might become wiser, freer, healthier, and better able to serve. The way of the child calls to me and I am given to respond, and when I do not respond there is an undeniable draught that begins inside, a drying up that results in rigidity, defensiveness, and unwillingness to grow.

In response, I must return to the deep well where the water of life and rejuvenation is found in beloved others who help us find our way back to the best sense of what is human and what is good. My wife is such a person to me. She walks in dignity and her voice illumines and makes whole the fragmentation so common to ordinary life. With her presence—confident, intelligent, courageous—she embodies a way of life inherent to the servant leader . . . that when confronted by life's ambiguity, injustice, or abusive tendencies, a legacy of love asserts itself through wisdom, foresight, and healing. She sees what is necessary for wholeness. She creates wholeness.

Viktor Frankl, the renowned psychiatrist and social critic who survived the death camps of Nazi Germany but suffered the loss of his parents and his wife, believed in the integral importance not of seeking what we might gain or gather in life, but rather of seeking the answer to what life asks of us. In fulfilling life's deepest questions, in answering to life's most unyielding problems, meaning accompanies our way in the world and draws us to the true wonder of the self and the beloved other. Frankl, considered the father of existential psychology, believed that we encounter meaning by creating a work or doing a deed, by experiencing goodness, truth, and beauty, by experiencing nature and culture, or by encountering the very essence of another unique human being—specifically, by loving that person. Our personal approach to unavoidable suffering then becomes the crucible through which our humanity is honed and refined. Frankl, having faced the fires of the Holocaust, affirmed Anton Wildgans's piercing affirmation regarding the call from life to greater life:

What is to give light must endure burning.[36]

Perhaps the most recognizable mark of true humanity is the sacrificial love given from one person to another, from one organization of people to the people served, or from nation to nation. Through love, by love, the servant leader leaves a legacy of legitimate greatness and power. In this light, the kiss of a child, the kind word of a friend, and the fortitude that wrests tyranny from the hands of the tyrant are one. The servant leader not only sees us whole . . . not diminished, not destroyed . . . the servant leader lives in such a way that we become whole, and in so doing, we bring wholeness, or a sense of that which is holy, to the world. The life of the child symbolizes a life of vulnerability, tenderness, vitality, openness to new experience, and the unbridled desire for growth. And so, Hesse's voice rings forth: *children live on one side of despair, the awakened on the other* . . . in other words, under the right conditions the child's existence is characterized not by despair but by joy and ascension, just like the life of a mature human being, regardless of circumstances. Even, or perhaps especially in difficult experiences, daughters and sons in healthy families, enveloped by meaning and love, are given the opportunity to realize their destiny. Whether that destiny, such as in the life of Vaclav Havel or the life of Nelson Mandela, led to the cold reality of a prison cell or to the very seat of government did not revoke the strength of the human spirit, but rather enlivened its robust inner beauty. The same realization of our destiny is required of us as we develop into adulthood. In Hesse's terms, we find our destiny in the mystery of transcendent grace, and from this grace we are *awakened*. If we are to bring healing to others . . . if we are to truly serve others, life asks us to embrace that which comes naturally to the child—vulnerability, tenderness, openness, vitality, and the desire to grow.

In people such as the Aquinos, King, Mandela, Tutu, Frankl, and Greenleaf, it becomes very clear: listening is essential to servant leadership. A sense of quietness, a sense of devotion to listening, individually and collectively, returns us to our belief in our children and our responsibility to the future. Down in the depths of the human crucible lies dormant a mature and lovely interior, and having emerged we walk forward like lions with the fierceness we need to serve the world. We fulfill Hesse's vision: our children live on one side of despair, and with stamina we persevere with them until we are all awakened to life on the other side . . . a life of purpose and undaunted joy.

Chapter 12

Martin Luther King Jr. and Desmond Tutu

Voices of Light in the Dark

Martin Luther King Jr. and Desmond Tutu, men who might also be called spiritual brothers, are essential voices. Hearing them in their own words, we find each with a cadence all his own, the reality of hard-won wisdom, and a balance of grace and expectation. Martin Luther King Jr. presented the timely notion that those who treat us poorly, harm us, or even seek to destroy us are worthy of our own luxuriant and abiding love. To frame the person we disagree with in a dark light was to King a poison, something he intentionally fought against. King's work is prophetic and revolutionary and provides an open doorway for the growth of the servant leader who forgives and lives a life of legitimate power:

> Now I am aware of the fact that there are those who would contend that we live in the most ghastly period of human history. They would argue that the rhythmic beat of the deep rumblings of discontent from Asia, the uprisings in Africa, the nationalistic longings of Egypt, the roaring cannons from Hungary, and the racial tensions of America are all indicative of the deep and tragic midnight which encompasses our civilization. They would argue that we are retrogressing instead of progressing. But far from representing retrogression and tragic meaninglessness, the present tensions represent the necessary pains that accompany the birth of anything new. Long ago the Greek philosopher Heraclitus argued that justice emerges from the strife of opposites, and Hegel, in modern philosophy, preached a doctrine of growth through struggle. It is both historically and biologically true that there can be no birth and growth without birth and growing pains. Whenever there is the emergence of the new we confront the recalcitrance of the old. So the tensions which we witness in the world today are indicative of the fact that a new world order is being born and an old order is passing away.[37]

King's inspired aim for a future of greater harmony has given light to the nations. He furthered the thought of the necessary growing pains involved in new life, and he positioned forgiveness as the spiritual imperative of our time.

> A . . . challenge that stands before us is that of entering the new age with under-standing and good will. . . . Virtues of love, mercy and forgiveness should stand at the center of our lives. There is the danger that those of us who have lived so long under the yoke of oppression, those of us who have been exploited and trampled over, those of us who have had to stand amid the tragic midnight of injustice and indignities will enter the new age with hate and bitterness. But if we retaliate with hate and bitterness, the new age will be nothing but a duplica-tion of the old age. We must blot out the hate and injustice of the old age with the love and justice of the new. . . .
>
> Violence never solves problems. . . .
>
> We have before us the glorious opportunity to inject a new dimension of love into the veins of our civilization. There is still a voice crying out in terms that echo across the generations, saying: Love your enemies, bless them that curse you, pray for them that despitefully use you . . .
>
> This love might well be the salvation of our civilization.[38]

For followers of King, even the most rabid racist is worthy of love, not because the racist deserves love, but because in loving, we see our own humanity in the humanity of the other and we are given strength to go forward and work to change destructiveness both in ourselves and in the systems around us. Tutu's wisdom reflects that of King:

> We are bound up in a delicate network of interdependence because, as we say in our African idiom, a person is a person through other persons. To dehumanize another inexorably means that one is dehumanized as well.[39]
>
> There is hope. There is hope because [we] are revealed as human beings, frail but with the capacity to do better if [we] get out of the self-justifying mode, the denial mode, and are able to say quietly, humbly, "I am sorry, forgive me/us. . . ."
>
> I came away with a deep sense—indeed an exhilarating realization—that although there is undoubtedly much evil about, we human beings have a won-derful capacity for good. We can be very good. That is what fills me with hope for even the most intractable situations.[40]
>
> In relations between individuals, if you ask another person for forgiveness you may be spurned; the one you have injured may refuse to forgive you. The risk is even greater if you are the injured party, wanting to offer forgiveness. The culprit may be arrogant, obdurate, or blind; not ready or willing to apologize or to ask for forgiveness. He or she thus cannot appropriate the forgiveness that is

offered. Such rejection can jeopardize the whole enterprise. Our leaders were ready in South Africa to say they were willing to walk the path of confession, forgiveness, and reconciliation with all the hazards that lay along the way. And it seems their gamble might be paying off, since our land has not been over-whelmed by the catastrophe that had seemed so inevitable.[41]

King and Tutu are examples of the new critical depth being discovered in the discipline of leadership, a leadership that balances power, seeks to honor both feminine and masculine giftedness as well as a grand diversity of voices, and moves people toward greater richness with one another. Nobel laureate Toni Morrison, her voice a national treasure, turns a rapier-like wisdom toward understanding the human spirit. In her novel *The Bluest Eye* she speaks of a young black girl who is plagued by the over-whelming opportunity that attends those who have blue eyes (white girls). In a final statement the black girl puts out her own eyes.[42] The symbol of one person, plagued by another, one culture plagued by another—in which that other is at worst blatantly or violently authoritarian and at best oppres-sively indifferent—is the story of leadership superiority and entitlement throughout history. Significantly, Morrison's antihero, seeking the oppor-tunity and privilege of her blue-eyed antagonists, loses her own vision in the process.

Under conditions that range from leader ignorance to leader dominance, a common component of the alienated relational environment is distorted vision. This cloudedness, or lack of assurance regarding hope, growth, and community, takes on the quality of voluntary blindness in the immature leader. The leader grows defensive, resisting or even refusing to grow. With an immovable, diseased heart such a leader infects the family, the workplace, the culture, and society as a whole.

Burns's transformational leadership, Komives, Lucas, and McMahon's relational leadership, and Greenleaf's servant leadership—the best expres-sion of a transformational, relational leadership style—are three examples of a shift in the conception of the development and use of power.[43] In these ways of thinking, power is harnessed not primarily for social, political, and economic purposes, though these are natural ends of better leadership. Rather, the leader understands power and develops it for the good of the beloved, and for the world. In the person able to be both a servant and a leader, love, with its dynamics of justice and mercy, is the most complete and appropriate form of power. The person who speaks love leads self and others well. The person who builds and furthers love is content.

In other emergent forms of leadership theory, the pursuit of excellence is realized through character elements such as discipline, modesty, and discernment regarding the subtleties of effecting change. With regard to leadership in contemporary research, thought, and practice, *The Leadership Challenge* by Kouzes and Posner, Bolman and Deal's approach to the artistry of the leader, *Good to Great* by Collins, Noddings's ethic of care, Block's work in stewardship, Cooperrider's appreciative inquiry, Zohar's focus on quantum theory and spiritual intelligence, and Bennis's attention to the best qualities of leaders all dovetail with servant leadership.[44] Yet in Greenleaf's approach I find a central focus on healing that is not present in the work of other thought-leaders. Helping others become more whole, and the bright raiment of healing that comes of reconciliation and forgiveness, are essential gifts of servant leadership.

King and Tutu walked through a desert of despair back to the revitalizing waters of love. Servant leadership calls people toward a communal effort with others that both invigorates the individual person and draws the community toward moral clarity; therefore, it requires a sustained effort at both personal and spiritual formation, the contemplative and active will to understand the inner life. This is the deepening and broadening of a person's character that then results, without undo force, in the deepening and broadening of the character of others. Such a course of action is not done quickly because to serve others requires uncommon staying power, a work not of minutes or days, but of years, decades. In a poignant example of this, a woman once devoted herself to a calling, a calling that would richly serve society and with lasting effect. Her calling was poetry, and in the name of this calling she forsook the typical trajectory of the modern life and devoted herself to the study of her art. Born in 1806 at Coxhoe Hall, Durham, England, Elizabeth Barrett was the first of twelve children. By ten years old she had read passages from *Paradise Lost* and a number of Shakespearean plays, among other great works. By the age of twelve she had written her first "epic" poem, composed of four books of rhyming couplets. Yet by fourteen Elizabeth had developed a lung ailment that plagued her for the rest of her life. Doctors administered morphine, which she took until her death. At fifteen, she also suffered a spinal injury.

Despite her physical setbacks, her mind continued to bloom and she consistently sought to bring healing to others through her writing. During her teens she taught herself Hebrew in order to better read the Old Testament. Later she turned to Greek studies, and her appetite for the classics was matched by a passionate Christian faith. At age twenty Elizabeth anonymously published *An Essay on Mind and Other Poems.* At twenty-two her mother died, leaving her bereft. The ongoing abolition of slavery in England and financial misdirection cut into her father's income, and in 1832, he sold his estate and moved the family to a coastal town, before settling permanently in London. While the family was living on the coast, Elizabeth's translation of *Prometheus Bound* (1833), by Aeschylus, was published.

As her star began to rise in the 1830s, Elizabeth stayed in her father's London house under his tyrannical rule. He began sending her siblings to Jamaica to help with the family's estates there. Elizabeth bitterly opposed slavery and did not want her brothers and sisters sent away. With her health waning, she spent a year at the sea of Torquay accompanied by her close brother Edward, whom she called "Bro." He drowned while sailing at Torquay and Elizabeth came home emotionally desolate. Her next five years were spent as an invalid and a recluse in her bedroom at her father's home.

In the face of despair she continued writing, however, and in 1844 produced a collection entitled simply *Poems*. In one of the poems Elizabeth had praised the poet Robert Browning, and he wrote her a letter. Together over the next twenty months the two exchanged 574 letters. Their love was bitterly opposed by her father, a man who wanted none of his children to marry. In 1846, Robert and Elizabeth eloped and settled in Florence, Italy, where Elizabeth's health improved and she bore a son, Robert Wideman Browning. Her father never spoke to her again.

Elizabeth Barrett Browning, the woman whose work was favorably compared to that of Shakespeare and Petrarch, died in Florence at the age of fifty-seven on June 29, 1861. Despite her crushing physical ailments and the total rejection she experienced by her father, in the following poem, a poem touched with beauty and grace toward her husband Robert, she leads others into a healed expression of love itself. In so doing, she expands our ways of knowing:

How Do I Love Thee? (Sonnet 43)

How do I love thee? Let me count the ways.
I love thee to the depth and breadth and height
My soul can reach, when feeling out of sight
For the ends of being and ideal grace.
I love thee to the level of every day's
Most quiet need, by sun and candle-light.
I love thee freely, as men strive for right.
I love thee purely, as they turn from praise.
I love thee with the passion put to use
In my old griefs, and with my childhood's faith.
I love thee with a love I seemed to lose
With my lost saints. I love thee with the breath,
Smiles, tears, of all my life; and, if God choose,
I shall but love thee better after death.[45]

Considering Elizabeth Barrett Browning's devotion to language, to the nuances of people and connection and to the hope of discovering self and others and the world, her words carry significant power. "I love thee with the breath, smiles, tears, of all my life." Her words echo a similar advance in the relationships formed by the servant leader: let us move toward an understanding of one another that leads us to know one another, to love one another. Now, in the present. For the leader who is dominant, distant, or needy, and far from both the interior of the self and the interior of others, the lack of such love is a void in which darkness dwells, a desperate place, fragile and lonely.

A person-to-person view of relating infuses servant leadership and becomes invaluable for people living and working in relational systems.[46] A relational system is a community, be it a two-person community, a family-sized community, or larger communities such as in business, politics, and religion. Gardner, a leading leadership theorist, offers a list of necessary ingredients for community, such as diversity, shared norms and values, free-flowing communication, an atmosphere of trust, effective participation in leadership, and an awareness of the larger systems to which the community belongs.[47] Komives, Lucas, and McMahon furthered Gardner's work by defining community as the "binding together of diverse individuals committed to a just, common good through shared experiences in a spirit of caring and social responsibility."[48] Greenleaf's ideas focus leadership theory and practice to an even more abundant end—that of drawing the self and others toward greater personal health, wisdom, autonomy, and freedom. Servant leadership as a way of life brings about a new definition of democracy, family, and work. The person who loves well finds the unique exceptionality of his or her family members, coworkers, and even those in authority, and then enhances this uniqueness. The servant leader does not detract from others. The servant leader encourages, or "builds courage" in others. Community depends on leadership that values inclusion and strengthens all members toward meaningful common purposes. King and Tutu provided servant leadership in times when such leadership was an urgent social necessity. The same imperative exists today.

Historically, leaders have tended to either attack when confronted by the relational environment, or run—both severely destructive responses. On an individual level, leaders who honor relationships reverse this, fulfilling the more personal promise of King's and Tutu's work. Rather than keeping people alienated or at a distance, such people draw us toward one another. They provide a cure for our hopelessness; they liberate us. Martin Luther King Jr. and Desmond Tutu sacrificed their own well-being for the well-being of others.

Early in our marriage my wife asked me to help her make the bed. Another time she asked me to help her develop a presentation she would be giving at work. On a third occasion she asked if I would like to go for a walk with her. My response to each of these requests was no. It wasn't that I wanted to say no; in fact, I believe I wanted to say yes. It's just that there was always some circumventing reason that took precedence, such as my need for rest, or my need to complete my own project instead of hers, or simply the undue importance I tended to place on my own agenda. It's not hard to see why my wife sometimes found me difficult to like. It was not until I grew more vulnerable, sacrificing my rigidity, that peace came to us.

Now consider the idea of people, leaders, who not only seek to say yes, but say yes and then follow through on the physical, emotional, and spiritual requests of their loved ones. They will be honored by their loved ones, their loved ones will speak well of them and desire to be near them. So too in the workplace. I have been a part of a group of men who have met weekly for the last fifteen years, good men devoted to the beloved people of their lives. We meet weekly to ask two meaningful questions and listen to one another: the first question—"Have you objectified your wife this week, treated her poorly, or failed to treat her with dignity and care?"; the second question—"What is one creative way you have related to your wife this week?" The marital commitment is a totality: emotional, sexual, intellectual, and spiritual. In this community of men who seek to build meaningful families, we ask forgiveness of each other when we fail in the commitments we've made. Many men around the world live cold and nearly purposeless inner lives, having given up a position of meaning in the most intimate circles of family, friendship, and humanity as a whole. Through the influence of the men I gather with I am learning to say yes to the promise of intimacy in self, family, and work and to realign myself by moving away from being a man of emotional deadness and defensiveness to becoming a man of listening, responsiveness, and gentleness.

Healing between nations and between people is found in the legacy left by servant leaders such as King and Tutu. In calling us to a greater sense of ourselves, Martin Luther King Jr. reminds us that "we must blot out the hate and injustice of the old age with the love and justice of the new."[49] Desmond Tutu echoes King's directive, saying, "There is hope . . . if [we] . . . are able to say quietly, humbly, 'I am sorry, forgive me/us.'"[50]

Chapter 13

The Question of Love and Power

Gratitude, Forgiveness, and the Conscious Cultivation of Servant Leadership

Feeling, thinking, seeing;
Love me in the lightest part,
Love me in full being.
Love me with thy thinking soul,
Break it to love-sighing;
Love me with thy thoughts that roll
On through living—dying.[51]

These words, also penned by Elizabeth Barrett Browning, are a fitting place to further consider servant leadership and the possibilities that exist in the paradox of power and love, which is also the paradox of justice and forgiveness. The tension of human conflict can be likened to a light born of heaven and seen in the perpetual gifts of human goodness . . . but also like a great fire reminding us of the hell we so often create by our interminable capacity for evil. In receiving the gift of life each person is confronted by forces undeniably mysterious, formidable, and unwieldy. If the nature of our daily encounter with existence could be captured in a directive, it might be precisely the one Elizabeth has given us:

Love me in full being.

The statement is of grave importance.

From the beloved women and men in my life, I have found that true living is ultimately tied to gratitude.

I recall walking as a boy with my father in the Beartooth Range along the eastern front of the Rockies in southern Montana. We wanted to catch the striking and elusive Golden trout, a delicacy of high mountain lakes and streams. The only problem, as I saw it, was a five-mile climb, near straight up, along steep, rugged switchbacks, rocky and severe. I was twelve years old, and when my dad told me of the hike, and how hard it would be, I wanted nothing to do with it . . . too much work, too much pain, and in the end we might not even catch any fish. My thoughts were consumed with excuses and even anger at my father for suggesting we go for Golden trout, rather than the Rainbows that filled East Rosebud Lake (no hike at all) or Mystic Lake (a comparatively easy hike over relatively flat terrain). But my father convinced me not only to go with him but to make the trip worthwhile, to enjoy the challenge together, receive the beauty of the Beartooths with wonder and respect, and not give in to everything in me that wanted to complain or blame. His own spirit of delight pervaded the air . . . he was in love with every aspect of encountering the mountains. He was present.

We began and he took me with him, keeping me in stride, waiting for me when we rested, helping me progress again. The hike was far and away the most difficult of the hundreds we took together, and many hours passed before we crossed a final up-slanted swath of mountain grasses, grabbing at the roots of windblown trees, scrambling slowly on all fours. At last the destination came into view and we pressed our hands into the earth, dug in our feet and went step by step until finally we crested the lip of a massive rock bowl and stood and looked down on Silven Lake . . . a blue gem encased in the heart of the mountains, reflecting the heart of the sky.

The right journeys are worth all the toil.

Servant leadership is just such a journey, one that at the outset is strewn with daunting obstacles, steep swings of overdone ego or lack of self-confidence, apathy or blind indifference, and a stubbornly embedded sense of anger and blame for self or others. But when we approach the life of the servant leader with awe and willingness, a remarkable pathway opens itself before us.

By the time we crested the jagged lip of the mountain, my thoughts had changed. Even now, decades later, when I think of my father and of the mountains of Montana, I think of gratitude, affection, confidence, love.

Servant leadership, when we surrender to the call humanity places on our lives, can lead us up through the difficult terrain of our own weaknesses, both individual and collective, and take us to places where we can look out and find again the beauty of life and not only the fulfillment of being well again, but also of leading others into their own longed-for sense of hope and well-being. In the bold mountains of Montana, the sun is big and shines bright in a seemingly endless sky. Our thoughts, too, are expansive and imbued with a natural capacity for grandeur. When the life of the mind receives illumination, our thoughts lead to a sense of humility and the desire to be present for the good of others.

Illumination has historically symbolized piercing vision, decisive knowledge, strong-mindedness, or a better approach to circumstances formerly viewed as irresolvable. Illumination is a sure and present light, the steady glow of a candle in darkness, the majesty of the sun at dawn. Our manner of thinking, too, can be blessed by illumination, and in this context, our thinking is vital to how we choose what to do with what poet Elizabeth Barrett Browning referred to as our *full being*. Natural logic says that the way we think is the type of thinking we are okay with, or willing to engage in . . . otherwise we would change our thinking. It follows that the quality of our thinking rises from our full being and is a binding part of what defines us.

Certainly thought is elusive, and before training our minds toward quality of thought, even the notion of developing, honing, or transforming our thoughts can seem slippery or beyond reach. However, a significant truth reveals itself if we follow the typical trajectory of our everyday thought life. If our thoughts are low-level, our minds tend toward an unconscious but sinister self-focus: unconscious because we have not called attention to the thoughts we think in order to change them; sinister because unexamined thought results in actions and impacts that can pervasively harm ourselves, others, and the world.

The life and work of Holocaust survivor and thought-leader Viktor Frankl define the wounded condition associated with being overly self-focused, and how the ascent into self-transcendence reveals what it means to live, to be fully alive:

> Consider the eye. The eye, too, is self-transcendent in a way. The moment it perceives something of itself, its function—to perceive the surrounding world visually—has deteriorated. If it is afflicted with a cataract, it may "perceive" its own cataract as a cloud; and if it is suffering from glaucoma, it might "see" its own glaucoma as a rainbow halo around lights. Normally, however, the eye doesn't see anything of itself.
>
> To be human is to strive for something outside of oneself. I use the term "self-transcendence" to describe this quality behind the will to meaning, the grasping for something or someone outside oneself. Like the eye, we are made to turn outward toward another human being to whom we can love and give ourselves.
>
> Only in such a way do people demonstrate themselves to be truly human.
>
> Only when in service of another does a person truly know his or her humanity.[52]

Though Viktor Frankl wrote over thirty books, he was no ivory tower scholar. He put his views of life into practice with thoroughness and integrity.

Born in 1902 in Vienna to a Jewish family of civil servants, he rose to become one of the leading neurologists in Europe, serving as head neurologist in the *Selbstmörderpavillon* or "suicide pavilion" of the General Hospital in Vienna. He treated more than thirty thousand women prone to suicide, and when the Nazis invaded Austria and he was relegated to practicing medicine only with Jews, he continued his neurology work, also worked as a brain surgeon, and succeeded in giving medical opinions that saved many patients from being euthanized during the program in which Nazis routinely found and killed people who were handicapped or mentally ill.

When the Nazi regime began to exert more and more influence in Vienna, Viktor's parents arranged for him to attain exile in America. Viktor, however, was not sure he should go. If he went to America, his parents would surely face a very difficult and painful future, but his life would be saved and this was their hope for him. If he stayed in Austria, he felt he might be able to act as a buffer to serve and protect them. He agonized over the decision whether to stay or leave and in the end told himself he would listen for a divine answer. At one point there were only days left before the window would close and he would be unable to leave the country. Viktor came home and his father was seated at the kitchen table with a piece of rubble in front of him. Viktor asked what happened and his father told him the Nazis had destroyed the temple that day. From where Viktor stood he saw a symbol engraved on the piece of broken rock, a mark his father had not yet noticed. Looking closely, Viktor made it out: the mark was a number from the Ten Commandments, the very number for the commandment *honor your father and mother*. Viktor found what he sought. He remained with his parents until he and they were taken from each other and shipped to separate concentration camps. In the concentration camps at Theresienstadt, Auschwitz, and Türkheim, though mandated to labor detail, even after being separated from his parents and his wife, Viktor Frankl continued until the final moments of the war to work to prevent suicide in his fellow prisoners and help cure them of despondency, depression, and weariness of life.

If we engage thought that resonates with transcendent values such as truth, mercy, goodness, beauty, justice, and love, our way of life becomes self-transcendent and we are given the opportunity to truly know our own humanity. Frankl felt there were only two races of people—either decent or unprincipled—and he found these two across all classes, ethnicities, and groups. He also found consciousness—the freedom to choose one's own quality of thinking regardless of circumstance—the factor that determines whether we are decent or whether we are unprincipled.

Nazism was not only a global atrocity, but it also precisely reflects the self-insulated and self-aggrandizing interior that each person must face and overcome. Selfishness, shown by degrading others through the use of manipulation, coercion, or force, happens daily in families throughout the world. And yet a false view of love must also be tested, and put through a kind of crucible. Yes, the abuse of power stalks us, but in a more subtle but equally insidious fashion, our humanity is also subverted by grave misunderstandings of the nature of love. Martin Luther King provides a picture of the struggle that lies in the center of existence, between the poles of love and power.

> Power properly understood is nothing but the ability to achieve purpose. And one of the great problems of history is that the concepts of love and power have usually been contrasted as opposites—polar opposites—so that love is identified with a resignation of power, and power with a denial of love.
>
> What is needed is a realization that power without love is reckless and abusive, and love without power is sentimental and anemic. Power at its best is love implementing the demands of justice, and justice at its best is power correcting everything that stands against love. It is precisely this collision of immoral power with powerless morality which constitutes the major crisis of our time.[53]

Those with the consciousness and personal maturity to generate moral power and powerful morality are those who heal the world. Humility and acts of deep compassion heal our selfishness, changing our degradation to confidence and lasting joy. Our way of thinking results in the actions we take in the world, and so who we are (in other words, our character) is directly tied to how we think. In light of this connection, good thinking becomes as valuable as good sight, and as indispensable as oxygen. In returning to Greenleaf's work of defining servant leadership, we can embrace the consciousness Frankl and King espoused and create meaningful and fulfilled lives. Author Stephen Covey said, "The deepest part of human nature is that which urges people—each one of us—to rise above our present circumstances and to transcend our nature. If you can appeal to it, you tap into a whole new source of human motivation. Perhaps that is why I have found Robert Greenleaf's teaching on servant leadership to be so enormously inspiring, so uplifting, so ennobling."[54]

Even when faced with the most heinous forms of human evil, there is a noble answer in the human heart. Again, Frankl points the way:

> Man is that being who invented the gas chambers of Auschwitz; however, he is also that being who entered those chambers upright, with the Lord's Prayer or the Shema Yisrael on his lips.[55]

Chapter 14

Before the Velvet Revolution

How We Begin to Deepen Our Consciousness

The level or type of thought we entertain determines the level at which we ennoble ourselves and others. Consider the plight of Czechoslovakia during and after World War II. Crushed by Nazism and then subsumed by the communist regime, after decades of subservience to an overruling power that severely suppressed human rights, the country threw off its shackles and gave the world a nonviolent new legacy. Václav Havel, the playwright and former dissident, one of the first spokesmen for the revolutionary group Charter 77, and a leading figure in the Velvet Revolution, became president.

Havel gives credence to the importance of our thought life not just as people, but as leaders who play a part in righting the wrongs of the world. Just as our thought life equates to our character, our character equates to the quality of our leadership. Havel's underground leadership of a nation bound by the negation and degradation of hard-line Soviet communism eventually led to the pervasive nonviolent awakening in Czech resolve that struck a chord in the collective soul of humanity, unseated a totalitarian regime, and gave the world a sense of freedom fought for and delivered by women and men of common purpose. Consider Havel's focus on the property of accountability with regard to one's own thinking:

Consciousness precedes being, and not the other way around, as the Marxists claim. For this reason, the salvation of this human world lies nowhere else than in the human heart, in the human power to reflect, in human meekness and in human responsibility. Without a global revolution in the sphere of human consciousness nothing will change for the better in the sphere of our being as humans, and the catastrophe toward which this world is headed—be it ecological, social, demographic, or a general breakdown of civilization—will be unavoidable.

> Hope is a state of mind, not of the world. Hope, in this deep and powerful
> sense, is not the same as joy that things are going well, or willingness to invest in
> enterprises that are obviously heading for success, but rather an ability to work
> for something because it is good.
> Hope is definitely not the same thing as optimism. It is not the conviction
> that something will turn out well, but the certainty that something makes sense,
> regardless of how it turns out.[56]

Yet the kind of thought Havel presented was long in coming. Before the
Velvet Revolution, before the onslaught of Western capitalism, before even
the long burden of communism that had followed the Prague Spring, at the
hand of Nazi Germany Czechoslovakia experienced a cultural annihilation
similar to that of the Cheyenne. I am reminded again of my grandparents on
my mother's side and their marriage in New York City during World War II:
my German grandfather, who died shortly after my wedding . . . my Czechoslovakian grandmother . . . whom we affectionately call The Great One. I
often wonder if every person's heritage is not one in which we must face the
vast history of our own personal and collective evil, and make a profound
reconciliation. I believe life asks us to free our children in a common effort to
overcome darkness with the light of forgiveness, responsibility, and love.

Forgiveness, responsibility, love. Such potent but elusive aspects of a well-
lived life are perhaps more divine than human, and when we embody them,
we become more present and more whole, or more *holy*, in the presence of
others. Listen to Havel's vision of the human condition:

> As soon as [people] began considering [themselves] the source of the highest
> meaning in the world and the measure of everything, the world began to lose its
> human dimension, and [people] began to lose control of it.[57]
> A modern philosopher once said: "Only a God can save us now." Yes, the
> only real hope of people today is probably a renewal of our certainty that we are
> rooted in the earth and, at the same time, in the cosmos. This awareness endows
> us with the capacity for self-transcendence. Politicians at international forums
> may reiterate a thousand times that the basis of the new world order must be uni-
> versal respect for human rights, but it will mean nothing as long as this impera-
> tive does not derive from the respect of the miracle of Being, the miracle of the
> universe, the miracle of nature, the miracle of our own existence. Only someone
> who submits to the authority of the universal order and of creation, who values
> the right to be a part of it and a participant in it, can genuinely value [oneself]
> and [one's] neighbors, and thus honor their rights as well.[58]

Love me in full being, the poet said, but when we lose sight of the Divine,
the voice of history is a clarion call: we do violence to others; others do

violence to us. Here, our capacity for inhumanity is appalling and our propensity for atrocity, shocking. I wrote the following description of a dark night in Czech history based on true events from *The Rise and Fall of the Third Reich* in order to honor those who suffered and died, and those who live well to create a new future for our children.

1942.

Over the wide gray ocean, back to Prague, situated on the River Vltava in central Bohemia, Europe's original high seat of learning, the city called the Mother of Cities, the Golden City, the City of One Hundred Spires, the City on the Threshold of Stars.

To Prague and Nazi occupation.

The world grew smaller and bigger at once, a heart of violence enthroned in the heart of nations. But also a new tongue for the song of women and men. A tongue to meet the violence of the old order and inscribe the new with consuming fire.

Jan Kubiš and Jozef Gabčík, sons of Czech, two born for a single day when the body rises and kills and the mouth long silent shouts vengeance to the sky.

People would say years later it was something of which they shouldn't speak, when in their great country of art and love so many lost their lives, and in the name of nothing. Useless, ugly, puffed-up, pompous, hatred from afar come to undo their ways and put out the light of their creative ones, to own the rest as slaves or idiots, imbeciles. Death, not life. Sorrow. And in the end, from the face of the earth, an entire city gone.

Even so, for the shamed city, people spent their lives to break the back of the foe. Such it was and so it stands, and from that day forward, they spoke freely of what they knew. They spoke not to forget.

In the summer of 1940, in secret the Czech king commissioned two men, Jan Kubiš, code-name Johannen, and Jozef Gabčík, code-name Courajien, officers, hidden and waiting, called to leave the country and travel nocturnally by foot and boat, over mountains and held by rivers through the dark west to England, across the channel to London, there to be trained by the old-century Royal Air Force, given the new science to return to their great besieged country, hunt, find, and kill the devil leader Reinhard Heydrich, the Nazi warlord. This their one act of retribution, their finality. And from it was wrought the end of Lidice, the small city, but also the redemption, finally, of their people.

City on a hill, Lidice, small Prague on the flatland just south of the high range of mountains called Pyratetten or Teeth of the Sky. Of Czech blood, vulnerable, laid bare, and borne of love: Who can lure the passion song of the world into a simple reed? Like the poet, Kahlil Gibran, who left his home country and made the world his home, Johannen and Courajien did the same. By faith the Czechs believed, and so it came to be.

In the summer of 1942, after their long study, Johannen and Courajien returned from their training and dropped by air into the heart of Nazi-occupied Czechoslovakia, in darkness, alone. This for their sons and daughters, their mothers, their fathers.

Nazi onslaught obscuring day, bearing night to the capital city of nations, Prague of the European empire, foreign tanks and airbirds, fears and terrors, skies filled of fire and screaming bombs, wind-cleavers and the cries of children, the mother's wail, and sirens, hospitals, mobs of people, no water, thirst, and as they gasped and held each other and suffered and waited for England, for allies, in the end their land was taken.

The unthinkable, to be lost to Germany.

Prague and her people, of proud nations very proud.

Occupied, the people sought the devil leader, Reinhard Heydrich, called "The Butcher of Prague" and "The Blond Beast." They sought him to take his life and return him whole to hell. A retaliation against the predator-face of the Nazi Order for its wanton slaughtering of Czech women and children, Czech men, and dignity. Heydrich, chief of the Security Police, deputy chief of the Gestapo, the implementing hand of the "final solution" that killed six million, countless Czechs among them, narrow-nosed man with haughty eyes, whose wife, dog-eyed and supple in postured ignorance, reminded the living of another Nazi frau who made lampshades of Jewish skin. "Hangman Heydrich" as he was known in the occupied lands, a man who adored power, secretly wanted his own boss Himmler's life, and came, under Hitler's authority, to be Acting Protector of Czech Bohemia and Moravia. In 1942 he took the ancient seat of the Bohemian kings at Hradschin Castle in Prague. Two months later, Czech sons Johannen and Courajien threw the bomb that tore his life away.

Johannen, of average height, thin-faced, serious; Courajien, taller and bigger, boisterous, wide-chested, a fighter—willing when called to forfeit their lives.

"Tomorrow we end it," said Johannen, staring at the floor. He spoke loudly to overcome the noise of the plane.

"Tomorrow," Courajien shouted, and smiled.

Johannen looked up into the eyes of his friend. "Are you afraid?"

Courajien took Johannen's face in his hands, firmly, as a brother might.

"If I die, I die happy."

Night drop orchestrated at low altitude in a British plane over forested lands, aircraft jet black, the quiet drone fading high above them. Wind in the air, blackened chutes opening like silk overhead, the two men on strings drifting down and down, in darkness the land below like a lost love, returned, *laskah*, the long awaited kiss, patient they fell, holy, into the body exact, enduring. They came to the earth effortless and made swift progress on the ground, subdued shadows in the dark, their forms near silent, near invisible and full of speed, intent, efficient, running as men run who know their enemy and whose desire is to devastate him, and being ready, men whose fate aligns them with their people so the ground of the world, water, wind, sky, lifts them easy as the morning bird to the appointed place so the deed is matched to the men, and the enemy, oblivious, receives his just reward.

Heydrich drove on a morning of May in 1942 in a top-down green Mercedes sports coupe toward the Castle in Prague. At a corner, concealed, the two men watched his approach and in a unified motion lofted their British-made bomb into the car, blowing the rear of the car to pieces, shattering Heydrich's spine so that the long nose of the man wrinkled in pain and groans were heard from the slit of his mouth while chunks of his flesh were set like objects among the car's remains.

"Smoke," whispered Johannen, and Courajien noticed the beauty, billowing, mixed with car fire, a black and gray column pervasive and all-consuming, and the men removed themselves slowly, concealed, and passed the man's body in the street and cursed him in his death throes, and left him to receive what they felt was of God's own making, vengeance to the face of the foe.

The face of the foe grew dark.

Johannen and Courajien reached the priests of the Karl Borromaeus Church in Prague and were given refuge.

Heydrich breathed for ten days, then died of his wounds.

Hitler and his Germans, savage in revenge, snatched up and executed 1,331 Czechs, 201 women among them.

Johannen and Courajien, along with 120 members of the Czech resistance, were besieged and killed in the Karl Borromaeus Church.

The Germans displaced 3,000 Jews from the "safe" ghetto of Theresienstadt, herded them East, and exterminated them.

When Hitler heard of the bombing, 500 of the 600 at large Jews in Berlin were imprisoned. On the day of Heydrich's death, 152 of them were executed as punishment.

In the small village, Lidice, near the mining town Kladno just outside Prague, the German hand rose to slay the Czechs for the death of Heydrich.

Though no evidence existed that Lidice's people had been involved in any way, the town stood only 12 miles from Prague and the order came directly from Hitler:

1. All men to be executed by shooting.
2. All women to be sent to concentration camps.
3. Children are to be concentrated, those capable of being Germanized are to be sent to SS families in Germany and the rest elsewhere.
4. The commune is to be burnt down and leveled to the ground.

Three days after Heydrich's death, on June 9, 1942, ten trucks of German Security Police led by Captain Max Rostock appeared and took formation around the village.

Nine years later his body hung by the neck in Prague for his misconduct.

But first, his days of infamy.

From the loudspeaker the electric voice of Rostock in the German tongue: "*Alles muss hier bleiben.*" Everyone stays.

"*Keine gehen.*" No one goes.

A twelve-year-old boy, afraid, ran five steps before a bullet took his life. Pierced through the upper torso he lay sprawled on wet earth, his shirt half-open, bands of ribcage exposed, the left hipbone motionless as a ledge of polished marble. A woman broke for the near field and they let her run, smiling before they shot her.

The Germans corralled every man and boy, herding most into the barn of Horak, a farmer, the town mayor. The rest they stored in Horak's cellars.

Night and darkness, whisperings of men and children.

The next day from dawn to dusk, boy and man were led to the garden behind the barn, ten by ten, and shot at close range by firing squads. One hundred seventy-two men and boys died, their bodies like loose change left on the ground. Nineteen more, found working in the Kladno mines, were also executed by firing squad.

The German police took seven Lidice women to Prague and shot them in public.

The remainder, 195 women in all, were hauled to Ravensbrueck concentration camp in Germany and there seven met the gas chamber, three "disappeared," and forty-two expired from concentration camp conditions. Of the Lidice women, an unlucky four were pregnant. These were taken to a hospital in Prague where the Germans murdered their newborns and shipped the empty mothers to Ravensbrueck.

The only humans left of Lidice were some few children, their fathers dead, their mothers prison wards of the Nazi state. The Germans reported they sent the children to a concentration camp, ninety all told, and of these, eight were less than a year old. The eight were taken by the Nazis, deemed sound by Himmler's "racial experts," and sent to Germany to be raised German with German names, ingested this way into the Fatherland, chosen for the Nazi program *Lebensborn*. The remaining eighty-two were shipped by train to Lodz, where they lived three weeks in a collection camp. The youngest child was one year and six days old, the oldest boys were under the age of fifteen, the oldest girls under sixteen. In early June the children were taken to a castle and told to undress. They were also told they could keep only their underwear, a towel, and a bar of soap, so they could shower before the journey to Chelmno concentration camp. They were squeezed into the closed bed of a truck modified to exterminate 80–90 people and killed by exhaust in eight minutes.

In 1945, at war's end, of the children of Lidice the Czech government stated in a report for the Nuremberg tribunal, "Every trace of them has been lost."

The Germans effectively removed Lidice from the earth. No trace of the village remained. All men killed, all women and children either killed, forsaken, or taken. The Germans bonfired the village, dynamited the ruins, and covered the remains with landfill.

The earth under storm and rain, snow and broken tree, wind, sun and fire.

Time and the hope for healing took Lidice, place of sorrow, and made it sacred. Sacred ground, and none beheld it, and none returned to it, covered over by Nazi ingenuity, and from the gaping wound of its dying day fields of flowers emerged in the quiet of coming years. The bells of the flowers, delicate, clothed in lavender and white, glowed in morning light.

As late as 1947, newspaper pleas after the war, pitiful but hoping, were sent through Allied-controlled media lines into post-war German homes, notes from the few remaining mothers of Lidice:

My city was lost. My child taken.
Please return my child.
I am from Lidice. Our husbands were shot.
Our children lost.
Have mercy on us.

And some few boy-children were delivered home, not knowing their mothers' names.

Now, long after the Nazi regime, long after the Prague Spring and the ensuing invasion in which Soviet tanks lined the streets of Prague, and finally, long after the vivid beauty of the Velvet Revolution, we return to Havel's conception of hope and consciousness:

> Consciousness precedes being . . .
>
> Hope is a state of mind, not of the world. Hope, in this deep and powerful sense, is not the same as joy that things are going well, or willingness to invest in enterprises that are obviously heading for success, but rather an ability to work for something because it is good.
>
> Hope is definitely not the same thing as optimism. It is not the conviction that something will turn out well, but the certainty that something makes sense, regardless of how it turns out.

If you visit Lidice today, you find a place of solemnity and quiet, a place of abiding reverence where the great Czech artists have erected elegies of sorrow and loss. Nearby is a city called New Lidice. A mayor of that city, now decades since the Nazi horror, was one of those few children taken to Germany as a child. *Lebensborn.* Stolen. Ingested. Returned finally to his homeland, where he grew to lead his people, in remembrance, in healing, in peace.

Chapter 15

The Practice of Consciousness

After considering the razing of Lidice alongside the Sand Creek Massacre, we are left with the despair and shame of being human. At the same time, both Black Kettle and Havel remind us of the grace of courageous leadership in times of crisis. There exists a worldwide crisis today having to do with our intricate dealings with one another. Our lack of sensitivity to each other in family, at work, in politics, and in churches, mosques, and synagogues has reached paramount levels. Servant leadership calls out . . . How often do we, men and women, ask forgiveness of others? How often do we actually choose to shake off our blindness and commit to the long good road of change and reconciliation? Do we ask forgiveness? Do we forgive? Are we healers?

If not, then perhaps we are not servant leaders.

Servant leadership echoes Havel's refreshing sense of the sacred with regard to consciousness and being. In so doing, servant leadership provides a thoughtful and active progression toward mature personhood. Havel's call is personal and global, and if it infuses the institutions, large and small, that constitute the daily work life of millions around the world, if it infuses both the individual and the collective, the result will influence significant trends of human interaction across all societal levels. Gratitude, forgiveness, and power accompany Havel's view of being and consciousness, a view of the life of the mind and spirit whose illumination is expressed in the body and breath, the elemental basis of what it means to be human. In this way we become present to others in listening, and touch, and quietness, and song, present to our deepest and most physical expressions of peace, love, and affection, especially in the aftermath of horror. We hear Parker Palmer's graceful call, and we respond by envisioning and living out "the most profound form of

Table 15.1. Below-the-Line Thinking

LEVELS OF CONSCIOUSNESS	HOW THE LEADER MOTIVATES
Stress and Effort	Pressure, Rewards, Punishments
Chaos or Crisis	Retribution, Control, Dominance
Unhappy, Insecure, Complaining	Guilt or Obligation
Troubled, Highly Fearful, and Angry	Fear and Threats

Source: Paul Nakai, *The Mindful Corporation* (Long Beach, CA: Leadership Press), 57.

leadership [we] can imagine—leading a suffering person back to life from a living death."[59]

On the other end of the scale, people who suffer under false leadership are bound by knots of ultra-self-focused thought whose foundation is ego and fear, and whose corresponding actions are oppressive to self, self-annihilating, and empty of regard for others. Consider the strands of consciousness depicted in Table 15.1 and the corresponding ways the leader motivates when he or she is bound by them.

In *The Mindful Corporation*, Paul Nakai presents a view of consciousness blessed with transparency. People of immature or undeveloped consciousness make poor leaders; however, in good leaders we find a complex nexus of personal responsibility, mature living, and self-transcendence. Consciousness can be envisioned as a fluid continuum in which the person or the collective experiences a steady advance toward increased thoughtfulness and greater maturity, or a pathetic stagnation in which the inner world is experienced as void of vibrant life. The lower levels of thought are intrinsically fortified and in certain cases intractable.

BELOW-THE-LINE THINKING

Nakai speaks of the totality of thought and how our grasp of our own thought and our responsibility for our own thought determine the light or shadow we cast in the world. At the lowest level our thinking is troubled and we find ourselves incapacitated, highly fearful, or tremendously angry. At this level we find relational functioning, work, and life itself extremely difficult. Our experience is often plagued by insurmountable failure or pervasive harm. Not everyone experiences this level, but most of us at one time or another have either lived in it for a time or encountered a system bound by troubled thought. For some the troubled thought life is so pervasive they never escape it. At the troubled level, anxiety or anger accompany us like unwanted visitors. Major depression or its counter, fully expressed rage, consume us. Our thoughts torque inward in an ever-deepening spiral; we face suicide. Our thoughts bend outward in uncontrolled explosiveness; we perpetrate homicide. Our self-focus is tirelessly inward or viciously outward: in undiluted narcissism, mentally and physically, we kill ourselves or kill others. We make very poor leaders, and, in fact, as people we are very hard to be around. We get our way by threatening others. Life in its most excruciating forms is caught in this web of thought, and degraded action and impact follow. Our lifestyle is entrenched in and bound by pain.

One level up from the troubled impulse is simple unhappiness. Unhappiness characterizes the thought life of those who tend to complain, rarely admit their own faults, and often point out the faults of others. Defensiveness also resides at this level, and in turn, insecurity. In other words, such thinking is often still laced by fear and anger, and it remains pervasively oriented toward externalization of responsibility for one's own choices, actions, and encounters with others. The unhappy person is unhappy, even when life is good. At this level, we may use our words to heap guilt on others, reminding them, manipulatively, of what we think they owe us. We make others feel obligated.

Above unhappiness is chaos. In chaos our thoughts center on the disruption and intensity of life, and even if a time of rest comes to us we feel uncomfortable and quickly orient our lives back to chaos. We tend to feel disordered and out of control; we live from chaos to chaos without a true sense of direction or consistency. In chaos we are definitely better than the levels below chaos, but our thought life remains tenuous because a given amount of chaos can tip the scales and send us plummeting back to unhappiness, fear, or anger.

Above chaos is stress and effort. At the level of thought in which we tell ourselves we are okay with stress and effort, our consciousness is oriented toward a hard work ethic and the compulsive push to press on, achieve, and never give up. A refreshing sense of accomplishment can accompany this level of thought, but our lives are also undeniably plagued by the haunting shadows of stress. Such shadows exhibit themselves through mental, physical, and relational breakdown. We tend to overdo it. We are rigid and defined more by efficiency and results than by creativity and exponential potential. Our attempts to motivate others are infused with control and dominance. We have a consistently high need for retribution.

Fear and anger, unhappiness, chaos, and stress and effort define the lower levels of consciousness. If there is a line between immature and mature thought, between intellectual unconsciousness and the thoughtful life, between unthinking reaction and conscious purposeful action, then fear, anger, chaos, stress, and effort are below this line.

ABOVE-THE-LINE THINKING

Above the line we find the fulfillment of the mind designed for beauty and selflessness. We are attended by elegant and decisive ways of thinking and living: contentment, grace and ease, gratitude, humor, wisdom, forgiveness, power, and love. Above-the-line thinking involves an immediate turn toward self-transcendence.

Contentment is the first level of thinking above the line (see Table 15.2). The contented person is not plagued by cynicism, blame, complaint, or nihilism. She or he is wonderful to be with. In this person's presence, we experience contentment, and it leads us to embrace our own self-responsibility for life and choices, and in doing so, we become more humble and more content ourselves. This contentment is not dependent on external circumstances, justice, physical health, or the avoidance of suffering. Contentment defines the life of a person who has come to terms with self, others, God, and world.

As we continue into more selfless ways of thinking, our thoughts become infused with grace and ease. We view others with grace, and we approach the complexity and uncontrolled aspects of life with openness and appreciation. Even during very difficult circumstances, we live in peace. We bring peace with us in daily life, and when external pressures intensify we embrace the ambiguity and provide a calming and salient influence. Even during oppression, injury, or unavoidable suffering, we lead others into a greater sense of peace. Relationships and common sense, not external circumstances, define our way of life.

Above grace and ease, we find gratitude and humor. People who live with gratitude bring a larger sense of life to bear. They are refreshing and undaunted. Viktor Frankl and Father Kolbe (whose story is detailed in Chapter 17) lived with tremendous audacity even while facing the sheer depravity of the Nazi regime. Father Kolbe was a source of nearly inexhaustible strength to those around him in the horrors of World War II. Frankl spoke of the healing powers of both gratitude and humor when confronted by humiliation and imminent

Table 15.2.   Above-the-Line Thinking

LEVELS OF CONSCIOUSNESS	HOW THE LEADER MOTIVATES
Love, Wisdom, Inspiration	Love, Discernment, Compelling life
Gratitude, Humor	Encouragement, Service to Others
Grace, Ease	Peace, Common Sense
Contentment	Self-responsibility, Humility

Source: Paul Nakai, *The Mindful Corporation* (Long Beach, CA: Leadership Press), 57.

threat to personal and collective life. In conditions of disease and death, Frankl and Father Kolbe drew themselves and others to a place of unshakable relationship and true respect through life affirmation and simple gratitude. Frankl's description of the eye is haunting in its metaphorical power, defining our purpose to focus on others, not ourselves. In service to others we live clearly. In service to self our life is plagued by relational blindness, lack of foresight, and self-defeat. Father Kolbe's example is striking. In the course of life he faced extreme brutality, yet his generosity to his fellow human beings remained unconditionally open.

On the upper end of the continuum of consciousness we find people who compel us to expressions of vitality and renewal that are luminous, and in a sense, eternal. Such people represent the divine or formless elements of our collective humanity, or what mystic Christianity defines as the Mystery, and branches of Hinduism, Buddhism, and the Tao define as soul force, life force, or life energy. The formless is that part of us we cannot hold down or easily control; it is wild and worthy, and in its presence we are drawn to a greater sense of ourselves. Love is the essence of the formless. Here, wisdom, inspiration, and forgiveness are love's attendants, and the healing that defines servant leadership is a way of life. The forms we take to express the formless are myriad—basic, complex, creative, direct—and we know them when we experience them. Power, then, resides in the ability to live in surrender, listening, persuasion, and obedience and to shun dominance, coercion, and control. In the true sense of human dignity, then, love is power. Table 15.3 represents the continuum of our potential for greater and more other-focused consciousness. The continuum, at its upper levels, reflects the mind and action of the mature leader.

Table 15.3. Above- and Below-the-Line Thinking

LEVELS OF CONSCIOUSNESS	HOW THE LEADER LEADS
Love, Wisdom, Inspiration	Love, Discernment, Compelling life
Gratitude, Humor	Encouragement, Service to Others
Grace, Ease	Peace, Common Sense
Contentment	Self-responsibility, Humility
Stress and Effort	Pressure, Rewards, Punishments
Chaos or Crisis	Retribution, Control, Dominance
Unhappy, Insecure, Complaining	Guilt or Obligation
Troubled, Highly Fearful, and Angry	Fear and Threats

Source: Paul Nakai, *The Mindful Corporation* (Long Beach, CA: Leadership Press), 57.

Truth is not a stepwise progression, but a spiral dynamic, both linear and circular. Contentment, grace and ease, gratitude and humor, wisdom, inspiration, forgiveness, healing, power, and love . . . these are the hallmarks of true personhood, true consciousness, and true leadership. In a spiral dynamic we may find ourselves in one moment afraid or angry, and in another full of grace. Reaching more mature levels of thought requires willing submission, or in other words surrender. When we surrender, our lives begin to take on a deeper and deeper devotion to the quality of being true. In this sense to be willing . . . to listen and obey . . . to submit . . . is not a burden but a heartfelt response to love. Not surprisingly, the word *truth* comes from the root word *troth,* or betrothal—to be faithful, devoted, loyal—to love another in the depths of his or her being. True leadership is love. People at mature levels of consciousness love deeply, and are deeply loved. They are not easily hurt. They are powerful, their power is legitimate, and they help others engage legitimate power.

From this place we return to Elizabeth Barrett Browning's directive:

Love me in full being.

Her voice is resonant with Havel's conception of consciousness, the interior tenacity of Frankl and Father Kolbe, and Greenleaf's great discovery that to listen well is to serve the heart of all. In her poem "A Man's Requirements," Elizabeth utters a radiant calling:

Through all hopes that keep us brave,
Farther off or nigher,
Love me for the house and grave,
And for something higher.

In Elizabeth Barrett Browning we find the bright nucleus of servant leadership—to love the world, to love others more than our own lives, to engage life and experience the grace of being deeply and truly loved—and from this emerges the consciousness that precedes being and the joy that accompanies a lifestyle devoted to what is good and what is essential. In this life we can enter together the crucible of human existence, with its ever-present capacity for good and evil, and emerge with a sense of refinement, wholeness, and holiness.

Chapter 16

Servant Leadership Consciousness and Listening

Servant leadership consciousness is particularly attuned to "above-the-line" levels of thought. The best description I've found of servant leadership consciousness and the character of the servant leader is provided by Larry Spears. In his seventeen years as CEO of the Greenleaf Center for Servant Leadership and in his current roles as CEO of the Spears Center for Servant Leadership and the Robert K. Greenleaf Servant Leadership Scholar at Gonzaga University, Larry Spears has been responsible for much of the movement of servant leadership in contemporary organizational life. Having met Robert Greenleaf shortly before Greenleaf's death in 1990, Spears helped collect, edit, and publish much of Greenleaf's work posthumously. As mentioned at the outset, Spears's content analysis of Greenleaf's writings resulted in his distillation of the ten characteristics of servant leadership, a classic of contemporary servant leadership thought. The characteristics—listening, empathy, healing, awareness, persuasion, conceptualization, foresight, stewardship, commitment to the growth of people, and building community—provide a distinctive look at servant leadership above the line.

I am grateful to Larry for contributing the foreword to this book, and for his ongoing work to help define and further servant leadership globally. In trying to gain an enriched understanding of the characteristics of servant leadership, I asked Larry if they are ordered in some way. His response astonished me and reminded me again of how frequently contemporary culture can sweep us into a form of breakneck pace and hyperspeed mentality.

"Are they listed in order of importance?" I asked.

"No," he replied. "Though one is the foundation for all the others."

The characteristics ran through my mind . . . is it building community? or stewardship? These probably reach the most people, I thought. Or maybe commitment to the growth of people? . . . or perhaps foresight because with foresight we see the way ahead and people, races, and nations can be saved from impending destructive forces.

"Listening," he said.

Listening is the source of the other characteristics. From his contact with Greenleaf's original work, he found that listening was the most foundational and most mentioned of all the characteristics. Listening is foremost, Larry declared, and in Larry's own writing he speaks to how listening must be maintained, for in listening we create the kind of lasting and informed relationships capable of meeting the great difficulties of the age:

> Leaders have traditionally been valued for their communication and decision-making skills. Although these are also important skills for the servant leader, they need to be reinforced by a deep commitment to listening intently to others. The servant leader seeks to identify the will of a group and helps to clarify that will. He or she listens receptively to what is being said and unsaid. Listening also encompasses hearing one's own inner voice. Listening, coupled with periods of reflection, is essential to the growth and well-being of the servant leader.[60]

Larry's words lead me back to the lived experience of those who listen, women and men whose lives are rich and generative because of the attentiveness of their listening and the actions they take from having listened well. From the Old Testament sacred text, Isaiah might well have been describing those who listen when he said, "In quietness and confidence shall be your strength."[61] Their lives demonstrate a highly developed capacity to hear and respond. They grow still. They seek more knowledge. Through listening, servant leaders discern the path ahead, and their interactions with others are then defined by the holistic embrace of empathy, healing, awareness, persuasion, conceptualization, foresight, stewardship, commitment to the growth of others, and building community. In listening, we surrender our ego and seek the above-the-line consciousness that results in a life lived for the greater good of others and the world.

FIRST THROUGH LISTENING

Earlier I mentioned Scott Peck's *The Road Less Traveled*, a book that was on the *New York Times* bestseller list for more than five years.[62] Delivering a profound challenge, Peck's thought requires great things of readers. Again, the first truth the reader encounters is this: life is difficult; therefore discipline is required. Receiving Peck's wisdom, readers experience a greater sense of life and love with each ensuing page. The book was informed by knowledge Peck gathered over the course of years, but specifically, one might ask, how did he accomplish a work of such great impact and reach? He attributed it at least in part to spending three hours in silence each morning *before* he began the day's writing.

Silence is elusive. The industrial, technological, financial, and media-driven machine of contemporary times is like a hungry beast, never satiated, never still, always on the move, noisy, and cloaked in the armor of desire, ambition, and addiction. But in the midst of all the noise an indomitable responsiveness can be found in the heart of those committed to finding answers. Greenleaf called such people true natural servants:

> I have a bias about this which suggests that only a true natural servant automatically responds to any problem by listening first . . . Remember the great line from the prayer of Saint Francis, "Lord, grant that I may not seek so much to be understood as to understand."[63]

Greenleaf further laid the foundation of one who listens by saying:

> Listening is a healing attitude, the attitude of intensely holding the belief—faith if you wish to call it thus—that the person or persons being listened to will rise to the challenge of grappling with the issues involved in finding their own wholeness.[64]

Peck's devotion to silence and Greenleaf's nod to true natural servants lead me to consider two more examples of deep listening: the Quaker clearness committee, and the spiritual formation of the Jesuits.

THE QUAKER CLEARNESS COMMITTEE

Quaker clearness committees create a devoted space of silence so that a person can discern a more confident current direction in his or her life.[65] The Religious Society of Friends known as the Quakers began in England in the seventeenth century. The word *Quaker* refers to a physical "trembling" in the presence of the Lord, a trembling early Quakers were noted for in their spiritual gatherings. From the start, Quakers were persecuted for their beliefs, but their resilience and fortitude kept the movement alive and growing, especially in the Americas and Africa. The influence of the Religious Society of Friends is notable in world history, perhaps especially because their way of life is just that: influential, or more precisely, dedicated to persuasion. Some examples: William Penn founded the state of Pennsylvania as a safe place for Quakers to live and practice their faith; Quakers have established strength and endurance in movements to abolish slavery, promote equal rights for women, and promote respect and dialogue over warfare; and Quakers have advanced the humane treatment of prisoners and the mentally ill while also forwarding education through founding or reforming various institutions.

From the original work of Gray Cox, Carolyn Crippen identified four fundamental beliefs that are interwoven in the Quaker tradition:

1. Truth is something that happens, it occurs. Truth is not a dead fact which is known; it is a living occurrence in which we participate.
2. Meaning is communal. Mind is a social activity; meaning is something we do together and share jointly. We may say many different things, and yet somehow speak with one voice.
3. Feeling and reason are viewed as continuous with one another. With feeling we touch, with reason we reach. Feeling is the aspect of immediacy, reason is the aspect of mediation or bridging.
4. The self is inherently social and transitional, becoming. People are aspects of communal processes.[66]

From these fundamental beliefs, five aspects of decision making help inform Quaker process: (1) quieting impulses; (2) addressing concerns; (3) gathering consensus or seeking clearness (coming together in worship with others is a quieting and a clarifying force); (4) finding clearness (here a strong conviction emerges and the person finds the resolve to embrace the truth of this conviction); imminent openness attends the seeker as a full palette of perspectives is considered; the seeker seeks wholeness and finds decision-making integrity; a central perspective is arrived at through multiple diverse perspectives; unanimity and a sense of presence characterize clearness; and (5) bearing witness—when clearness is found, the seeker is compelled toward private or public action.[67]

In Chapter 18, the Quaker John Woolman's work to abolish slavery will be presented, but first it is good to consider the role of listening in the Quaker clearness committee. Parker Palmer defines the purpose of the clearness committee as helping one another practice a process that protects the sanctity of the soul.[68] The person (the discerner) who calls the committee generally does so in order to gain insight and direction on a problem or some complexity he or she is facing in vocation, family, or another facet of life. People are chosen to participate, and the gathering meets for two to three uninterrupted hours. The discerner is the center of the group process. Silence and listening are the primary components. Committee members do not speak unless they feel they can add to the process by asking the discerner an open, honest question. The discerner may answer or pass on any question. Advice or oversimplification by committee members is forbidden. Two levels of confidentiality are held to: no speaking outside the meeting of what was said in the meeting; and members may not make comments or suggestions to the discerner either during or after the process. The process is infused with prayer, both corporate and individual. A convener facilitates both process and prayers, keeps track of time, and toward the end of the session asks the discerner if she or he would like to do some "mirroring." If not, the members continue with questions. If so, what the discerner said or did, but what might be out of present awareness, is reflected back. For example, members might make comments such as: "Your body seemed heavy when you spoke of . . .", or "Your face looked alive when you said. . . ."

The experience is an embrace of wisdom in the self, others, and God. From listening comes clarity, and from clarity, action. The abolition of slavery, the promotion of human rights, and the opportunity for education and thus, greater understanding, all have their roots in the Religious Society of Friends' devotion to quietness and resolute commitment to communal listening.

THE JESUITS

The Jesuit order of the Catholic priesthood has also exerted great influence toward the betterment of humanity. Dubbed by Chris Lowney as the 450-year-old company that changed the world, the Jesuits, or "little Christs," have injected into the bloodstream of humanity an approach to education, formation, and discovery that is characterized by resplendent internal and communal ideas such as *cura personalis* (care for and education of the whole person: heart, mind, and spirit) and the *magis* (among many possible good choices, let us choose together the ultimate good). Chris Lowney speaks to the quiet power of the Jesuits as founded not on the flashy mystique of popular leadership, but on enduring pillars of substance such as self-awareness, ingenuity, love, and heroism.[69] In the last five centuries Jesuits have been leaders in philosophy, science, poetry, and exploration. In so doing, they built relationships founded on deep care, wisdom, and prayer and became confidants to European monarchs, the kings of Spain and Portugal, and the Holy Roman Emperor, as well as China's Ming emperor and the Mughal emperor in India. Jesuit explorers were among the first Europeans to cross the Himalayas and enter Tibet, paddle to the headwaters of the Blue Nile, and chart the Upper

Mississippi River. Founded in 1540 by ten men, today the order has twenty-
one thousand professionals who lead two thousand institutions devoted to
education and social justice in more than one hundred countries.

Ignatius of Loyola, the founder of the Jesuits and a humble and dedicated
leader, helped develop the Jesuits' life-affirming essence. Through bonds of
"mutual affection" he wanted himself and his Jesuit brothers to go forth and
"help souls."

Perhaps the quintessential aspect of the Jesuit presence in the world is
listening. In each Jesuit's personal formation, a decade-long process, the
Jesuit embarks on specific interior journeys devoted almost solely to listening. Based on the spiritual exercises Ignatius formed in the 1500s, even today
each Jesuit enters at least two encounters of *thirty days of silence* in which a
spiritual director, a kind of mentor or father, helps the journeyer travel deeper
into the experience of his own shadow and light. Awareness of faults, weaknesses, and gifts comes to the fore, and this enriching internal inventory is
honed by a thrice-daily contemplative moment called the *examen* in which the
journeyer continues to experience greater love for God, others, and self while
weeding out attachments that confine, reduce, or distort the soul. The result
of this highly attuned sense of listening is a more refined ability to discern the
difference between the spirit of life and the spirit of death in the world, and
how to become more aligned with the spirit of life.

As the Jesuit moves through his own personal development from the time
of his first calling even unto his death, the thrice-daily examen draws him
closer and closer to life. Greenleaf named listening as the foundation of serving others and the mark of all who seek to heal the heart of the world. Talking
too much, like being too busy, is a form of failing to be present to the essential
human journey. Greenleaf's message, written in the legacy of servant leaders
the world over, draws us into a sacred quietness and reminds us to listen first
and listen well:

Many attempts to communicate are nullified by saying too much.[70]

From listening, the world can be transformed. Consider the Jesuit Father
Pedro Arrupe, a man who listened well and discerned a call to action in the
South Pacific during World War II. In 1938, when his superior sent him
to Japan for work as a missionary, Arrupe went wholeheartedly. While in
Nagatsuka on the outskirts of Hiroshima on August 6, 1945, he experienced
the devastating effects of atomic warfare. "I was in my room with another
priest," Arrupe said, "when suddenly we saw a blinding light, like a flash of
magnesium." A large sound came, a "formidable explosion" like the "blast
of a hurricane," and suddenly doors, windows, and walls fell on Arrupe and

his companion as well as on the rest of the priests in the building. After they picked themselves up and went into the streets to try to help others, Father Arrupe recorded what he witnessed:

> I shall never forget my first sight of what was the result of the atomic bomb: a group of young women, 18 or 20 years old, clinging to one another as they dragged themselves along the road. One had a blister that almost covered her chest; she had burns across half of her face, and a cut in her scalp caused probably by a falling tile, while great quantities of blood coursed freely down her face. On and on they came, a steady procession numbering some 150,000. This gives some idea of the scene of horror that was Hiroshima. We continued looking for some way of entering the city, but it was impossible. We did the only thing that could be done in the presence of such mass slaughter: we fell on our knees and prayed for guidance, as we were destitute of all human help.[71]

From the abyss of anguish, they listened and responded. When he and his colleagues rose, Father Arrupe, a man who trained as a physician before entering the Jesuits, converted their communal living space into a hospital and cared for people suffering wounds from the bomb and the aftereffects of radiation poisoning. His experience helped form in him an astounding love for humanity, which led to his later being elected as the Superior General of the Jesuits, a leader who many feel returned the order to its devotion to social justice, love, and finding God in all things. When he led the Jesuits, he helped the order listen and reflect, and take action. The Jesuit calling, in response to Father Arrupe's healing presence, was to reconcile people to God, knowing that the only way divine reconciliation happens is when we, as people, reconcile with each other, and that the only way we can truly reconcile is through setting things right again . . . through working to attain social justice for all, and especially for the least privileged and the most oppressed. Here, forgiveness, power, and servant leadership are kin. The following counsel, a kind of guiding prayer written by Father Arrupe, creates a resonant recognition in the heart of the servant leader of just what is required to help heal the heart of the world:

> Nothing is more practical than finding God, that is, than falling in love in a quite absolute, final way. What you are in love with, what seizes your imagination, will affect everything. It will decide what will get you out of bed in the morning, what you will do with your evenings, how you spend your weekends, what you read, who you know, what breaks your heart, and what amazes you with joy and gratitude.—Fall in love; stay in love, and it will decide everything.[72]

Part III

A Narrative of Hope and Responsible Action

The strong of soul forgive.

—Kahlil Gibran[1]

Chapter 17

The Inward Road

For Greenleaf, listening occurs both in one-to-one relationships and in the context of a higher order more concerned with the life of the community as a whole. In person-to-person encounters, a servant leader is "concerned, responsible, effective, value oriented." At the same time, on a more global level the servant leader is "detached, riding above it, seeing today's events, and seeing oneself deeply involved in today's events, in the perspective of a long sweep of history and projected into the indefinite future."[2] Legitimate power is achieved by persuasion and example. Forgiveness is embodied first by asking forgiveness and restoring one's integrity through necessary change, as well as by granting forgiveness and working toward a just resolution. Just as the servant leader is servant first, the servant leader asks forgiveness first and does not wait for the "other" to take the initial steps toward reconciliation. Hope and responsible action animate our lives.

In servant leadership, the listener becomes a person who sees more clearly his or her own faults, works diligently to overcome them, and understands then how to bring healing to others. For the seeker, this portion of the road is an inward road, often fraught with confusion, halts, and starts. Yet with mentors and patience we find other travelers, and greater clarity and direction. From the core of listening, Greenleaf's journey into legitimate power and greatness is vitalized, and the ten characteristics of servant leadership become a unified way of life. The characteristics help form the consciousness of the servant leader. A closer look at the characteristics, illustrated by true life examples, will shed light on servant leadership *as a way of being* in relationship with others. Listening is first. Empathy, healing, and awareness follow.

EMPATHY

Empathy is the compassionate gift of seeing life through the eyes of another, and in seeing clearly, to extend tenderness. Servant leaders recognize people for their "special and unique spirits," assuming the good intentions of others and not rejecting people, even when they may be forced to refuse to accept patterns of behavior, attitudes, or larger systemic fault lines evident in the world.[3] The most successful servant leaders are those who have become skilled empathetic listeners. The empathic listener sees the heart of the other and values the heart of the other. In conditions imbued with human gravity, the listener hears and values the life of the other even more than his or her own life.

Prisoner 16670, Father Maximilian Kolbe, was a Polish priest condemned to the death camp at Auschwitz when the Nazis' Final Solution was in full effect. With charred bodies, monstrous experiments performed on the living, countless mass graves, a string of death camps across Europe, and endless smoke rising from the chimneys of human incineration, the Holocaust had ramped to horrific proportions. In this cauldron of dislocation and anguish, Maximilian Kolbe listened earnestly to the call of life.

When a prisoner escaped from Auschwitz, the Nazis chose ten others to be killed by starvation as vengeance. On just such a day in Auschwitz one of the men selected to die started crying, "My wife! My children! I will never see them again!" Immediately, Father Kolbe walked forward and asked to die in his place. The Nazis switched the two men, and as Kolbe and nine others were led off to the death block of Building 13, the priest supported one of the others who was nearly unable to walk. None of the ten survived. Kolbe was the last to die.

Kolbe's life became an elegy to the human spirit. At the beginning of the ordeal he and the other nine were thrown into the pit of Building 13, an underground death chamber where hunger and thirst made the days so ravenous men reportedly drank their own urine and licked moisture off the dank walls. Father Kolbe prayed with the men, recited psalms, and led them in songs and meditations. Two weeks later, the songs were still rising from the death block at Building 13 and the Nazis grew impatient, greedy to use the cell for more victims, hating Kolbe and the other prisoners for their tenacious resolve. The camp executioner, a common criminal named Bock, was called in, and when he entered the cell he found five men dead. He found Father Kolbe singing and holding the four who were still alive. Kolbe was the only one still fully conscious. The executioner injected a lethal dose of carbolic acid into the left arm of the four. He turned to Father Kolbe. Still singing, Kolbe raised his arm to receive the injection.[4]

HEALING

The practice of empathy is seamless in the heart devoted to healing. Spears said, "One of the great strengths of servant leadership is the potential for healing one's self and others. Many people have broken spirits . . . servant leaders recognize that they have an opportunity to help make whole those with whom they come in contact."[5] The source of healing is love, and while healing one's self is a daunting process in which we are often unsure and filled with confusion or fear, love can make the process one we welcome. My wife Jennifer is the primary place where I encounter love and healing. I've often wondered at her gifts, so effervescent, creating wholeness in others. She finds pathways out of her faults into a more whole and healed way of life. She does this by seeking out those she loves, asking them how she might improve, asking forgiveness easily and gracefully, and changing. Then she leads others into the same enriched sense of themselves. In the heat of a conflict, even when there is a power imbalance, she remains calm, and most often she achieves the underlying truths of all mature relationships—care, affection, forgiveness, justice. So how does one learn to live in that way, to live well? Books, insights, and experiences are all indispensable and inform Jennifer's way of life, but primarily she attributes her learning to the influence of her parents. Her parents, on the other hand, were raised in chaotic, often troubled homes and were compelled in their own lives to find gifted mentors to lead them. Close connection to others who live well is the bridge to healing.

I saw this early in our marriage during a drive to Seattle from Spokane. Jennifer and I accompanied her father and mother, and shortly into the trip her father said, "I'd like each of you to tell me one of my faults, so I can change, and strengthen my relationship with you." What I noticed immediately was not just the shock of the question (most fathers don't commonly embrace vulnerability!), but the fact that Jennifer and her mother received his words easily, and with a sense of confidence. They knew he would hear what was said, he wouldn't block their influence, and they knew he would follow through on their requests. After we all gave him input, Jennifer's mother asked the same question. Jennifer and I followed, and this was the beginning of a progression. In the coming years I experienced something so many individuals, families, organizations, and nations lack: the ability to come together and approach our deep-set faults in order to overcome them. In healing, we face our faults, and we change.

AWARENESS

The atrocities of human conflict seem literally to beg for hiddenness, silence, deceit, and denial, but the realm of truth is a realm of voice, and by giving voice to the pain and suffering endured in atrocity we see again the human will not just to survive but to be fully alive and restored to the best sense of ourselves. Awareness is the counter to denial, and in awareness we encounter the imagination and determination necessary to turn atrocity into meaning, and meaning into transcendence. In the award-winning film *Grbavica* by acclaimed writer and director Jasmila Žbanić, atrocity is the black under-line to a story of voice and hope. During the Serbo-Croatian conflict from 1990–1995, in addition to mass genocidal killings, rape was used as a weapon of war. Twenty thousand women, primarily Muslim, were systematically gang-raped by Serbian soldiers in order to humiliate the women and produce further destruction of their ethnic group. Jasmila Žbanić lived through the war, and her film tells the story of a Muslim mother named Esma. Her child Sara is twelve years old in the film. Sara was conceived when Esma was raped in a Bosnian concentration camp, and Esma frantically tries to conceal from her daughter the knowledge of the rape. In the movie, Žbanić uncovers the real truth of post-Bosnia women, among the worst sufferers of the war. She shows an intimate portrait of the life of Muslim women by freeing people to see a humane reflection of one woman who struggled with many years of hatred for her victimizers, while conveying to the world how it is impossible to hate one's child even if she was conceived in violence and horror. At home, as the truth unfolds, Sara confronts her mother Esma. Esma finally breaks and speaks the whole brutality of her experience. Suddenly Sara realizes she is the child of violation, and yet the truth draws mother and daughter closer. In the end, Sara is pictured on a school bus waving to Esma at the last moment, while the children on the bus are singing a popular tune about Sarajevo called "Land of My Dreams." As Sara looks courageously forward and starts singing with the other children, the film leaves viewers with the hope of healing.

Jasmila Žbanić is an image of the artist as reconciler—she reflects artists throughout human history whose fearless work shows genuine and natural servant leadership. Such artists draw us back to reality from the abstract planes associated with nihilism, the worship of nothingness, and the despair of life that often accompanies a darkened lens of engagement with the world. Czeslaw Milosz is another such artist, the Nobel Prize winner and Polish poet who loved the world enough to help us face reality and emerge with a greater sense of the future. Milosz's thoughts in *The Witness of Poetry* unabashedly question contemporary art filled with emptiness or life-negating expressions of meaninglessness: such art emerges from the artist who flees reality, rather than the artist who remains purposefully connected to this world, to people, to concrete detail, and being present. For Milosz, the artist who remains present to reality succeeds finally in giving witness to meaning. Milosz prophesies a turn, humanity having been given enough distance, and therefore grace, to move from meaninglessness up through the heart of human atrocity into something new that can meet the people of the world in an intimate and ultimate space: a movement Milosz calls "humanity as an elemental force conscious of transcending Nature."[6] He is referring to one's own nature, our enduring fallibility, and encourages artists not to fear and not to flee, but to live in and through memory toward a sense of renewed hope.

This brings us back to Havel, Czech president and playwright, who referred to suicides as the sad guardians of the meaning of life. Again, we hear his echo, "consciousness precedes being," a refrain that calls us to a real encounter with one another and the very human challenge of being a healing presence in the lives of others. Here we find possibility, and even more, miraculous possibility: a reconciliation that leads down through the abyss of evil, terror, and vacuousness, and up again to a vista from which we see one another whole and worthy of care and concrete purposeful action. Just and collective decision making accompanies this journey, as well as the kind of democratic and sacrificial good will that is the essence of life and love. From such consciousness we become willing to lay down our lives so that others may be free.

Consider Jan Palach, the university student who witnessed the will of his country severely tested when two hundred thousand communist troops invaded Czechoslovakia and two thousand tanks rolled into the streets of Prague. After the Prague Spring of 1968, the invasion that occurred in August of the same year meant the death of many who tried to resist, and in effect the fall of the entire country. Seeing his nation drop into a kind of sleep in the aftermath of such militarism, Palach and a group of like-minded university students decided to try to awaken the heart of the people in order to throw off the chains of the oppressive regime. The students made a pact and drew straws. Palach drew the first straw, went to the central square of Prague, and lit himself on fire, burning himself alive.

Self-immolation: *to burn oneself to death*. The very word *immolate*—to kill by sacrifice, to kill by fire—causes a restless gestation, and sends us into the open maw of that part of our collective humanity that cries out for justice. Some twenty years later, Palach's death had birthed the underground tremor that was fully realized when nearly a million people flooded the streets of Prague and brought about the Velvet Revolution—unseating a regime of terror, lies, and human regret and fulfilling a new and justly imagined democracy. The Velvet Revolution illumined for the world once again the elegant and powerful sense of who we can be, who we were meant to be. With uncommon insight Greenleaf observed, "Awareness is not a giver of solace—it is just the opposite. It is a disturber and an awakener. Able leaders are usually sharply awake and reasonably disturbed. They are not seekers after solace. They have their own inner serenity."[7]

A true encounter with love and power results in healing one's self and in turn healing others, even at the cost of complete self-sacrifice. Awareness, then, leads through an often fearsome doorway into a crucible that burns away chaff and results in one's own healing and inherently also the healing of the world around us. Touching again on the Jesuit ethos, we find the resolve to face ourselves. Early in the 1500s in the tiny Spanish town of Manresa, Ignatius of Loyola experienced an epiphany that "left his understanding so very enlightened that he felt as if he were another man with another mind."[8] Yes, he became the founder of the Jesuits, but it is noteworthy to remember that his life had been marked by failure, his leg nearly blown off in war by a cannon ball, his direction and aspirations at a standstill. When awareness struck him at Manresa, it impacted him so strongly that he who had come from a noble family left a life of privilege and wandered as a penniless beggar for nearly two years. Eventually, at age thirty-eight, he attended the University of Paris, the seat of higher learning of that day, and drew some of the brightest young minds of Europe to devote themselves to God simply for their desire to engage the composed and potent personhood Ignatius emanated. His gift was not his personal leadership qualities; it was the way his self-understanding allowed him to discern and bring forth in others their own latent leadership potential. Self-understanding had forged an attractive vitality, which he credited to encountering God in the quietness of Manresa, and the spiritual exercises Ignatius wrote became the program of meditations and interior practices that have energized and given life to Jesuit intelligence, spirit, and social justice throughout the world. Over the span of nearly five hundred years now, Ignatius's way of life has resulted in Jesuit advancement of science and medicine, fearless exploration, and the founding of hundreds of the world's finest universities. Through a purposeful process to engage the inward journey, self-understanding becomes balanced maturity, and human resilience becomes an art form.

Spears echoed this vision of a greater reality when he stated, "General awareness, and especially self-awareness, strengthens the servant-leader. Awareness helps one in understanding issues involving ethics, power, and values . . . to view most situations from a more integrated, holistic position."⁹ From the Serbo-Croatian conflict to the Velvet Revolution, and from the epiphany at Manresa to the complex nuances of being present to others today, the servant leader who is aware gives light, life, and healing. All around us we see a world fraught with numbness, addiction, and failures of relationship that come in a myriad of forms. Closing our eyes to the pain, it is as if night has fallen and we find we have been lulled into a deep and seemingly endless sleep. But in the morning, when the sun returns, the servant leader awakens the world.

Chapter 18

The Illumined Nature of Persuasion

The below-the-line fear mentality so evident in the power imbalances of life, work, and family shows the hard-rooted grip of manipulation and oppression, rather than the harvest brought to fruition by servant leadership. Listening leads us further into the characteristics of servant leaders, giving the journeyer a new understanding of persuasion, conceptualization, and foresight.

At our worst, when trying to get our way, we often resort to the use of manipulation, pressure, and violence. But in a life attuned to beauty and healing, persuasion achieves mutual respect and healthy results without coercion. The life led by persuasion and example is true. In like fashion, the true life is intrinsically persuasive and legitimately powerful.

PERSUASION

"The servant leader seeks to convince others, rather than coerce compliance. This particular element offers one of the clearest distinctions between the traditional authoritarian model and that of servant leadership."[10] From the 1700s in colonial America, the life of John Woolman proves to be an invaluable model.[11] As a boy he passed beneath a tree and spotted a robin's nest with a mother robin and her hatchlings inside. Being impetuous, he started throwing stones at the nest and ended up killing the robin. Immediately he was struck with immense sorrow, knowing the baby birds could not survive without their mother. He removed the nest from the tree and quickly killed the baby hatchlings, convinced it was the most merciful course of action. From this brief encounter with his own shadow, he felt both horror and shame. The incident inspired in him love and protectiveness for all living things for the rest of his life.

Raised in a family of Quakers, Woolman quietly became a major influence on the Quaker movement, genuinely attuned to the Friends' traditions of seeking the Spirit of Christ for guidance, and waiting with an abiding and patient will for unity in the Spirit with other Quakers. Woolman saw slavery as a horror against God and humanity, gave up his career as a tradesman, and traveled from one Religious Society of Friends meeting to another, devoting the last twenty-seven years of his life to convincing Quakers to free their slaves and choose abolition as a life course. In his travels, when a slaveholder gave him food and lodging, Woolman paid the slaves for their work in attending him and would not eat with silver utensils, cups, or plates because of his conviction that slaves were forced to dig precious minerals from the earth to feed the greed of the rich. For nearly thirty years Woolman went by foot or horseback up and down the East Coast, sitting down to talk with Quaker slave owners. He did not coerce or dominate them. Instead, he simply tried to persuade them by asking questions: What does owning slaves do to you as a moral person? What kind of institution are you binding over to your children?

He was a gentleman, and a person devoted to the well-being of others. Through this patient process, one Quaker gathering after another became convinced of the evil of slavery and began to write condemnation of the practice into their meeting minutes. In 1790, eighteen years after Woolman's death, no Quakers owned slaves, and the Religious Society of Friends petitioned the United States Congress for the abolition of slavery.

A rich sense of persuasion in everyday life can change the world. Persuasion in our beloved relationships, in our organizations, and in our contact as nations is frequently the difference between that which gives life and that which deals death.

CONCEPTUALIZATION

To see beyond, to see what may need to be seen so that others can grow and experience goodness and love, conceptualization is required. Greenleaf observed that servant leaders dream great dreams and that great achievements are the result of great dreams. During the year following the 9/11 World Trade Center disaster, only one airline made a profit. Long before the tragedy, the leadership of Southwest Airlines had established concrete conceptualization practices.[12] When people stopped flying and economic scarcity hit the airline industry, Southwest Air was prepared. Unlike other major airlines,

Southwest had kept a large portion of its earnings fluid, holding a significant cash reserve specifically for the unlikely onset of an economic drought such as that brought on by 9/11. But beyond this, and significant to the recovery of the country as a whole, Southwest Air conceptualized lasting relational practices—care and love held the highest importance in its corporate culture.

Administrative leaders at Southwest took 20 to 30 percent pay cuts to show respect for employees and to avoid having to cut people's jobs. Incredibly, the employees themselves, those not in the administrative leadership tier, donated money back to the company in a mutual effort to support Southwest Air, an organic show of loyalty that alone raised $3 million. Southwest Air even gave of its largesse to help other airlines. Showing the ingenuity inspired by real-life conceptualization, in the aftermath of 9/11, while others were forced to make major cuts, Southwest did not lay off a single employee.

At Southwest Air, as in other organizations purposefully seeking to serve society, there is a primary difference in focus and power, just as in individuals and families capable of healing others. Here, women and men come together to conceptualize and then to persuade, and freedom is the result. Greenleaf gives direct expression to the difference:

> In a complex institution-centered society, which ours is likely to be into the indefinite future, there will be large and small concentrations of power. Sometimes it will be a servant's power of persuasion and example. Sometimes it will be coercive power used to dominate and manipulate people. The difference is that, in the former, power is used to create opportunity and alternatives so that individuals may choose and build autonomy. In the latter, individuals are coerced into a predetermined path. Even if it is "good" for them, if they experience nothing else, ultimately their autonomy will be diminished.[13]

In a more graphic and arresting motif, present-day Rwanda, having suffered one of the world's bloodiest genocides, has begun to imagine a future free of the hatred and violence that result from extreme forms of coercive power. Of necessity, conceptualization in the aftermath of such devastation takes on increased importance. When the plane of Rwandan president Juvenal Habyarimana was gunned down in 1994, a killing spree of such wanton lust was unleashed that the country saw nearly a million deaths in one hundred days, a butchery performed by the Hutu population against the Tutsis and largely done by machete. In a small space, a lush and natural paradise, the country became a place where "victims knew their attackers, and attackers knew their victims," reported Ellis Cose in *Newsweek*. "The country is like one huge extended family. That's what made the violence particularly unfathomable."

Yet the people of Rwanda conceptualized hope in the wake of atrocity. Cose's article is informative. With those still alive a mix of victims and oppressors, and with twenty-five thousand Tutsi women having given birth after being raped by Hutus during the genocide, Anglican bishop John Rucyahana and many with him saw the work of reconciliation as a work of optimism and urgency, a work in which Rwandans could not afford to wait "until the pain [was] over." Rucyahana viewed the process as one in which God would work in the Rwandan people to use the "humility, the broken-ness, the ashes to set an example for other counties. . . . If Rwanda can recover from this . . . other nations can recover." When the bishop started the work, one of his first experiences brought the reality of the terror home and sealed his resolve to be a part of the healing. He took ten other pastors in a minibus on a journey to survey the damage. What they saw they never forgot. They made their way to Nyamata, near Kigali, the capital of Rwanda. "We saw mass graves," he said. "We saw dead bodies. In one home, we found 27 dead bodies, including a cat and a dog. . . . Some of the pastors couldn't sleep; they spent all night crying. . . . Two of them had to be taken back home."

Ellis Cose's article illustrates the work of Bishop Rucyahana to conceptual-ize a future for Rwanda. Two of the bishop's endeavors have become a beacon to other countries seeking to recover from the horror of genocide, and Cose's words in this regard craft a stunning narrative:

> One of his [Bishop Rucyahana's] first tasks was to build a boarding school for orphans: "Having lost a million people, lots of babies were left behind." The school in Musanze, near the Volcanoes National Park, opened in 2001. It is now one of the best schools in the country. It is called Sonrise, which Rucyahana explains, "means the Son of God rises into the misery, into our darkness."
>
> But the Bishop is reaching out to perpetrators as well as to victims. His prison ministry encourages those who participated in the genocide to accept re-sponsibility and repent. He has also built reconciliation villages whose primary purpose is to bring victims and perpetrators together. I visited one not far from Kigali and spoke to several residents, including Jeannette, who lost seven family members to the genocide. What was it like for her to stand beside a neighbor who admitted killing women and children? "In the beginning, it was very dif-ficult," she said. "But now I forgive him."
>
> I asked a pastor who works in the village whether there was a secret to creat-ing trust among former enemies. "They have to learn," he said, "that life goes on. So instead of dwelling on the past, they embrace the future. And if their faith is strong, they even embrace the people who killed their children, destroyed their homes and left them traumatized and afraid."[14]

FORESIGHT

Foresight is often referred to as the least explored area of servant leadership. Some believe foresight is more an innate trait than a quality to be learned, and even Greenleaf at times seems to lean more toward the mystery involved in foresight than the possibility that foresight, like forgiveness, love, and the appropriate artistry of power, might be not only an important facet of learning but perhaps the direct responsibility of each person and each collective in order to secure the future health, autonomy, wisdom, and freedom of others. Spears refers to foresight as deeply rooted within the intuitive mind. But perhaps below the abstract function of intuition is solid ground. Perhaps intuition, like the mystery of grace, is made more visible in the context of humble but purposeful pursuit.

John Gottman's work in relational health reflects this elusive earned quality of foresight.[15] In learning from and submitting to the truths of Gottman's research, people gather strength in their families and more accurate vision in all relational interactions. The primary findings, worthy of personal and collective investment, create the capacity to heal ourselves and others. Gottman can predict divorce at a 95 percent rate after only a few brief minutes with a couple. The foresight involved in such unprecedented accuracy seems to border on something magical, but Gottman's history decries this. According to Gottman, essential alienation between two people, and by extension between groups, or even between nations, has to do with two interlocking systemic concepts: (1) contempt and (2) the unwillingness to receive influence. Gottman looks for the facial, behavioral, and vocal manifestations of these two components between people, and when the amount and intensity of these manifestations reach overload, prediction accuracy is guaranteed. Gottman's thirty years of robust empirical research to reveal the guideposts of love and affection are grounded in highly concrete assertions associated with foresight. Notably, once the nexus of contempt (severe dislike) and unwillingness to receive influence (stonewalling) became clear, Gottman refined his ability to detect these two elements in the faces of research participants. He did so by going to France to study under one of the world's facial expression masters, for more than a year.

From this and other methods to develop and extend foresight, Gottman developed a precise mechanism for detecting and healing human alienation. The alienated life is plagued by what he called the Four Horsemen of the Apocalypse: contempt, stonewalling, defensiveness, and criticism. People who enact these forms of consciousness against the self and others orient themselves and their relationships toward disintegration. A relational exchange can be any expression of thought, action, attitude, behavior, voice tone, facial expression, touch, or lack thereof. Gottman's research reveals that people whose relationships are in a state of critical disarray fall prey to what he called *negative sentiment override*, meaning they experience five to ten negative exchanges to every one positive exchange. Not surprisingly, as referred to earlier, people whose relationships are in a state of ultimate generativity experience what Gottman called *positive sentiment override,* meaning they engage in five to ten positive exchanges to every one negative exchange. From this foresight, even greater foresight surfaces regarding the systemic dance of human interactions. The painful disunity of people trapped in a downward spiral is evident in all increasingly alienated interactions, be these interactions within the individual, between people, or among nations. In a pattern of circular viciousness, stonewalling evokes contempt, contempt evokes stonewalling, and in like fashion criticism and defensiveness perform their own recursive *dis-eased* and diseased circuit.

Gottman also gave a specific, very daunting grid for people to recognize in the context of divorce: 80 percent of men who divorce all share one thing—they don't receive the influence of their wives (they stonewall); and 80 percent of women who divorce all share one thing—they severely dislike their husbands (they harbor contempt). The work of Shirley Glass validates this potent foresight regarding relational breakdown.[16]

Foresight can help us take such fear-invoking knowledge and turn it to hope. By working out a reliable and earned sense of the counterparts of the Four Horsemen, we enter a life of possibility. Conciliatory potential then, if we apply Gottman's foresight, has to do with devotion to countering the Four Horsemen through what might be called the Four Angels of Our Better Nature, to continue an earlier theme from Lincoln's illumined body of work. I have named the counterparts gratitude, invitation, affirmation, and brokenness. In light of unleashed human potential, gratitude heals contempt, invitation heals stonewalling, affirmation heals criticism, and brokenness heals defensiveness.

When we embrace a servant-led lifestyle, we acknowledge and pursue above-the-line thinking. Gratitude toward the beloved other entails an undaunted belief in each person, despite the terrifying violence or frailty of his or her actions toward us. Martin Luther King Jr.'s love for the racist, and in fact for all enemies, is an astonishing and a richly textured example. As relationship is pursued and acknowledged, contempt cannot exist in the presence of gratitude.

Inviting the beloved into our inner life heals our desire to stonewall. When we turn toward the other rather than away, even in the midst of conflict, disagreement, and painful interactions, we build a road of intimacy rather than rejection, and we invite the beloved's perception of the world to engage with our own in a mutual pathway of change and renewal.

Affirmation strengthens our will to face the difficult complexities of intimacy with buoyancy and resolve. When we affirm a divine presence in the beloved, a commitment to unconditional encouragement informs our interactions, and we forgo the need to criticize. The affirmative life persuades; it does not criticize; it does not coerce.

Finally, our own willing submission to the legitimate desires and hopes of the beloved other calls us toward personal brokenness. Sincere acknowledgement of our own brokenness, our own weaknesses or shadow, heals our defensiveness and produces the desire to change. We surrender willingly to the definitive call love places on our lives.

The Four Angels of Our Better Nature seem logical in the context of love relationships, but what of the enemy, what of the one who maliciously brings us harm? Martin Luther King took comfort in remembering the words of Jesus Christ. "Love your enemies," Christ said, a singular response to the hateful hostilities we sometimes encounter in life, as well as to our own inner hatefulness. Gratitude, invitation, affirmation, and brokenness help us see through the inhumanity of ourselves and others to the core of our shared humanity—to a vision of people that affirms unity and reminds us we are children of God and that we have the capacity for wholeness with one another despite human evil. When we hear about or witness the atrocities of which we are capable, shame consumes us. We lose our will to rise, and lose sight of heaven. Our legs bent beneath us, our bodies belabored by loss, hope seems outside the realm of possibility. An angry, fearful, and depressed self holds us hostage, and often we either try to fight or run before exhaustion takes us, pressing us closer to the earth. We fall, and we ask again, "How can we ever rise?" Here in our most naked sense of surrender, Palmer reminds us that the way to God is not by looking to the clouds but by placing our feet firmly on the ground, and that to listen to the self in the very foundation of the heart is to listen to heaven:

> It is the self planted in us by the God who made us in God's own image.
>
> When I was finally able to turn around and ask, "What do you want?" the answer was clear: I want you to embrace this descent into hell as a journey toward selfhood—and a journey toward God.
>
> I had always imagined God to be in the same general direction as everything else that I valued: up. I had failed to appreciate the meaning of some words that had intrigued me since I first heard them in seminary—Tillich's description of God as the "ground of being." I had to be forced underground before I could understand that the way to God is not up but down.

The underground is a dangerous but potentially life-giving place to which depression takes us; a place where we come to understand that the self is not set apart as special or superior but is a common mix of good and evil, darkness and light; a place where we can finally embrace the humanity we share with others. That is the best image I can offer not only of the underground but also of the field of forces surrounding the experience of God.[17]

To openly pursue the "moral arc of the universe" requires foresight, and to bring about genuine healing involves cultivating the lifestyle of the broken person, willingly surrendered—the life of the seeker listening for the answer that is subtle, and ultimate. Through listening to more mature, more intimate viewpoints, servant leaders seek healing and seek change. Annie Dillard has told us and we recognize with trepidation that "in the deeps are the violence and terror of which psychology warned us." But on the other side of our fear we listen deeply to the song sung softly in darkness and we discover with her and Parker Palmer that "if we ride those monsters all the way down, we break through to something precious—to "the unified field, our complex and inexplicable caring for each other."[18] History becomes charged with meaning, and people who develop the inner life become people of foresight capable of envisioning, or conceptualizing, a way through. Such people then persuade others to come together and begin the journey that does not go over or around, but down and through the devastation that attends human existence. From the lives of those who've gone before, from loved ones, mentors, sponsors, counselors, rabbis, pastors, priests, and friends, we are given the gift of greater wisdom.

May we seek together, and may we find what we seek.

Chapter 19

People of Self-Transcendence

Greenleaf's view of the servant as leader leads to a hidden but important vista in families, organizations, and nations in which people in all roles—mothers, fathers, sisters, brothers, line workers, politicians, businesspeople, civil servants, laborers, blue-collar workers, white-collar workers, directors, staff, and trustees—hold their work in trust for the good of humanity and commit fully to the growth of others and to building community. Stewardship, commitment to the growth of people, and building community rise from a natural servant leadership consciousness and form the strategic and concrete groundwork of societal change. Education, in its best expression, does this fluently with people young and old. Greenleaf commented on the need for two additional fields where he felt that if servant leadership took root and flourished, a great distance would be traveled toward healing society: the business world (organizations large and small) and the world of theology (the seminaries). He envisioned educational, business, and spiritual cultures throughout the world gathering to thoughtfully choose how to serve humanity. In such communities, forgiveness and power undergird the work of healing in the world.

The servant leader transcends himself or herself to become the steward of others, capable of raising up future generations, and confident in building community. Greenleaf associated this protracted effort toward bettering society with the paradox of living with a sense of oneness toward the mystery of existence as well as generating practical ways of working together.

Greenleaf said of his friendship with the rabbi Abraham Joshua Heschel, the great scholar, writer, and teacher, a European Jew and survivor of the Nazi regime, that his bond with Heschel was on the level of the religious experience of the unknown, what Heschel called the "feeling of awe and wonder and amazement." Greenleaf said, "When I was in the presence of this good and gentle rabbi and was suffused with the warmth of this feeling, I was lifted above all the differences that divide people."[19]

Greenleaf's words beg the question: How *do* we overcome the differences that divide us? In considering the stewardship of future generations, a global example is necessary, and national awareness is a good place to begin. Consider the history of slavery in America alongside the degradation and decimation of America's first people, her Native Americans. Of course there are many other examples in U.S. history of race atrocity: the myriad pervasive violations of black Americans before and after emancipation; the mass displacement of Japanese Americans during World War II in which 120,000 U.S. people of Japanese descent were removed from their homes and put in internment camps by the U.S. Justice Department; the grim severity of deportation and labor inequities with regard to Hispanic Americans—President Eisenhower's so-called "Operation Wetback" of 1954 is one such event, in which approximately 1 million Mexican Americans or "Mexican-looking" people were deported and sometimes shipped 500 to 1000 miles into Mexico—the list goes on. Many Americans today might consider it absurd to apologize for acts committed centuries ago, or decades ago, *even* if there remains a stubborn systemic desecration of the less privileged in American society by the more privileged—for example, consider the inequities in education, socioeconomic advancement, housing, and all the more full expressions of upward mobility Martin Luther King Jr. so eloquently pointed to.

Yet alongside a suffocating lack of will in the dominant culture to take responsibility for historic wrongs against the nondominant culture, something elegant also rises. The desire to make amends and reconcile remains a potent force exerting itself in every generation. In my experience, there are many Americans today who feel a sense of personal shame and guilt over the current inequities of the larger systems of U.S. society, as well as the acts of their ancestors, even if their own family line cannot be directly traced to slaveholding, atrocities against Native Americans, or the dark undertow of civil rights violations either subtle or deadly against races not their own. Many people have begun to follow Desmond Tutu's resolute call to the nations: "The most effective way to build a new world community is for the perpetrators or their descendants to acknowledge the awfulness of what happened and the descendants of the victims to respond by granting forgiveness."[20] Tutu states unequivocally that there is no future without forgiveness. Asking forgiveness and acknowledging the horrific nature of what happened is a crucial first step.

Tutu's statements ring near to the heart on the international level and lead to a sober reckoning. Graceful and responsible approaches to our failures can help our children live well, especially when they grow tall and are eventually confronted by the seriousness of evil in the self and in the world.

A global case in point from Israel's relationship to Germany is poignant for Americans and people throughout the globe. Political activist and Holocaust survivor Elie Wiesel has become a symbol of the kind of stewardship that heals our children. When Wiesel received the Nobel Peace Prize in 1986, the Norwegian Nobel Committee referred to him as a "messenger to mankind" and lauded his character in transcending "his own personal experience of total humiliation and of the utter contempt for humanity shown in Hitler's death camps." The committee commended his "practical work in the cause of peace" and recognized the bravery and power of the message "of peace, atonement and human dignity" he had delivered to humanity.[21]

In his writings Wiesel has said:

> Sometimes I am asked if I know "the response to Auschwitz"; I answer that not only do I not know it, but that I don't even know if a tragedy of this magnitude has a response. What I do know is that there is "response" in responsibility. When we speak of this era of evil and darkness, so close and yet so distant, "responsibility" is the key word.[22]

As one might imagine, many Germans or people of German descent feel disgrace and mortification over the atrocities their German ancestors committed against the Jewish people. A large part of being human is to feel shame, but more importantly, to feel responsible in some way and to desire to make amends. As our own personal experience can attest, another large part of us is unfortunately made of denial and our fear or unwillingness to face ourselves, let alone to face our own deepest forms of collective inhumanity. Though substantial financial reparations have been made to Israel from the people of post-World War II Germany—more than $70 billion from 1952 to 2009—what can be done, truly, with horrors of the like perpetrated by Hitler and the Nazis? Before the original postwar agreement between Germany and Israel, in September 1951 Chancellor Konrad Adenauer of West Germany addressed the German parliament, saying, "Unspeakable crimes have been committed in the name of the German people, calling for moral and material indemnity." He recognized that material reparations can never substitute for German moral reparations, but he hoped that good faith material reparations over the years might ease the way toward a "spiritual settlement of infinite suffering."[23]

In 2000, Wiesel helped the two countries take steps toward that spiritual settlement. Wiesel gave the German people the open opportunity to face their history when he spoke at the dedication of the Holocaust memorial in Berlin.

Wiesel spoke a fierce truth: "No people ever inflicted such suffering as your people on mine in such a short period. Until the end of time, Auschwitz is part of your history and mine." He then urged the German parliament to pass a resolution formally requesting, in the name of Germany, forgiveness from the Jewish people for the crimes of Hitler. "Do it publicly," he said. "Ask the Jewish people to forgive Germany for what the Third Reich had done in Germany's name. Do it, and the significance of this day will acquire a higher level. Do it, for we desperately want to have hope for this new century."[24]

A month later German president Johannes Rau came to Jerusalem to appear before Israel's Knesset (the Israeli parliament) and ask forgiveness. Rau stated:

> I bow in humility before those murdered, before those who don't have graves where I could ask them for forgiveness. I am asking for forgiveness for what Germans have done, for myself and my generation, for the sake of our children and grandchildren, whose future I would like to see alongside the children of Israel.[25]

Many Jews do not believe that the living have a right either to ask forgiveness or to forgive on behalf of those who were killed. Even so, the question of atonement was asked, and the reverberations were felt the world over.

Elie Wiesel and many others, by living their lives in devotion to the future of the world, have inspired and refined our attention to the human condition. Wiesel's will for peace has given the children of the world the gift of total honesty, the hope for unity, and the deepest possibilities of atonement, forgiveness, and reconciliation. Rau's speech before the Israeli parliament echoes Wiesel's and Greenleaf's call to be stewards and healers of our children.

STEWARDSHIP

The steward holds values and proper action in trust for the greater good of society. Such stewardship is sometimes difficult to see in the contemporary era, but a close look at family reveals an intimate picture. In truth, the life of a child can call forth our richest forms of stewardship, reflecting one of the most robust human archetypes of care, wisdom, and sacrificial giving. Servant leadership evokes love, and love evokes forgiveness. My mother and father are primary servant leaders to me, as are my wife, my mother-in-law, and my father-in-law. Because of them, I try to embrace an intimacy that tills the soil of healing and stewardship. Three brief stories from my life with my daughters when they were young remind me of the nature of stewardship on an elemental level.

Story 1. I returned to the house one afternoon when my daughter Natalya was five years old. Seated on the kitchen floor she had paper and crayons spread around her. With a face of delight she looked up and held high a colorful piece of paper she had folded in half.

"I made a card for you!" she exclaimed.

I sat down and put my arm around her and she opened the card. On white paper I saw a blue sky with bright gold stars. "Look what I wrote," she said, and then she read the scrawling words: "You are the best Daddy in the stars!"

She kissed my face and hugged me and I said, "Thank you! What a beautiful card! How did you think of such lovely words?"

"Oh," she said with a matter-of-fact look, "I didn't know how to spell *world.*"

Natalya's quick, sure answer conveyed the confidence and trust we feel when we are at peace with those we love.

Story 2. On another day some years later I had just finished a great wrestling match with Natalya's younger sister Ariana. I was lying on the floor, spent. I had a big smile on my face as Ariana, seven years old at the time, stepped up onto my chest and stood proud announcing her triumph. She hopped down, and when I rose and walked into the kitchen to pour us some water she saw me approach her mother, Jennifer, and give her a kiss on the cheek.

"Do that again, Daddy!" she said.

I turned to Ari and said "I'd love to!" and turned back to Jennifer and kissed her on the lips.

"Yay!" Ari said, shouting her approval.

We call Ariana, Ari. Her classmates call her Ari Ferrari. Ari means "lion" in Hebrew, and Ari lives up to both names, fast and fun, and strong as a lion . . . loyal, fierce in her protection not just of those she loves, but everyone.

Hugging Jennifer, I said, "Why do you like it so much, Ari, when I kiss your mommy?"

Beaming a big smile at both of us, she said, "It means you love her. It means you love me."

Even now, remembering the delight in Ari's voice reminds me of how it feels to be surrounded by love.

Story 3. On still another day some years later, I was seated with Natalya's and Ariana's younger sister Isabella on my lap. Shimmering with sun, the water of Deer Lake spread before us—a bright blue oval west of the Rocky

Mountains near our home in Spokane. The lake, a vibrant fish hatchery, is home to eagles and osprey, ducks, loons, and geese. Isabella, four years old, was hugging my neck and kissing my cheeks while singing a delightful song she'd just created. Suddenly, she released from me and ran around the picnic table to sit with Jennifer and eat some corn Jennifer prepared for her. As I watched her with her mother I felt filled with life, just as I had countless times before either with Isabella or with her two sisters.

"Isabella," I said, drawing close, and staring into her eyes. "Why do I love you so much?"

"I don't know," she said, chewing emphatically and looking at the food on her plate.

"No, really," I said as I reached out, touching her face, "Why do you think I love you so much?"

She stopped chewing for a moment, looked into my eyes, and said the following:

"Because God made you to love me."

Isabella's response resonates with the most meaningful expressions of love, culture to culture, person to person, across humanity: in such moments we encounter transcendent or divine love with one another. The primary role of the steward is to meet others in the center of existence where the most intimate needs of people are revealed—those of love, care, connection, and authentic life. Stewardship is born of love, and it calls us to answer the most pressing current needs of those around us, their highest-priority needs, as well as their essential future needs. Servant leaders notice their own faults, promote reconciliation not only in the family but across races, cultures, and creeds, and unswervingly seek to see in others their great capacity . . . their hidden and arrestingly beautiful potential.

Servant leaders hold this potential in trust and help bring it to fruition.

COMMITMENT TO THE GROWTH OF OTHERS

When he was forty-six, Nelson Mandela was imprisoned by the political leaders of apartheid for acts deemed subversive to the South African government. Considering that at the time a country of only 3 million whites ruled and violently oppressed more than 40 million blacks, many saw Mandela's actions as not only appropriate, but necessary. At forty-six, he was no novice to the fight for freedom. But none guessed he would remain in prison for the next twenty-seven years, many of those years spent at Robben Island, a high-security facility constructed on a largely barren rock within sight of Cape Town, the South African coastal city whose exquisite seaside location set against the backdrop of Table Mountain rivals those of the great cities of the world.

Mandela did not rise from nowhere. His mentoring from within his own culture, his royal lineage among the Thembu dynasty, a branch of the great Xhosa Tribe, his long endurance to become a lawyer and found the first black South African law firm, and his humble and lasting relationship with Walter Sisulu, the man Mandela called his "spiritual father" (Sisulu was imprisoned before Mandela), coalesced to form the heart and spirit of Mandela, one of the truly great servant leaders of the contemporary age.

While in prison Mandela was noted for many acts of humility and legitimate power, such as raising the consciousness of all prisoners, so much so that the prison authorities eventually erected a giant wall between political prisoners and common criminals because they felt Mandela was converting the criminals into beacons of intelligence and social action. Mandela is also known for raising the consciousness of the guards and befriending many of them. In a reversal of the logic of vengeance and a furthering of the inherent wonder of reconciliation, Mandela invited many of his captors to stand with him on the inaugural stage after the world witnessed the fall of apartheid. Mandela's magnanimous spirit as he was elected president of South Africa remains a lodestar of hope to all who struggle against oppression.

A simple story illustrates the heart of the man, in the fist of captivity, behind the prison walls. Even here, his will to give dignity remained true. When one of the other prisoners became ill, so ill he could not take care of himself and manage basic human functioning, Mandela came to the man and went away with the man's chamber pot, emptied it, cleaned it, and returned it to him. The man felt embarrassed because Mandela was his revered elder, and he felt he should serve Mandela, not the other way around. The man implored Mandela, asking why he had done this, saying he was unworthy to be served by Mandela.

Mandela comforted him, saying "It is nothing."[26]

Mothers and fathers, sisters and brothers, coworkers and CEOs would do well to emulate the true natural servant we find in Mandela. In living to serve others over self, Mandela demonstrated one of the inviolable truths of authentic human contact: "Servant leaders believe that people have an intrinsic value beyond their tangible contributions."[27]

BUILDING COMMUNITY

Greenleaf said, "All that is needed to rebuild community as a viable life form for large numbers of people is for enough servant-leaders to show the way, not by mass movements, but by each servant-leader demonstrating his or her unlimited liability for a quite specific community-related group."[28] In reading Greenleaf's quiet discovery we know the responsibility to build community should not be taken lightly.

In building an essential community, dialogue is necessary and represents the will to listen and evoke listening, the will to build a mutually influential conversation from which all parties emerge changed for good. Not a spirit of war, but a spirit of peace pervades the heart of dialogue. In this sense, we cannot be antagonistic toward one another if we are to liberate one another. Hatred cannot exist in dialogue, and in the words of Freire, "Dialogue cannot exist without humility. Dialogue cannot exist . . . in the absence of a profound love for the world and its people."[29] In being with others on the person-to-person level, dialogue is the revolutionary unifier, especially when cynicism and lack of movement begin to take root. "Some may think that to affirm dialogue—the encounter of women and men in the world in order to transform the world—is naively and subjectively idealistic. There is nothing, however, more real or concrete than people in the world and with the world, than humans with other humans."[30]

One of America's most iconoclastic and gifted leaders did not seem destined to be a community builder. But as he grew to adulthood, he helped transform a nation through his intrepid dialogues with others. Born into poverty in a one-room log cabin on Sinking Spring Farm in southeast Hardin County, Kentucky, he appeared to be one of the most unlikely candidates for even local, let alone national, servant leadership. His hardworking mother and father were uneducated, and farm life, though rich with ingenuity, was bare existence in the early 1800s in America. The family became impoverished and lost their farm when he was six. His mother died when he was nine. Later, his first love died before he could marry her. When finally he married at thirty-four, the marriage was blessed with four sons, but of the four, three died before the age of twenty. He loved deeply, and deeply grieved the loss of those he loved. He taught himself law through rigorous study of borrowed law books as well as by observing court sessions, and he was eventually admitted to the Bar. He became a renowned and convincing litigator, noted for his impassioned and potently reasoned stances against social injustice.

At age twenty-five he was elected to the state legislature. At twenty-seven he made his first protest against slavery, saying the institution was founded on injustice. Over the next two decades of his life he continued to outline, define, and eventually present the moral basis for his economic and political arguments against slavery. In 1860, at age fifty-one, he was elected president of the United States. Three years later his Emancipation Proclamation legally ended slavery in America. Abraham Lincoln is unanimously recognized by historians and scholars as one of the greatest American presidents.[31]

Although he was famous for his role in helping to end slavery, one of his most meaningful contributions as a servant leader was his ability to build a humane intellectual and political community that could sustain formerly unattainable goals of morality and conviction for the betterment of humanity. "How does one build community?" we might ask him, and Lincoln's reply might be found in his response to a reporter who questioned Lincoln's appointment of Edwin M. Stanton as secretary of war, one of the highest cabinet positions. Stanton had been a vindictive, even hateful opponent of Lincoln during Lincoln's bid for the presidency. Even so, Lincoln stated, "He is the best man for the job," and then said, "Besides, if you make a friend of an enemy, do you have an enemy any longer?"

To the end of Lincoln's life Stanton was among Lincoln's strongest supporters, saying of Lincoln after Lincoln's assassination, "Now he belongs to the ages. There lies the most perfect ruler of men the world has ever seen."[32]

Lincoln was refined by the suffering he endured, sifted and made to undergo a crucible of life and leadership that resulted in greatness. His own words carry the lasting portent, imagistic grandeur, and care for humanity that are a hallmark of servant leadership everywhere. Lincoln's Gettysburg address stands as a fitting reminder of the love that emerges like tempered steel as a result of giving of oneself for the betterment of others.[33] The speech remains an imprint of wisdom in the wake of war and reveals the internal gentleness and sharp reasoning of a man who had suffered the death of so many loved ones and reconciled himself to build community and be a healer of humanity:

> Four score and seven years ago our fathers brought forth on this continent, a new nation, conceived in Liberty, and dedicated to the proposition that all men are created equal.
>
> Now we are engaged in a great civil war, testing whether that nation, or any nation so conceived and so dedicated, can long endure. We are met on a great battle-field of that war. We have come to dedicate a portion of that field, as a final resting place for those who here gave their lives that that nation might live. It is altogether fitting and proper that we should do this.
>
> But, in a larger sense, we can not dedicate—we can not consecrate—we can not hallow—this ground. The brave men, living and dead, who struggled here, have consecrated it, far above our poor power to add or detract. The world will little note, nor long remember what we say here, but it can never forget what they did here. It is for us the living, rather, to be dedicated here to the unfinished work which they who fought here have thus far so nobly advanced. It is rather

for us to be here dedicated to the great task remaining before us—that from
these honored dead we take increased devotion to that cause for which they gave
the last full measure of devotion—that we here highly resolve that these dead
shall not have died in vain—that this nation, under God, shall have a new birth
of freedom—and that government of the people, by the people, for the people,
shall not perish from the earth.[34]

Lincoln's project was to preserve a union based in democracy, and having
done so, in many small and not so small ways, in the ensuing century and
beyond, his work helped infuse democracy and human freedoms into the
social and political landscape of the world. After the American Civil War
ended, Lincoln carried himself with great flexibility and generosity toward
the South, and toward all who suffered. Forgiveness, legitimate power, and
servant leadership form a three-strand cord that is not easily broken. Lincoln's
second inaugural address ended with words that serve as an anthem to his way
of life and to the sense of community he envisioned for others:

With malice toward none, with charity for all, with firmness in the right as God
gives us to see the right, let us strive on to finish the work we are in, to bind up
the nation's wounds, to care for him who shall have borne the battle and for his
widow and his orphan, to do all which may achieve and cherish a just and lasting
peace among ourselves and with all nations.[35]

Chapter 20

Shadow and Light

Forgiveness, Power, and Love in Practice

Every person, every culture, and every nation is haunted by the hope for light and the reality of shadow. Coinciding with this notion, the greater the gap between a nation's embrace of transcendent moral values and its actions of secrecy, oppression, and abuse of privilege, the greater that nation's capacity to be fragile with regard to human interests and highly fortified in the will to enact grave harm.

With this understanding, it is imperative to observe that above- and below-the-line thinking is rooted in the collective mind, and that the collective mind is various and multifaceted. Shades of difference can range from stark contrast to near fusion. Take, for example, the ethical side of our response to oppression. Stark contrast can be found between nonviolent resistance and taking up arms against the oppressor. On one end of the continuum is the unconditionally pacifist stance of certain forms of Christianity (Mysticism, Quakerism, etc.), Hinduism, Buddhism, Jainism, and Taoism, as well as forms of pacifism found in traditionally retributive-oriented traditions such as Judaism and Islam. On the other end of the continuum we find the strongly justice-motivated military engagements that are also found in the history of Christendom, Judaism, and Islam, as well as in geographic regions in which the official ideology was Buddhist, Hindu, or Taoist. Consider the human paradox: evidence of pacifism and tolerance exists in the historical record of every major religion, as does evidence of war and atrocity. Forgiveness and true mutual power then become the architecture of humanity aimed at love and servant leadership in order to forestall atrocity and human evil.

A historical divide in Western philosophy and theology provides further direction. The divide marked the advent of modernism and the continuation of both intellectual and popular thinking into what became characterized as postmodernism. Before this divide, people lived largely in the afterglow of the Enlightenment and Romanticism, an ever-weakening light whose waning was not quickly apparent, but over time exerted itself in the collective's over-willingness to exalt the ideal. For centuries the Islamic, Jewish, and Christian philosophical ground, and the ground of Classical intelligibility represented by transcendent values, was largely unquestioned. Yet beneath the ideal, and often beneath a thick veneer of sentimentalism, the dark horse of our own failures, hypocrisy, and personal and collective hiddenness came running, strong and warlike. Modernism and postmodernism began a protracted struggle for the human mind.

Modernism commenced a pervasive critique of the values that had directed the West throughout the Enlightenment, the Romantic period, and beyond. Postmodernism, the child of modernism, then exerted itself in the glorification of relativism, irony, and exaltation of the absurd. But like all quality progressions of philosophy, postmodernism not only reveled in critique, it revealed a deeper wisdom . . . the need to unseat power abuses and the unthinking regimes that had oppressed the human spirit, suppressed autonomy, and entrapped people in often despotic hierarchies.

Because of the appropriate need to debunk the thoughtlessness of abusive power structures, the great divide arose. Immanuel Kant (1724–1804) set a profound path to the summit of this divide. Nietzsche (1844–1900) stood on one side, pointing out the ferocious will to power to which humankind is given, claiming all values as mere fictions set up to keep the masses inert, dumb, and subservient. Kierkegaard (1813–1855) stood on the other, also recognizing the fragile consciousness of humanity, but rather than rejecting transcendent values, he called for a more refined recommitment to them, a form of humble fear and trembling characterized by razor-like discernment with regard to the potential for falseness in ourselves, others, and the collective.

Notably, Nietzsche's rise to prominence as a man of thought did not develop from others ranking him a leading philosopher, but rather rose from how his writings helped inspire Hitler's National Socialism.[36] Nietzsche, in effect, was writing in a vein common to German philosophical thought at the time, and he is not considered among the strongest intellectuals of the day. Nevertheless, since he is recognizable by lay readers and philosophers alike, he is a good figurehead for the purposes of this discussion. Certainly some have critiqued the connection between Nietzsche and Nazism; however, the fundamental rigidities embedded in Nietzschean thought remain, and aim toward debunking traditional life values.[37] Not surprisingly, though Nietzsche's critique of religion rails sharply against an unthinking group mentality, he tends to make sweeping generalizations, ad hominem attacks, and largely thoughtless pronouncements about views opposed to his own. Consider his stance on morality from *The Will to Power*:

> How far psychologists have been corrupted by the moral idiosyncrasy:—not one of the ancient philosophers had the courage for a theory of the "unfree will" (i.e., for a theory that denies morality);—no one had the courage to define the typical element in pleasure, every sort of pleasure ("happiness") as the feeling of power: for to take pleasure in power was considered immoral;—no one had the courage to conceive virtue as a consequence of immorality (of a will to power) in the service of the species (or of the race or *polis*), for the will to power was considered immorality.
>
> In the entire evolution of morality, truth never appears: all the conceptual elements employed are fictions . . .
>
> Moral philosophy is the scabrous period in the history of the spirit.[38]

Also redolent of a personhood that degrades others, throughout many of Nietzsche's writings he has the audacity to uplift his own thought, even to the level of shameless self-aggrandizement. Ego statements run rampant. He denies the intelligence of others and forwards himself. Chapters in his books are titled, "Why I Am So Wise"; "Why I Am So Clever"; and "Why I Write Such Good Books." In 1888 he said of himself, "It is not impossible that I am the greatest philosopher of the century."[39]

A generation before Nietzsche, Kierkegaard, a Danish philosopher and theologian, began to critique the undiscerning and often dark side of Christianity such as the church's misuse of power, the politicization of religion and the accompanying underlying hypocrisy, and the pervasive self-absorbed distortion or perversion of the revolutionary teachings of Christ. Kierkegaard's work paved the way for the healthy skepticism that would become the hallmark of modernism and early postmodernism.

Like separate families the two squared off. Nietzsche was resolutely atheist and oriented against values (eschewing all values and positing them as "falsifications" and "lies" imposed by illegitimate, unthinking authorities), while Kierkegaard, on the other hand, was devoted to faith and oriented toward rigorous consciousness regarding transcendent values such as love, beauty, goodness, and truth.[40] In effect, both thinkers were forerunners who helped expose the monolithic regimes of religious and nonreligious hierarchy that had kept people subjugated everywhere. As one can imagine, even from before the time of Nietzsche and Kierkegaard to today, philosophers, scholars, and scientists have aligned themselves on one side of the divide or the other.

Those aligned with a Nietzschean concept often support many aspects of Kierkegaard's philosophical views but criticize and reject his religious views. Those aligned with Kierkegaardian thought affirm some of Nietzsche's assertions but tend to reject his anti-God stance.

Regardless, healthy skepticism arose, followed by a hermeneutics of suspicion, or the need to intellectually question or dismantle all so-called "truth," as well as the need to deconstruct the "master-" or "metanarratives" to which people had been bound like "slaves" to the "herd mentality" (Nietzsche's conception of the numb, unthinking populace) like members of a docile and ignorant mass. Today, nothing escapes the sharp eye of skepticism, be that mass driven by patriarchy, religion, racism, gender bias, communism, capitalism, consumerism, or even scientific method.

Yet skepticism, with its ceaseless indelicate questioning, its tendency to focus almost exclusively on the dissolution of overarching order, ironically has begun to chain people to something perhaps equally as egregious as wanton power abuses: humanity's chains often appear now as the fundamentalist dogmas of the cynic, the nihilist, and the atheist. Not so clearly apparent in these dogmas is a fatalistic ethos that often unconsciously includes the near worship of negativity, a belief in nothing, and the quiet exaltation of self-defeat and self-loathing. From here, the more despairing arm of the atheist collective claims that suffering is meaningless. A black hole of despair is the result.

Neither Nietzsche nor any single philosopher or writer, for that matter, is responsible for the human condition with all its attendant subjectivity, demand for answers, and calcification of the seeking process. Yet, there is something to individual and collective responsibility that calls to each one of us. From Immanuel Kant to Georg Freidrich Hegel to the Russian philosopher Michael Bakhtin, the struggle over individuality in the context of the collective, infused by the transcendent or the Divine, carries great responsibility and considerable moral weight. Certainly every person, and humanity as a whole, must face what C. G. Jung pointed at and what German and Jewish philosopher Gotthold Lessing called the "ghastly abyss," which is made up not only of the gravity of evil, but also the seemingly "accidental temperament of history, sacred or profane."[41] Whether one faces that abyss by finding meaning through loving and serving others, or by making conclusions that reside in meaninglessness, survival, and the will to power, determines the shape we make of the world around us.

The "ghastly abyss" is inescapable, especially when one considers the daily denial of basic human rights worldwide. But skepticism in the face of human suffering, and the ready cynicism and nihilism so often found in skepticism's wake, often lead to individual and collective despondency, dejection, and desolation.

On the other side of the great divide, away from Nietzsche and toward a legitimately life-affirming ethos, we discover concrete thought and action, and we find ourselves capable of being present to help and heal in the midst of suffering. A look at the thought of noted Jesuit philosopher Bernard Lonergan, and a return to existential psychiatrist and Holocaust survivor Viktor Frankl, can provide solid footing. Lonergan's masterwork, *Insight*, a tome that delves into the major fields of inquiry in order to discover the substance of our inherent quest to know, honors the nature of questioning in its ability to unravel abusive and inappropriate regimes.[42] In the end of Lonergan's magnum opus, he arrives at love as the essence of all knowing, an essence that calls us to be aware, and caring. Lonergan's "transcendental precepts" engage the heart, mind, and spirit to be attentive, intelligent, reasonable, and responsible—not as a call to formulated rules but as a gesture to the interior elegance and fortitude required for anyone who transcends the self and lives in reality. To live in reality is to attain "total surrender to the demands of the human spirit." For Lonergan, to be, in the real sense of being, is to be in love.[43]

Frankl, too, places love at the foundation of what it means to be human. Though he went through the depths of the "ghastly abyss," in the face of the absolute evil of the Nazi regime he did not grow self-absorbed. Instead he posed essential questions: What does life ask of me? And what is my response, especially when confronted with unavoidable suffering? Frankl felt that Nietzsche's will to power was too narrow and far too narcissistically defined to sustain people. He also felt that Freud's pleasure principle, or trying to suppress the darker emotions (stress, anxiety, fear, anger, etc.) by enacting pleasure, was in like fashion too narrow and narcissistically defined.

Philosopher Jon Stratton delivers a striking look at the constitution of evil, the obfuscation of God performed by people consumed by evil, and the response to evil made by mature people such as Frankl:

> Evil does not afford a turn to God because no one is capable of withstanding its force. This, I believe is the central aspect of evil. Thus, the atheist is one who is beset with evil—in some way. I agree that even in the presence of evil, God is present, and calls to us. If God's face is turned from us, it is because God—in our experience—has turned away. Ironically, we are so immersed in the force of that which turns us from God that our experience is thoroughly that God has turned from us. I believe it is very important to capture that aspect of the experience of evil; it is as if God has turned from us. Yet I believe that evil, in fact, has made it that we cannot turn to God.

God, as inherent in the world, as immanent, experiences our turn and calls to us. But we are not capable of making that re-turn. The "death camps" were precisely scientism's environmental construct. Living human beings were categorized as if they were nothing but measurable data. There was no hope there. The survivor Frankl shows us that in the absence of hope, some individuals could manufacture an approximation of hope. Some could momentarily find the call of The Spirit within a living blade of grass or a kind gesture. This courageous and wise discovery was the result of being open to the heart of life in the presence of evil.

Remarkable. Heroic. Exceptional.[44]

Frankl proposed the will to meaning, or the pursuit of life meaning, as an answer not only to the wretched conditions imposed by Nazism, but to life itself. He felt that every person must find life meaning in order to have a complete and verdant life, and from this stance it follows that the "ghastly abyss" we face in the darkness can and must be crossed. For Frankl, the answer to life's most entangled questions is found in giving oneself to beloved others in a completely unselfish act of knowing them through unconditional love.[45] This giving is accomplished not by shutting down the self, or by concluding the search for truth, but by maintaining a stance of revolutionary openness to life's most ultimate demands.

LOVE IN TIMES OF EVIL

Love leads us to a confrontation with our own darkness, and calls us to stand face to face with evil in order to overcome evil with good. Evil goes on, unaccountable and full of fury, chaos, and trouble. But love finds order in chaos and asserts the eternal over the temporary. Jesuit Father Pedro Arrupe's confrontation with the results of atomic warfare introduced a mending touch to a great rift in the fabric of humanity. Taking this healing further, I'd like to consider two additional accounts of war. The first gives greater detail to the dropping of the atomic bombs on Hiroshima and Nagasaki.[46] The second speaks of one woman's response to the horror she experienced in the context of U.S. involvement in Vietnam. Remaining faithful to historical facts, each account is set in narrative form.

Account 1: *Telegraph Report of the Firebombing of Japan and Eventual Atomic Warfare*

STOP. 1945. People walked the streets of industry looking overhead and listening. A whistle of sound came like a torch-fire to the bone behind the ear. The powerless, the dispossessed, fragile of body and fearful of mind, at war with foreign foes who occupied air and sea, the citizens of Japan had been invaded, and overhead a near constant droning accompanied squadrons of enemy planes. Delivery, disaffection, detonation. Time bends forward and back and eternity goes on forever.

STOP. Then, men fueled B-29s. Superfortress 1 and 2.

STOP. "With the help of the United Kingdom and Canada, the United States designed and built nuclear bombs under the codename The Manhattan Project, creating weapons of mass destruction in the desert at Alamogordo, New Mexico, in the face of Nazi and Japanese threats overseas."

J. Robert Oppenheimer, whose work defined the atomic age, observed the desert spectacle at Trinity Test Site: a flash of tremendous light along with the ominous deep growling shudder of motion and sound. Instantly he recalled words from the Bhagavad-Gita:

> If the radiance of a thousand suns were to burst at once into the sky, that would be like the splendor of the mighty one. Now I am become death, the shatterer of worlds.[47]

STOP. "U.S. said purpose of nuclear weapons: for use as war deterrents."

STOP. "Gadget, the first nuclear device, was detonated at Trinity Test Site near Alamogordo, New Mexico. The Hiroshima and Nagasaki bombs were the second and third detonated, and the only nuclear warheads ever used as weapons."

STOP. "Before dropping the bombs on Japan, United States president Harry S. Truman and other allied leaders made the Potsdam Declaration:

> The might that now converges on Japan is immeasurably greater than that which, when applied to the resisting Nazis, necessarily laid waste to the lands, the industry and the method of life of the whole German people. The full application of our military power, backed by our resolve, will mean the inevitable and complete destruction of the Japanese armed forces and just as inevitably the utter devastation of the Japanese homeland. . . .

> We call upon the government of Japan to proclaim now the unconditional surrender of all Japanese armed forces, and to provide proper and adequate assurances of their good faith in such action. The alternative for Japan is prompt and utter destruction.

STOP, the feature article from major U.S. news outlets:

> On the morning of August 6, 1945 the United States Army Air Forces conducted the first nuclear assault mission and dropped the nuclear weapon "Little Boy"

on the city of Hiroshima. Three days later the "Fat Man" bomb was detonated over Nagasaki, Japan. In both cases, depleted Japanese air assault forces did not expect the weapons, and to conserve weaponry were not engaging small enemy air forays, and so gave no resistance.

Little Boy, a gravity bomb, a gun-type fission weapon containing 60 kg (130 pounds) of uranium-235 was carried 6 hours in flight by the B-29 bomber *Enola Gay*. Photographs of the destruction were shot from sister plane *Necessary Evil*. The attacks came off exactly as planned; the bombs performed as predicted. Little Boy was dropped over the center of Hiroshima and exploded 600 meters (2000 feet) above ground, a blast equivalent to 13 kilotons of TNT, instantly killing 70,000 people. The radius of complete destruction was 1.6 kilometers (1 mile), and ensuing fires covered 11.4 square kilometers (4.4 square miles). Ninety percent of the buildings in Hiroshima were damaged or completely destroyed.

STOP, forgetting. After Hiroshima, President Truman's voice to the world:

"If they do not now accept our terms, they may expect a rain of ruin from the air the likes of which has never been seen on this earth."

STOP. More reports from the major news media outlets:

On the morning of August 9th the B-29 Superfortress *Bock's Car* carried the nuclear assault weapon codenamed "Fat Man." At 11:02 a.m. Fat Man, housing a core of 6.4 kilograms (14.1 pounds) of plutonium-239, was let down over Nagasaki's industrial valley. The weapon detonated 469 meters (1540 feet) above ground, and 70,000 of Nagasaki's 240,000 residents immediately died. The radius of complete destruction was 1.6 kilometers (1 mile). Fires raged over the northern portion of Nagasaki, consuming 3.2 kilometers (2 miles) of city.

Together Little Boy and Fat Man killed 140,000 people instantly. An additional 100,000 died the following year from radiation poisoning, burns, necrosis, and other bomb-related injuries. In the years to come, more deaths ensued.

STOP. The news articles, raiding even our dreams:

In the span preceding August 6, 1945, the United States bombed Japan using conventional firebombs killing 100,000 people in Tokyo alone, and 400,000 more throughout the country. Conventional firebombing destroyed 60 cities.

DEATHS by firebombing, 500,000.
DEATHS by nuclear assault, 400,000.
Albert Einstein and Leo Szilard, who initiated the first bomb research in 1939, sent a jointly written letter to President Franklin D. Roosevelt. Szilard,

who played a major role in the Manhattan Project, argued: "If the Germans had dropped atomic bombs on cities instead of us, we would have defined the dropping of atomic bombs on cities as a war crime, and we would have sentenced the Germans who were guilty of this crime to death at Nuremberg and hanged them."

Previous to the detonation of Little Boy and Fat Man, many scientists, American nuclear physicist Edward Teller among them, reported the following:

"The destructive power of the bomb." STOP.
"Could have been demonstrated." STOP.
"Without the taking of lives." STOP.

Account 2: *Does One Forgive Warfare?*

YES. Fast forward nearly three decades to the U.S. role in the civilian life of Vietnamese people during the Vietnam War. Some historians say the Vietnam War began in 1945, the same year we commenced atomic warfare against Japan. The Vietnam War officially ended in 1973.

YES. On March 16, 1968, U.S. Army forces conducted the mass murder of nearly 500 unarmed citizens in South Vietnam. The victims were all civilians; some were women and children. The atrocity came to be known as the My Lai Massacre.[48] U.S. military sexually abused, beat, tortured, and maimed the victims, mutilating some of the bodies. Of twenty-six U.S. soldiers charged with criminal offences for their actions at My Lai, only one was convicted, and sentenced to life in prison. He served only three years of his sentence.

YES. On June 8, 1972, combined U.S. and South Vietnamese military forces rained napalm over the village of Trang Bang, forcing children and their families to run from the city down Route-1, their bodies burning with chemical fire. One young girl became engraved onto the memory of the world through the photograph taken by Huynh Cong Nick Ut, an AP photographer. The girl's name was Phan Thi Kim Phúc.[49] She lived. Two of her cousins died.

YES. The photograph showing Phan screaming in pain and fear of death became an international symbol of antiwar sentiment. The photograph is considered one of the most striking images in the last 150 years of photo journalism for its unyielding severity and heart-wrenching ability to inspire compassion and human rights throughout the world. The London *Observer* named the photograph "the most haunting image of the horror of war since Goya."[50]

Third-degree burns covered more than half of Phan's body. In the hospital she faced a pronouncement that her burns were so extreme she could not

possibly survive. She went on to endure fourteen months of excruciating rehabilitation, including seventeen surgical procedures in Saigon. She wrestled
with years of despair, loneliness, and loss after overcoming the tragedy, and
though small in stature physically, her faith and strength of character fused
to make her one of the strongest voices for peace in the contemporary age.
Phan Thi Kim Phúc is now a Goodwill Ambassador for the United Nations
Educational, Scientific and Cultural Organization (UNESCO).

Even more miraculous is Phan's personal reconciliation with a past that
had haunted her from the day the photo was taken. Today she greets life with
profound joy. As she works with groups throughout the world, she states that
though burns had covered most of her body, her feet remained unburned, and
this allowed her to run, escaping the epicentre of the bombing. She describes
this simple truth as a gift of God.

Growing up, Phan had felt convinced no man would love her, but in adulthood she married and now tells others how her husband's love healed her and
helped her find a better view of her wounds. When she gathered the courage
to ask him if her scars bothered him, he responded by saying her scars made
her more beautiful, and that knowing what she'd been through only made him
love her more.

Often even in adult life when she looked at her wounds, she questioned,
"Why me?" But she began to believe more and more fully in a complex interplay of love and fate. She felt cared for in an ultimate sense and found that
a life verse she'd chosen seemed to return to her like a healing song, even in
her despair:

For thou hast delivered my soul from death:
Hast thou not delivered my feet from falling;
That I may walk before God in the light of the living?—Psalm 56:13

YES. Phan chose faith rather than desolation and by choosing faith she
embarked on a journey to forgive those who had wounded her, even those
who had dropped the bombs on her village. Her spiritual quest continued
when she gave a speech at the Vietnam Memorial in Washington, D.C. on
Veterans Day in 1996.

With hope in her heart she met a crowd charged with raw emotion. She
looked out, and in the eyes of the people she saw sorrow and shame, guilt
and bitterness and anger . . . even hate. She rose and delivered the following
speech:

Dear Friends:
    I am very happy to be with you today. I thank you for giving me the opportu-
nity to talk and meet with you on this Veterans Day. As you know I am the little

girl who was running to escape from the napalm fire. I do not want to talk about the war because I cannot change history. I only want you to remember the tragedy of war in order to do things to stop fighting and killing around the world. I have suffered a lot from both physical and emotional pain. Sometimes I thought I could not live, but God saved me and gave me faith and hope.

Even if I could talk face to face with the pilot who dropped the bombs, I would tell him we cannot change history but we should try to do good things for the present and for the future to promote peace. I did not think that I could marry nor have any children because of my burns, but now I have a wonderful husband and lovely son and a happy family.

Dear friends, I just dream one day people all over the world can live in real peace—no fighting, and no hostility. We should work together to build peace and happiness for all people in all nations.

Thank you so much for letting me be a part of this important day.[51]

YES. John Plummer was in the audience.

YES. Plummer was an American pilot who helped coordinate the air strike on Trang Bang.

YES. After the speech, Plummer approached Phan, told her who he was, and sought her forgiveness.

YES. Phan Thi Kim Phúc forgave John Plummer.

Phan willingly opened her heart to forgive and reconcile. She became a servant leader to the world, and today as she promotes peace her personal message resounds across the ages:

"I can never forget, but we cannot change the past.

Because I have lived with hatred, I know love, hope, and forgiveness."

Today she asks people to reconsider the iconic photograph of her as a young girl in the death grip of the Vietnam War.

"Do not see me calling out in pain," she says.

"See me calling out for peace."

Chapter 21

A Cree Man's Journey

On Mother Loss and Mother Love

In taking the last steps of a journey, sometimes we encounter the most intimate forms of existence. Here where the shattered nature of contemporary life can completely overwhelm us, the servant leader brings healing . . . the servant leader heals others. In facing ourselves, especially in the darkness of our experiences of unavoidable suffering, love can touch even our deepest wounds. Often those wounds are held very close to the heart, in the place reserved for mother or father. I am reminded again that this book is a book about the transcendent nature of humanity: our will to love, our will to heal, and our will to give meaning to our children so they may overcome the evil that walks the earth, making itself known. Viktor Frankl conceived of three elements every person must face in life, and in fact must *resolve* in order to find life meaning. Frankl's tragic triad is composed of pain, guilt, and suffering.[52] How we face these generational and humanity-wide inner crucibles with determination, individually and in community with others, builds our capacity to heal and be healed, and affirms our capacity to love and be loved. In coming to a better understanding of our own existence, we must pass through the history of our mothers and fathers, and our choices in this regard are of paramount importance.

A friend of mine, in one vital moment, revealed the beauty of such choices.

If you knew Sheldon McLain at his strongest and most authentic, you not only knew a man of intense interior discipline, but a physical specimen worthy of the great images of the masculine passed down through the ages. Half Cree, he stood six feet four inches tall and looked intimidating, his face and eyes darkly striking, his muscular frame lithe, quick, and powerful. Sadly, he died much too young, in his thirties, in a car accident on the winter roads of the Hi-Line in northern Montana. He had been a close friend, a complex person of a very mercurial bent, at times confusing, at times lovely . . . inherently hard to understand and stubborn enough to be difficult about it. Capable of grave harms, he lived a double life wrought by generational cycles of abuse and pain. Yet in Sheldon's most noble moments he evoked deep compassion, and the best of the human heart.

With respect for his death I tell this story of his life.

Shel and I first met as boys on the Cheyenne reservation in southeast Montana.

My father was the head basketball coach and high school principal at St. Labre, the students a combination of Cheyennes from Lame Deer, Busby, and Ashland, and those from the Crow tribe bussed in from a distance, from towns such as Crow Agency, Pryor, and Lodge Grass.

I found out from Sheldon that his father had died from drug-related events just before I arrived on the Cheyenne reservation. As young boys, Sheldon and his older brother George were left in the care of the state and eventually were adopted by a white family in the small milltown that bordered the reservation. Ironically, Sheldon attended a white grade school while I attended a Cheyenne grade school.

We saw each other often, we loved basketball, and we played the game all-out. Our heroes were the players who starred for my father's team: young men with names that matched the joy and originality they showed on the court— Juneau Plenty Hawk, Fred and Paul Deputy, Stanford Rides Horse. We grew up admiring them and trying to emulate them . . . and then my family moved, and Sheldon and I lost touch.

Years later, both of us having left the reservation, having lived in totally different geographic regions, we met again and discovered common ground and formed a lasting friendship. We both pursued collegiate basketball and ended up spending a decade of summers coaching younger players on the summer basketball camp circuit. We also both pursued graduate degrees in psychology and spent countless hours talking about the inner life . . . about the nature of family and the nature of God. Sheldon's life reflected a vibrant truth I had found in my readings on personal and collective healing: "The need for forgiveness arises when someone has acted in such a way as to bring about a fundamental disruption to the wholeness or integrity of one's life. Initially, on a deep, almost organic level, there is a tearing of the fabric of one's life, one's world."[53] The mother loss and father loss Sheldon had experienced, both of great depth, formed a complex network of internal pain and the desire to overcome. Near the end of my own doctoral degree in psychology, when I began my central research on touch and forgiveness, I asked Sheldon to participate in the research.

His story, printed below in his own words, is one I carry with me.

When I was three years old my parents were divorced and myself being the youngest of three boys I was raised along with my two older brothers by my father. He was a single parent and as a school teacher we had the opportunity to spend quite a bit of time with him. So I developed a really strong relationship with my dad and I loved him a lot. I just felt loved by him. When I was three my parents divorced and my mother went up to Canada. They divorced because my father was physically abusive and my mother was an alcoholic.

She just went up to Canada and lived her life up there away from us and made no contact with us at all—she never wrote, she never called. So I really felt abandoned. I felt a lot of hatred toward her. I had a strong need to be loved by my mother and to be denied that was very painful for me. I hated my mom as much as I loved my dad. I was hurt. It was like she was dead or we were dead. There was just nothing there.

When I was nine years old my father died and I was scared that my mother was going to come down from Canada and try to get custody of me. But she never came, she never even made an attempt and that was even worse; it cemented my feelings that she didn't care about me and she just didn't love me . . . and because of that I hated her.

The first time we ever talked on the phone I was sixteen—it was a really strange, awkward conversation—there wasn't much speaking involved. Just a lot of silent times on the phone, and a lot of moments of hesitation, of not knowing what to say and not knowing what to ask and just the basic uneasiness and discomfort. Shortly before that she had called my stepfather, who was my legal guardian. She'd called him at work and said in a drunken voice, "I want my sons back." Then she had called me and I was terrified. At the end of it she said, "I love you, Son," and I could tell that it was kind of a searching statement, like she was trying to give me a cue to say I love you Mom, or something along those lines. I didn't have it in my heart to say that. I just said, "Yeah, I gotta go now." I said goodbye and as I did I heard her swearing as she slammed the phone down. That was pretty traumatic for me because I felt that I should have been able to say I love you Mom, but it was just at that point I was unable to. She was just a stranger to me; it would have been an empty statement. It would have meant nothing to me.

So I was sixteen the first time I had any contact from my mother. That was not the first time I had tried to make contact though. When I was in the seventh grade I had gone to a basketball camp and a speaker there said some things that hit me hard. One thing he said was that the thing you hate the most is the thing you will become. Knowing I had deep hatred for my mom, and knowing that she was an alcoholic and the fact that I'm a Native American

Indian may predispose me to become an alcoholic, I really feared I might become like her if I didn't work through my feelings. Unless I chose to forgive her then I would most likely become like her. So I wrote her a letter.

I was pretty young at the time and I probably could have done a better job of saying what I did but that's probably the best way I knew how to say it at the time. As the years have gone by I've had to come to terms with different aspects of that forgiveness and reconciliation with my mother. I had the opportunity to come to a place where I was in contact with a lot of people who really knew how to love, and a lot of people that really loved life, and lived life strongly and knew the aspects and principles of forgiveness. They were beginning to heal my heart and so I was able to get some kind of mild counseling growing up. But when I was sixteen, even though I had written this letter as a seventh grader I still had a lot of feelings and a lot of hurt there, unresolved emotions. There were some issues there that needed to be settled. And I never once said I love you to my mother, I just said I forgive you. And I think those are two different things for me. I really believed that I could forgive her but that didn't mean that I loved her.

When I was eighteen, after my mom had called me maybe two to three times between the ages of sixteen and eighteen, an opportunity came for me to see her. My older brother was getting married. A month before the wedding she called and said she'd be coming down for the wedding. I was really fearful of that. I was fearful of this issue of saying I love you to her and I felt I needed to be able to say that to her because I had written to her and said I had forgiven her.

I had been dealing with those emotions of resentment and abandonment the years between writing as a seventh grader and then the possibility of seeing her at eighteen. There was a lot of years there, a lot of gradual healing took place, and as I got older, I think I was able to work through some of those feelings slowly and by the time I was eighteen, yes I was afraid, but I had pretty much come to terms with a lot of the abandonment. I had been given a home. Through the state I had been blessed with two parents who cared for me, provided for me, gave me opportunities to succeed in life, and I had been around other people that also furthered that and really focused their love to meet my needs and to help me in my areas of weakness. Areas such as the insecurity that comes from abandonment. I'd started to believe in myself and not be ashamed but accept and actually be proud of my past. As a Native American Indian I had a heritage to be proud of. I needed to stay strong and be a breaker of stereotypes. It may be true that some of the stereotypes of Native American Indians are based on fact. But there are exceptions and I wanted to be an exception.

But I was afraid.

She called me and said she was coming to the wedding. So she came down four weeks later. And during those four weeks—in between the time she called and the wedding—I prayed every night. My prayer was along the lines of, "God, I really need your help in this, I need your love because I don't have any love for her in my own heart. I want to be able to say I love you Mom, to her. And I want that to be genuine and I want it to be strong—not something that is just said. So I just ask you to give me your love so that I may be able to show her your love and that you would just work in me and do whatever it takes."

I prayed this prayer every night before falling asleep, for a month. At the end of the time she came down to the wedding, and I was taken aback by her appearance. I remembered her as a little child would, when I was three years old; that was the last time I'd seen her. I remembered her as being young and pretty, and she had long black hair and she was tall and she had a beautiful face, and being Native Canadian Indian she had dark skin and dark eyes, and she was a pretty lady. But the first time I saw her at the wedding it was amazing. I was taken aback by the changes. Her face showed a lot of pain, a lot of years. Her face was just haggard—it was hard and there was no light in her eyes. Nothing that showed joy. There was nothing that showed happiness. And that was a day that she should have been rejoicing; her son was getting married. She was hardened. Like she just didn't show emotion, it was just harsh. She'd had a hard life as evidenced by her face; she's got a lot of scars you know. And a lot of those scars are because of what she did, because of the pain of living without your son. She's a fairly tall lady, about 5'11" and she still had long black hair. You could tell that she'd been pretty once, but there was nothing now that would really be attractive. She kind of stooped when she walked and there was no confidence in her. That weekend we probably spent about six to seven total hours together, during which I smelled alcohol on her breath constantly. I remember the night after the wedding we went back to the hotel room. She had to pick up some clothes, and when I walked into the hotel room it smelled like a liquor store. It was the stench of alcohol, of hard liquor, the same that was on her breath. I remember walking out of her hotel room and just saying to myself, it's no big deal you know, no big deal.

The next day she was leaving and it was about 10:30 in the morning. I remember standing in my foster-parents' living room. Everyone had gathered there to say their goodbyes, and she was nervous, you could tell. She was kind of hesitant, shifting back and forth, and I was also pretty nervous. I was praying the whole time to myself, just, God, I'm going to be strong, I'm going to be strong. I was pretty emotional, I was ready to cry. My mom stood across the room and . . . here's her eighteen-year-old son. She's never been a part of his life, she's had no contact whatsoever, and she's never heard the words I love you come out of his lips. And I'm sure she's scared of rejection. I'm sure she's scared of a lot of things. We've never talked openly about her alcohol or anything like that, it was just kind of a skirted issue. Then she said, "Well, we've got to be going now, we've got a long road ahead of us. We have to drive back to Canada and it's about a nine-hour drive." She was making small talk and she was kind of at a standstill, she didn't know what to say. I walked across the room, took about three steps and put my arms out and she took a step towards me. I embraced her and said, "I love you, Mom."

It was the only time I had embraced her and it was a real strong moment. My left arm was underneath her right arm and my right arm would be on top of her shoulder. Her hair was kind of in my face, it was real close. So our bodies were close to one another and I remember having my hand on her back and just drawing her to me, and holding her strongly for a while. I made sure it felt strong, not weak. It was like the ending part of the story of forgiveness—for my forgiveness of her you know.

It was just healing for me to reach out and say, I love you, Mom.

It was like saying I forgive you, I love you . . . it's okay.

The embrace had a lot to do with forgiveness of all those years of abandonment and pain, and hatred towards her. The touch was an acknowledgement of the relationship that existed between us as a son and a mother. That bond had been re-established and recognized and acknowledged in the eyes of others. If I was giving her something, I was giving her her son back . . . in the sense that I was giving my heart to her as a son and looking at her as my mother. I was acknowledging that she was my mother, yet realizing at the same time she most likely wouldn't act on that and she wouldn't involve herself any differently after we touched. I gave her the freedom and the opportunity to be there. And for that moment in time she was my mother.[54]

Chapter 22

The Nature of the Forgiving Touch
On Father Loss and Father Love

In the end, forgiveness and servant leadership are personal, and are meant not merely to challenge the heart and soul, but to give deep comfort. Fittingly, this book's final encounter with forgiveness is also personal and comes from the life of my father-in-law, giving witness to some of the difficulties he experienced as a boy and leading to the choices he made in life that resulted in surrender and tenderness for his daughter, Jennifer, the woman I fell in love with and married. In my research on touch and forgiveness, I've been honored to interview many people who have made the choice not only to forgive but also to ask forgiveness. When I spoke with Jennifer's father, I was reminded of the joy of having him as a mentor all these years, and how the richness of true relationship becomes a priceless tapestry woven across the generations. His attention to forgiveness and true mutual power with and for others are equaled by an unfailing devotion to servant leadership. Family to family, in all cultures, father loss and father love infuse many of our most deeply held dreams of life and relationship. The time spent with Jennifer's father in interviews I conducted with him years ago reminds me today of the gift of presence, of being present with others. For from such presence understandings arise that astound us, and in the end, if we listen, we give our lives to changes that are daunting, but also necessary and unfailingly good.

Searching the literature on touch and forgiveness, I was awed by the nature of touch and the essential role of touch with children. Without affection in the life of the child, the results are devastating. All the way back to Frederick II, the emperor of the Germanic lands in the early 1200s, the facts are undeniable. Frederick wanted to find out what language a child would speak as an adult if no one spoke to the child beforehand. He conducted his own crude experiment in which he prevented foster mothers and nurses from speaking to or showing affection toward a group of children. He wondered if the children would end up speaking Hebrew, the oldest language, or Greek, Latin, or Arabic. He hypothesized they might even speak the language of their parents to whom they were born. But his experiment yielded no results. All the children died.[55]

The significance of touch cannot be underestimated. In a classic study from 1958 that helped define the nature of touch, experimental psychologist Harry Harlow revealed the need for young animals to experience touch from the outset of life. He found that when baby rhesus monkeys were raised in a bare wire mesh cage, the monkeys survived with difficulty, or did not survive at all. The baby monkeys did better when a wire mesh cone was introduced. Finally, baby rhesus monkeys thrived and were healthy and husky if the wire mesh cone was covered with terrycloth, thus making contact comfort a profound step involved in survival. Harlow reported, "Contact comfort is a variable of overwhelming importance in the development of affectional responses."[56]

Notably, under touch deprivation rhesus monkeys die at a much lower rate than humans. The more primitive the animal, the less the consequences of touch deprivation. The human infant suffers the effects of touch deprivation quicker and with greater threat, and though we are often capable of hiding the emotional damage that accompanies our life, when we come from a heritage that lacks affection, we suffer. Montagu projected the effects of touch into adult life: "To be tender, loving and caring, human beings must be tenderly loved and cared for in their earliest years."[57]

The resounding importance of this truth became evident in the foundling homes designed to care for orphans during and after World War II. The pioneering work of René Spitz showed the gravity of the love object (mother and father) to the development of the child. Conducting research in a hospital for abandoned babies, babies whose fathers and mothers were absent, Spitz found that though the infants were well fed and kept in a fully sanitary environment, they had very high death rates as a result of the disease called *marasmus*: a wasting away with no apparent medical cause. In Mexico, Spitz investigated an orphanage in which conditions were often unsanitary, but babies were happier, more alert, and did not cry as much. He proposed that the condition of the babies had much to do with the women who came in from the village each day to sing and talk to them. As the women talked and sang, they rocked and held the babies. In later years, when the war resulted in thousands of orphans, Spitz observed that touched babies were not deficient in growth, while those left alone in bassinets often became ill and developed profound growth deficiencies and intellectual defects.

In Spitz's research on children who experienced partial emotional deprivation, he stated, "Recovery is prompt when the love object is returned to the child within a period of three to five months." However, in cases of total emotional deprivation and lack of touch, Spitz discovered that "if one deprives children during their first year of all [love] relations for periods lasting longer than five months, they will show the symptoms of increasingly serious deteriorations, which appears to be, in part at least, irreversible." In 1945 Spitz observed total deprivation and its consequences in a foundling home that housed ninety-one infants. Here, children were breastfed by wet-nurses for their first three months. During these three months the children demonstrated the developmental level of normal children of the same city. After the third month the children were no longer breastfed and reentered the usual system of care at the foundling home. The children were well taken care of in every bodily respect: food, hygiene, medical care, medication. However, only one nurse was given to care for eight to twelve children. In the words of Spitz, because of the lack of touch and affection the children were "emotionally starved." Spitz felt that the infants received about one-tenth of the normal amount of touch provided in the usual parent-child relationship. After the separation from a primary source of love and affection the children deteriorated progressively, motor retardation became fully evident, and the children became completely passive, lying still in their cots, incapable of exerting enough motor control to turn to the prone position. Of the ninety-one children observed in the foundling home, thirty-four died by the end of the second year. The children who survived showed a progressive decline in development, explicitly referred to in Spitz's comment that "by the end of the second year, the average of their developmental quotients stands at 45 per cent of the normal. This would be the level of the idiot. We continued to observe these children at longer intervals up to the age of four years . . . by that time, with a few exceptions, these children cannot sit, stand, walk, or talk." The result, Spitz concluded, was "a spectacularly increased rate of mortality."[58]

Spitz's research caused major change throughout the world in the way children are cared for in hospitals and orphanages. Consider the clarity of the truth he revealed: love and affection, in the form of good loving touch, help children thrive. Without affectionate touch, children are prone to experience great difficulty.

As we turn our attention to fathers, the picture is often bleak. The infrequency of affectionate touch between fathers and their children is a factor all too common in the present day. In the Western world, in my own experience as a family systems psychologist, I classify the lack of appropriate and full expression of touch from fathers to their sons or daughters as approaching epidemic levels. Distant, rigid, and emotionally frigid fathers appear to be the norm in struggling families, not the exception. From this lack, children suffer, and in the end, the heart and spirit of the world are greatly diminished.

In conducting systematic hermeneutic phenomenological research involving in-depth interviews with people regarding touch and forgiveness, discoveries came from mining the rich oral histories of individual people. In many cases, they had experienced brutal harm physically, emotionally, and spiritually, and in listening to the pain in their stories I often felt deeply saddened. Significantly, the intensity and focus of the harm were due in large part to their experience of father loss or mother loss. The absence of abiding love and affection, from either mother or father, shook the foundations of the individual's life. Yet as the interviews went on I was struck by the refreshing sense of hardiness or resilience found in so many of those I interviewed. Rising from this resilience came the choice to forgive, to forgive and hold tenaciously to it . . . forgiveness as fully rendered in the life and action of people who hoped for a better life for their own children. In the end, the many resolute ways people reengaged relationship and restored even their perpetrators to healing left me with a renewed sense of the human capacity for love and greatness.

From the research process on the forgiving touch, certain themes emerged having to do not only with the notion of unconditional or ultimate forgiveness, but on a more elemental level with the human capacity to heal one another.[59] In the end, five of these themes were most salient and revealed that the moment of the forgiving touch symbolizes the opportunity for:

1. The restoration of a loving bond.
2. The restoration of character.
3. The lifting of past relational pain.
4. The lifting of the burden of shame.
5. The restoration of oneness.

In the presence of either violence or neglect, for those who had the determination not only to forgive but also to purposefully go and offer a forgiving touch to those who had formerly harmed them, a powerful sense of self emerged. From this sense of self, the ability to refocus the interior life toward self-responsibility, forgiveness-asking, and reconciliation became a reality. And in becoming people of integrity and forgiveness, they stepped forward and brought healing to others, and in effect, helped others envision what had been lost . . . a responsible and loving sense of life together.

In surrendering to the grace involved in healing the self, those who envisioned perfect forgiveness went forward and brought healing to others, and in so doing they fulfilled Greenleaf's best test of servant leadership:

The best test, and difficult to administer, is: Do those served grow as persons? Do they, while being served, become healthier, wiser, freer, more autonomous, more likely themselves to become servants?

And, what is the effect on the least privileged in society; will they benefit, or, at least, not be further deprived?

Such a test is not momentary; it endures throughout the lifespan. Perfect forgiveness is of the same vein, giving vitality to the course of our lives, reminding us of the responsibility involved in making choices toward servant leadership, and legitimate power, and how affirming such choices are in grounding us again in human love and spiritual growth. When we truly encounter authentic human love and spiritual growth, we cease to do violence, and we are able to overcome violence with confidence and faith in our ability to overcome. Similarly, in the gift of forgiveness and the work of reconciliation, we return to one another wholeheartedly, and we give our children the opportunity to dream their own great dreams.

Touch then, especially in light of our collective capacity for darkness, takes on new meaning. Forgiveness requires courage, asking forgiveness requires courage, and living a new life that eventually restores our broken relationships requires even greater courage. The following story, set in the words of my father-in-law, Fred Crowell, reveals the subtlety and awareness necessary to set our children free from the chains that bind us.[60]

When you have a negative experience with touch I think it takes a longer time to make it a positive. There has to be growth . . . change . . . it has to be gradual. One of the ways that I believe in parenting is that you never physically touch your children in negative ways with your hands . . . or with your body. For example we believed in spanking when they were young. But we wanted to use a neutral object so they wouldn't associate the hand with an instrument of pain, but would see the hand as an instrument of love. I feel very strongly about this based on the fact that my father used his hands a lot to slap you . . . or slug you . . . or hit you. I can remember even in my twenties when someone reached over to just pat me on the shoulder my first reaction would be a flinch like I expected to get hit. Like a dog does with an owner who slaps it with his hands.

So I look back on getting slapped or hit because of discipline, usually in anger. Those were basically the ways of touch in my family. There wasn't much hugging or positive physical forms of expression. When you hit somebody, it's pretty hard to turn around and put your arms around them.

There's a violation of a relationship when, for example, you get into a fight with somebody . . . there's a big difference between a word fight and a physical fight. I almost feel like there's a boundary there. And when you cross that boundary, you really injure that relationship. Once you cross the line of physical contact in a negative way it builds a wall of hurt and mistrust and violation. So first of all I look at touch from a negative standpoint. From the negative in my youth. And it took me personally a long, long time to feel comfortable in positive touch.

Forgiveness starts inside. Forgiveness starts when you are willing to say, I choose to forgive you. I choose to hold it against you no more. That's a release. When you don't get that there's tension. When you are mad and bitter, and there is unforgiveness, you not only want emotional separation, you also want physical separation. The question is do you want to be right, or do you want to forgive and be forgiven. Do you want the relationship or do you want the fractured life. And if you want to be right more than you want the relationship, then you will lay there in your anger. The beautiful part of the touch is that moments before you go and touch the person, you are in a place of isolation and alienation and darkness. In the right conditions, touch illumines love, and sets you and your loved one free.

When forgiveness hasn't taken place we often want emotional and physical separation because tender touch and kindness and softness are expressions of the heart. You have to be an incredible liar to be really tender during unforgiveness, that or out of touch with what's going on. There is incongruence there, to have tremendous anger or bitterness or conflict with someone and yet touch them tenderly.

When there is no forgiveness the relationship either stands still or it reverses. There are times when the problem gets worse and worse and worse, and that's why you have to have commitment to forgiveness or eventually the unforgiveness overcomes you, you just can't find forgiveness in your heart. I think if you let anger run for a period of time, it becomes very difficult to stop. You have to stop it and choose a new course of action and expect new things. Rather than an on and off switch, it's more like a river that cuts a new path. That's why when you teach young people a given lifestyle, they need to be really aware of those patterns, because they are difficult to change. There are times when I'm so angry about an issue and I choose to forgive or to let go of that anger, yet I have to work on it, sometimes for a great while. Or I've been mad at a person who wronged me, and I'll choose to give that up, and then five minutes later I'm back chewing on it again and I'm angry with that person again in my mind. When you're angry at someone, your mind highlights their weaknesses, and when you really truly forgive and love someone you highlight their strengths.

Touch takes it to another level. Touch is a very delicate and critical issue and if you ever violate it physically . . . I mean you can say something very harsh to somebody, but slug that person in the face and the impact is incredibly different. I remember mentoring a family one time, this woman asked her husband to forgive her and he forgave her and then he just gave her a love tap on the shoulder and it hurt. It negated everything that was said. He didn't mean it that way, but it produced pain. The manner in which touch is handled is crucial.

You have to use your touch moments to build what you are trying to accomplish. For example, let's say that my wife and I have an argument and we ask each other forgiveness and we embrace and kiss and hug and we have some tears and it really means a lot, but we don't correct the irritation that caused the problem to start with. If we don't correct it we will get right back to that irritation and if that irritation continues, at some point, it's very likely we will no longer get to the embrace, the forgiveness, the touch, because we didn't use the tender moment to build upon another level of relationship. The tender moment of forgiveness and touch can open the relationship to deeper levels.

Out of a situation of touch and forgiveness I think the growth of the relationship can come to life in a powerful way. I mean it could be the difference between harmful words and beautiful words, between wanting your loved one to be in the same room or not even wanting to be in the same house with him or her. It's the difference between having a wonderful two-hour conversation nonstop versus sitting in a restaurant not saying a word to each other.

When resentment is going on, I think it dehumanizes, destroys; it's destructive. You are feeding on each other's weaknesses and there are shrugs, and look aways, the evil eye . . . sarcasm. There is no intimate touch. There may be a harsh touch. Abuse. No intimacy. There is no softness of touch. The touch and the forgiveness give certain things to the relationship . . . honesty . . . trust . . . oneness of heart and mind. Your own personal character is enhanced because you know the person values your character and you find when you enter the deep work you again feel worthy. You are willing and capable to do the disciplined and necessary work of forgiveness and change. Unforgiveness basically says I don't believe you can change, or I don't believe you want to change, or I don't believe you care about me. And when we trust we are saying . . . I believe. When you ask forgiveness with sincerity and authenticity and follow-through, you are saying I want to be trusted again. I want you to believe in my character. I want you to care about me as a person.

When there's forgiveness and peace and a commitment for intimacy, the touch grows and expands . . . it becomes common. Holding hands. Arms around each other. A pat on the back. When there is genuine forgiveness and touch, further touch is welcomed. When there is a lack of forgiveness, touch feels dishonest. Offensive. The forgiveness and that ensuing touch can some-times take touch between significant people from something that's offensive to something that's welcomed.

When you have anger and bitterness and you have let that build, then you have a period of destruction going on between two human beings. And that destroys you. Or at least you're being made to feel you're being destroyed. So there's a wound. And some wounds are quite severe. Why do we need authentic touch? I don't know the answers, I just know we do. And I know I see the satisfaction, I see that with people. I see it with children. They want to be touched. They want to be touched appropriately. It's affirming them as a person in terms of—I am special, I am unique, I am cared for, I am loved. Touch in forgiveness closes the gap between two people. It takes away the distance. Touch, during forgiveness, bonds together. At its best, the touch communicates I'm so glad you're a part of my life, I really need you, I really want you to be a part of my life. I want the best for you.

It's powerful. I think if every boy and girl had that there would be a lot less pain.

Usually the touch of negative is associated with negative emotions, vio-lence . . . anger . . . bitterness, resentment; and positive touch is associated with calmness, gentleness, and kindness. When I began to associate myself with people who had a balance with God, with people, and with themselves, I was attracted to the patience, the discernment, to the ability to handle things without flying off the handle and throwing things, and screaming and swearing. Gentleness, with firmness and discernment, fosters trust, support, encouragement, and those things lead to a pat on the back or to an embrace.

The big breakthrough is with children. To have your own children and to see how much they enjoy jumping around and wrestling. Then as they grow older it's just a natural extension of that.

Both my wife and I came from families where scores were kept, and there was bitterness. When my dad went off and broke something like a high chair, or threw something, or hit you . . . he would laugh about it later on, like, "What a fool I was for acting so stupid." But he would never say, "I'm really sorry I did that, could you forgive me?" It made you have more bitterness. There was no ownership.

I remember one time when I was about six years old. My dad was out washing his car. He was very fussy about his car. It was a real nice warm day and my brother and sister and I were out in the yard. He went to get his nozzle to put on the hose and he couldn't find it. His immediate response was that one of the kids took that nozzle. He just went absolutely ballistic. He would have hit us if we would have been close enough. It was just a tirade of swear-ing, and storming around. About five minutes later, and I can still see it, I'm standing in the yard and I can see the nozzle on the windowsill high enough that none of us kids could have put it up there. And he saw it. Then he thought that was kind of funny you know, because he realized that he had put it there. He didn't turn around and say, gee guys I'm really sorry. And I just thought, you idiot, why don't you grow up.

If my dad would have stopped and said, "Would you forgive me, I really crossed the line," I think his behavior would have changed. When you start humbling yourself and turn to the other person to take ownership, then you discover you don't want to put yourself in that embarrassing situation again.

I remember when my daughter Jennifer was about eighteen months old. I had disciplined her in anger and usually when she did something wrong I would be very calm, firm but tender. But I hadn't done it the way I thought I should and a part of me said I needed to ask forgiveness. So I picked her up and asked her to forgive me for being angry. We were living in an apartment and it was afternoon or early evening. She was doing something that I didn't want her to do and I spoke harshly, angrily. I pushed her aside and she had a real hurt look on her face. At that point I realized I was being kind of like my dad.

I believe with little kids you should be on the same level . . . your face about the same height, and so I brought her up to me. I picked her up, put my arms around her, held her face maybe six to eight . . . maybe ten inches away from my face. She looked directly at me and I said, "Jennifer, I'm really sorry I was angry with you. Would you please forgive me? I was wrong." And she didn't say anything. Her vocabulary wasn't big at that time. She just put both arms around my neck and gave me a hug. That was a special touch. What I remember about it was, "at eighteen months you really understand and you received the forgiveness." This turned a very painful situation on my part into a very positive one.

The touch she gave said, "I really love you. I trust you."

Chapter 23

Healing the Heart of the World

My father-in-law grew up in a difficult, angry, and entrenched system in which abuse and illegitimate uses of power caused children to be constantly afraid. Sheldon McLain was born into a family system of sheer agony between woman and man. When we restore our lost sense of the feminine and the masculine—our mother loss and our father loss—we become healers of our children, and when we heal our children we heal the future. Here, in an age of atrocities as personal as they are global, forgiveness and servant leadership exert great influence and rouse the power of love in the world. Hope and responsible action define the life of the servant leader, and draw us to challenge what stands in the way of a more concerted and humane response to suffering and loss.

In some of the most direct and arresting works of human freedom in recent history, bell hooks and Paulo Freire shake our foundations and lead us toward a holistic sense of each other:

> Like most men, most women are taught from childhood on that dominat-
> ing and controlling others is *the* basic expression of power. . . . they, along
> with male ruling groups, and most men, believe in the dominant ideology
> of the culture.
>
> —bell hooks[61]

Domination reveals the pathology of love: sadism in the dominator and masochism in the dominated. Because love is an act of courage, not of fear, love is commitment to others. No matter where the oppressed are found, the act of love is commitment to their cause—the cause of liberation. And this commitment, because it is loving, is dialogical. As an act of bravery, love cannot be sentimental; as an act of freedom, it must not serve as a pretext for manipulation.

Liberation is thus a childbirth, and a painful one. The man or woman who emerges is a new person, . . . which brings into the world this new being: no longer oppressor, . . . [no] longer oppressed, but human in the process of achieving freedom.

—Paulo Freire[62]

In any system in which power is used willfully at the expense of others, oppression and injustice take root. Hooks and Freire, like Greenleaf, Mandela, King, and Tutu, do not commend a placating or passive response to such injustice, but rather a form of intensified and soulful purpose in the presence of atrocity.

An important question presents itself: Can there be leadership without healing?

In my experience the answer is both luminous and inevitable. False leadership does harm. True leadership heals the heart of the world. Jung reminds us, "Everyone carries a shadow, and the less it is embodied in the individual's conscious life, the blacker and denser it is. At all counts, it forms an unconscious snag, thwarting our most well-meaning intentions."[63] In becoming conscious, in living above the line, grace and ease guide us from contentment toward wholehearted love for the world and the people of the world. Again, Jung delivers a poignant challenge: "As far as we can discern, the sole purpose of human existence is to kindle a light in the darkness of mere being."[64]

Palmer echoes Jung's call, saying:

A leader is someone with the power to project either shadow or light onto some part of the world and onto the lives of the people who dwell there. A leader shapes the ethos in which others must live, an ethos as light-filled as heaven or as shadowy as hell. A good leader is intensely aware of the interplay of inner shadow and light, lest the act of leadership do more harm than good.[65]

For a moment in time Sheldon McLain deeply recognized his mother, and as Fred Crowell came into adulthood he made intentional choices that resulted in lasting changes. King's "beloved community" actively pursues the restoration of the human heart and spirit. This view of human nature recognizes the propensity for violence—against self and others, physically, emotionally, intellectually, culturally, spiritually—in every person. People who uncover their own forms of oppression become leaders who seek and build relationships of mutual respect with others, with authority figures, with women and men, and with their own children.

In our inmost being, when we obey the call of life, our experience of the journey toward servant leadership, forgiveness, and legitimate power is uplifting and liberating. In the center of our most beloved relationships we find real answers for today and for the future, a flourishing and thriving even in the shadowed complexity that attends the human experience.[66] The development of spirituality free of the diminishment of self or others is the hope of the servant leader. People of maturity then live from a sense of creative wholeness in light of faith, and the difference in their character is a notable difference— their countenance, their personhood, is as strong as it is loving and kind. Such people are powerful *and* gentle, and ultimately they live a meaningful, forgiving, and fulfilling life. For the leader who is unapproachable and isolated, fortified and remote, a return to a real self and to the welcoming embrace of loved ones is deeply refreshing. This person, one who loves well and is well loved, becomes the natural servant and leader of others. Such people recognize their own woundedness, and through surrender and discipline they become people of integrity. With love and power, they heal the lives of those around them.

In the contemporary age, an age of such inhumanity between people, family to family, culture to culture, and nation to nation, I consider with wonder the daily natural progression that after the dark of night, the sun appears, breaking the edge of the known world and bringing light. When atrocity rises to suffocate and destroy, I consider again the hard-won belief of those who have gone before and led the way so that even in our most dreadful moments we can embrace the better angels of our nature. I believe God does not become absent, but immanently more present in such times. A passage from sacred scripture speaks to the reality of God in the midst of human suffering:

He gives wisdom to the wise and knowledge to the discerning.
He reveals deep and hidden things.
He knows what lies in the darkness, and light dwells with Him.[67]

Greenleaf echoes history's hope for a justice that draws us into the light, restoring us to one another through acceptance, forgiveness, and love. "We have known this for a long time in the family. For a family to be a family, no one can ever be rejected."[68] Such love takes personal and collective responsibility, not only for our wrongs but also for the greatness of our dreams. "Love is an indefinable term, and its manifestations are both subtle and infinite. But it begins, I believe with one absolute condition: unlimited liability! As soon as one's liability for another is qualified *to any degree*, love is diminished by that much."[69]

In the crucible of people, faith, and life there are many dualities and hypocrisies. We often reveal our national tendency to condemn, criticize, and diminish others rather than striving to articulate our own emptiness, our own abiding sense of personal weakness, or our need for help and wholeness. But at the bottom of our quest for human connection "our heart glows, and secret unrest gnaws at the root of our being."[70] In our most genuine conceptions of life together we know, even in our darkest hours, that our hypocrisy can be turned into the lived experience that moves us past simple answers into a lasting and soulful sense of existence.

The following story helps us look with new eyes and see what needs to be seen. King David of Hebrew lore, one of the most beloved of all the kings of history, was said to be the friend of God. He was considered a man after God's own heart. This seems to be an ugly irony considering that in scripture David is also shown to be an abuser of power, a murderer, and an adulterer. Such a desperate paradox, though extreme, is not unfamiliar to the lives of leaders everywhere.

David had become complacent; he was letting others fight battles he should have fought. One day, while looking down from the heights of his castle he saw a woman bathing. Her name was Bathsheba. He found her beautiful, and he was struck by the sudden desire to have her. In his passion David impregnated Bathsheba. Upon discovering she was married to Uriah, one of David's most loyal and skilled soldiers, David became distressed. Through a devious succession of events David succeeded in having her husband Uriah killed on the front lines by withdrawing Uriah's surrounding warriors in the heat of a bloody conflict. David proceeded to hide what he'd done, acting as if the balance of his kingship, morality, and relationality remained noble. The lifestyle he exemplified at this time—a lifestyle of dominance, greed, the abuse of power, manipulation, and pervasive hiddenness—is the lifestyle of leaders locked in the command-and-control mentality. In a turn of grace, but not without terrible cost, David moved from command and control to personal surrender, willing to hear of the great wrongs he had done, willing to try to make amends and move with renewed care for the human community. In the perseverance and eventuality of this turn, he was brought again to a place of integrity.

Like David, and like others who aspire to lead, we are people, and therefore fallible and beautiful at the same time. It is in facing the dark tragedies of life, facing death or the threat of death in the self, in others, and in the community, that we are given opportunity to create a vessel that is sound, and worthy. It is good to consider again Greenleaf's great insight:

> To be on with the journey one must have an attitude toward loss and being lost, a view of oneself in which powerful symbols like *burned, dissolved, broken*

off—however painful their impact is seen to be—do not appear as senseless or destructive. Rather, the losses they suggest are seen as opening the way for new creative acts, for the receiving of priceless gifts. Loss, *every loss one's mind can conceive of*, creates a vacuum into which will come (if allowed) something new and fresh and beautiful, something unforeseen—the greatest of these is *love*. The source of this attitude toward loss and being lost is *faith*: faith in the validity of one's own inward experience; faith in the wisdom of one's history, events in which one's potential for nobility has been tested and refined; faith in doubt, in inquiry, and in the rebirth of wisdom; faith in the possibility of achieving a measure of sainthood on this earth from which flow concerns and responsibility and a sense of rightness in all things. By these means mortals are raised above the possibility of hurt. They will suffer, but they will not be hurt because each loss grants them the opportunity to be greater than before. Loss, by itself, is not tragic. What *is* tragic is the failure to grasp the opportunity which loss presents.[71]

The refining fire of life is undeniable. From this fire, human vitality emerges. Throughout the world people have not only forgiven, but invited their enemies back to the center of the community, calling one another brother, and sister, loved one, and friend. Ramsey's breakthrough research reminds us: it is not usually the repentance of the perpetrator that builds the necessary bridge to reconciliation and healing, but the unconditional forgiveness granted by those who were harmed.[72] The manifestations of love are as varied and wonderful as individual people, and when the light of love returns there is an end to darkness.

An interior recognition of the struggle between darkness and light, an honest accounting of our own darkness, and the choice to approach and humbly seek light may be the most intimate expression of relational fortitude. Leaders who give themselves over to the most hope-filled wishes of the human community, the most deep-felt dreams, become servant leaders who walk in such a way that others become wise, healthy, and free.

In our own country the bloodline of violence runs deep. The poverty of our age is the exaltation of the self, the objectification of the other as a product to be used, a consumable to be consumed—too often a philosophy of self-gratification supersedes the consideration of the other as beloved, as sacred. And it is in this poverty of mind that we first commence to do violence to one another. Consider our society and our great attraction to addiction, borrowing and lending, and the denial so common to the mediocre life. Consider the rate of sexual addiction in our society, the violence in our schools, and the emotional and intellectual violence associated with our familial, organizational, and political cultures. Violence in its most insidious forms shrouds the interior of our nation. The servant leader, devoted to the moral and loving depths of the interior, becomes a light to the generations, bringing hope and direction amidst the confusion. It is in the heart of forgiveness that the heart of violence is brought to its appointed place, a place of mercy and restoration. When my eldest daughter Natalya was seven years old, she came to me and sat on my lap while I was typing at the computer.

"Can I write a story?" she said. "You type it in, Daddy."

"Sure," I said, and holding her I typed the words. This is what she asked me to write:

> And sparkles came out of her eyes. And then she looked out the window and darkness clouds came out of the sky and then the next morning the sun came out and she was surprised, and she glimmered in beauty and long hair, she became the beautifullest, prettiest girl in town.

The vision I have for my three daughters is that their beauty is not only physical, but beauty of the heart, the mind, and the spirit. In this vision I take courage in the inimitable voice of Martin Luther King Jr., who said, "I believe that unarmed truth and unconditional love will have the final word in reality."[73] Human evil is a darkness that has accompanied humanity from the beginning of time, yet light in its natural vividness cannot be subdued, and when it comes it fulfills its purpose, taking away our fear, leading us to the grandeur of humanity, giving us a new vision, surprising us. The servant leader lives a life of illumination, and others are drawn to their own great significance by being in the presence of the servant leader. I believe it is because of the heroic resilience of the human spirit, the bright interior of the servant leader, that the words of the Lebanese poet Kahlil Gibran still ring so true:

> "The strong of soul forgive."[74]

Acts of Courage and Clarity

Afterword by Margaret J. Wheatley

The world's dilemmas and terrors have again cast their long shadows. We continue to be confronted by the complexities of our interconnected fates, resisting solutions. Our hearts continue to be challenged by the terrible things that humans should not be doing to other humans. Our Western worldview of material ease and endless progress has been shaken. Economic failures have worsened life not only for ourselves but everywhere in the world, among those who knew abundance and those who knew only poverty. Many of us have worked hard for many years to create a better world. We have worked for a world where more people would be free from suffering—the physical suffering of poverty, disease, and loss, and the emotional suffering of ignorance, misperception, and invisibility. In this time of rekindling hope, we must also acknowledge that suffering everywhere, both material and spiritual, has increased. For me and most of my colleagues, life these days is a roller coaster ride between hope and fear, oscillating wildly between what's possible and what is. Like all roller coasters, this one is both exhilarating and terrifying, often simultaneously. We are fully engaged in being part of the solution, and then we plunge into despair at the enormity of the challenges and the fear that our efforts will fail.

Life now insists that we encounter groundlessness. Systems and ideas that seemed reliable and solid dissolve at an increasing rate. People who asked for our trust betray or abandon us. Strategies that worked suddenly don't. Groundlessness is a frightening place, at least at first, but as the old culture turns to mush, we would feel stronger if we stopped searching for ground, if we sought only to locate ourselves in the present and do our work from *here*.

Freed from anger, aggression, and urgency, we are able to see the situation clearly, take it all in, and discover what to do. This clarity reveals "right action"—those actions that feel genuinely appropriate in this moment without any concern about whether they will succeed or not. Vaclav Havel describes hope as an attribute we carry in us always, a state of being that is not dependent on outcomes. He led his nation, the former Czechoslovakia, to freedom from Soviet rule in the "Velvet Revolution." As a poet-playwright-activist leader, he has given the world many choice and compelling insights. His awareness affirms that hope is not related to accomplishment. It is, quite simply, a dimension of being human. To feel hope, we don't have to *accomplish* anything. Hope is always right there, in our very being, our human spirits, our fundamental human goodness.

If we know that we *are* hope, it becomes much easier to stop being blinded or seduced by hopeful prospects. Instead of grasping onto activities that we want so desperately to succeed, we can see clearly and simply what to do. Grounded only in who we are, we discover those actions that feel right, rather than those that might or might not be effective. We may not succeed in changing things, but we choose to act from the clarity that this is right action for us. People who endure and persevere for their cause describe clarity as a force arising within them that compels them to act. They express this by saying, "I couldn't *not* do it."

Many years ago, I abandoned all hope of ever saving the world. This was extremely heart-wrenching for me, more difficult than letting go of a love relationship. I felt I was betraying my causes, condemning the world to a terrible end. Some of my colleagues were critical, even frightened, by my decision. How could I be so irresponsible? If we give up saving the world, what will happen? Still today, I have many beloved colleagues who refuse to resign as savior. They continue to force their failing spirits and tired bodies back into action one more time, wanting angry vehemence to give them vigor.

I didn't give up saving the world to protect my health. I gave it up to discover right action, what I'm supposed to be doing. Beyond hope and fear, freed from success or failure, I'm learning what right action feels like, its clarity and energy. I still get angry, enraged, and frustrated. But I no longer want my activities to be driven by these powerful, destructive emotions. I've learned to pause, come back to the present moment, and calm down. I take no actions until I can trust my interior state—until I become present in the moment and clarity emerges undimmed by hope and fear. Then I act, rightly, I hope.

It isn't outcomes that matter. It's people, our relationships, that give meaning to our struggles. If we free ourselves from hope and fear, from having to succeed, we discover that it becomes easier to love. We stop scapegoating, we stop blaming, and we stop being disappointed in each other. We realize that we truly are in this together, and that's all that matters. I know this to be true from my work, through the Berkana Institute, with colleagues in very desperate places. Zimbabwe has been the most compelling teacher—watching our friends and colleagues there deal with the descent of their country into violence, terror, and starvation, the result of a dictator gone mad. We've stayed in close contact by e-mail, phone, and periodic visits. We've learned that no matter how despairing the circumstance, it is our relationships that offer us solace, guidance, and joy. As long as we're together, as long as we feel others supporting us, we can persevere. A Zimbabwean, in her darkest moment, wrote: "In my grief I saw myself being held, us all holding one another in this incredible web of loving-kindness. Grief and love in the same place. I felt as if my heart would burst with holding it all."

We are consoled and strengthened by being together.

We don't need specific outcomes. We don't need hope. We need each other. Liberated from hope and fear, we find ourselves receiving the gift of patience. We abandon the pursuit of effectiveness and watch as our urgency fades and patience appears. Patience is, perhaps, this journey's destination. St. Augustine taught this infuriating truth: "The reward of patience is patience." Years ago, the Dalai Lama counseled a group of my colleagues who were depressed about the state of the world to be patient. "Do not despair," he said. "Your work will bear fruit in seven hundred years or so."

Can we do our work without needing to see results? Can we be content that our work *might* bear fruit, but not in our lifetime? Can we cheerfully plant seeds with little concern for the harvest? Consider the visionary leadership of Moses and Abraham. They carried promises given to them by their God, but they also knew they would not live to see these promises fulfilled. They led from faith, not hope, from a relationship with something greater beyond their comprehension.

I was recently struck by Greenleaf's admonition to "do no harm." I've been saying to a number of colleagues that doing no harm is becoming exceedingly difficult. It's not just about doing "good"; it's actually avoiding harm. We don't see the consequences of our actions. America is in the midst of a huge "wake-up call" about what is the cost to the rest of the world for us to be living the life we are living. It isn't about terrorist activity; it's about noticing that we put an extraordinary demand on the rest of the world for resources and energy, and that our way of life does not work well for most other people because of the demands we put on them. So that's what I've been feeling about "doing no harm"—we don't even know what we're doing that's causing harm. I know Greenleaf wrote that in a much simpler time, but I was really struck by that idea this time through.

I have been asking: "What is the leadership the world needs now, and what are we learning about leadership from actually being followers?" By this I mean that some of us who have been leaders are now followers, watching our government and our military trying to lead us. What are we learning about all this? I think the questions are writ large. "What are you learning now that you are a follower? What makes for effective leadership?"

Now more than ever, we have to fundamentally shift our ideas of what makes an effective leader. We have to shift them away from this secretive, command-and-control stance of "we know what's best." We have to leave all that behind, even though it may be effective in the moment. I'm certainly learning that there are different needs at different times when you are a leader. Different styles, different modalities. But what I find in servant leadership that I still find missing in the world is this fundamental respect for what it means to be human. And I think that right now the greatest need is to have faith in people. That is the single most courageous act of a leader. Give people resources, give them a sense of direction, give them a sense of their own power, and just have tremendous faith that they'll figure it out.

We need to move from the leader as hero to the leader as host. Can we be as welcoming, congenial, and invitational to the people who work with us as we would be if they were our guests at a party? Can we think of the leader as a convener of people? I am realizing that we can't do that if we don't have a fundamental and unshakable faith in people. You can't turn over power to people who don't trust. It just doesn't happen. So what I think I'm learning from September 11 is that it's possible that people really are motivated by altruism, not by profit, and that when our hearts open to each other we become wonderful. The level of compassion and gentleness that became available, taking a little more time with each other—all of that, I think, has shown me the things that I have treasured for a long time in people. But I think it's very clear, and so we have an opportunity to notice how good we are. If you don't have faith in people, you can't be a servant. I mean, what are you serving? If you're not serving human goodness, you can't be a servant. For me it's just that simple. There is no greater act on the part of the leader than to find ways to express that great faith in people.

The other part about the timelessness of servant leadership is, what do you do if you can't control events? There is no longer any room for leaders to be heroes. I think one really needs to understand that we have no control, and that things that we have no control over can absolutely change our lives. I think it will take a little while for Americans to really accept that there is no control possible in this greater interconnected world. There are lots of things we can do to prepare, but there is no control. One of the great ironies right now is that no matter how good you were as a business before September 11, no matter how skilled you were at planning and budgeting, everything has shifted. The only way to lead when you don't have control is to lead through the power of your relationships. You can deal with the unknown only if you have enormous levels of trust, and if you're working together and bringing out the best in people. I don't know of any other model that can truly work in the world right now except servant leadership.

Even within the military, *command and control* is not what's making it work right now, and it hasn't for a long time. I was just reading about a huge fiasco with the Delta Force as they went into Afghanistan at the start of our military action there in October 2001. Instead of their normal procedure, which is to operate as small teams in quiet and stealth, they were parachuted in—one hundred of them—because that's how central command decided they should be used. And they were furious, absolutely furious! They nearly got killed, they got out by the skin of their teeth, and they had several casualties. They exclaimed, "You can't do this to us! We know how to fight. You can't create these huge theatrical events and you can't have centralized control and expect us to do our job." So, even under the facade of command and control, one of the things I've always noticed in the military is that it works on the basis of deep relationships, long-term training, and reliance on every individual soldier—especially in special operations. I can't think of any other model than servant leadership that works in times of uncertainty. That time is now! Recent events regarding Osama bin Ladin's capture and the role of our Special Forces attest to this.

There is such a thing as the human spirit. It's an awareness that people have something beyond the instrumental or the utilitarian. People have deep yearnings, a quest for meaning, and an ability to wonder.

When did we forget this, about being human? When did human beings become so instrumentally viewed, and when did we start to see ourselves as objects, just to be filled with information and sent to work? When did we lose that awareness? It's just mind-boggling if you think about it. I feel the same sort of puzzlement at the whole focus on emotional intelligence now. When did we forget this? It really shows you the bizarre side of our Western civilization that we have to relearn what is so obvious in other cultures.

When spirituality became connected with the workplace in the 1990s, it was initially just another way to motivate people. There were many of us saying, "Be careful here." If the only reason supervisors are going to acknowledge that people have a spiritual life is to figure out how to get more work out of them, and if they don't get more work out of them, are they then going to forget the fact that we all have spirit?

Then we had a nice shift to the idea that if you don't acknowledge that people have spirit, you really can't have a productive workplace. It wasn't using spirit for productivity; instead, it was acknowledging who the person is, who the whole person is. Now I see our spirit in the questions we're asking. People are questioning the meaning of life. The meaninglessness of just working harder, consuming more, becoming disconnected from your children—these large questions have started to well up in people. *We do all have spirits.*

In terms of organizations, I look to see those organizations that describe back to me a real understanding of what is a human being. They don't have to use the words *soul* or *spirit,* but I get from them that they have a deep appreciation of fundamental creativity and caring, that they really rely on the wholeness of the people who work there. I haven't seen it in a lot of large corporations recently. Even those that had those strong values have been whipped around in the past year. But I consistently hear this from smaller manufacturing companies. I've had some wonderful conversations with those folks because they really understand and rely on the people who work there. They do all sorts of innovative things without consciously talking about spirituality in the workplace. What they talk about is human beings. That's more than enough for me! You know, if we can just understand what it means to be human, then that brings in our spirits.

What I think about crisis is that it's an easy opportunity to see how good we are, spontaneously. But if you look at life in organizations, it's amazing how fear-based they are, so that we are afraid of spontaneity. We are afraid of people's spirits, actually. We are afraid that if we give people any room they'll go off on some crazy direction with the work. I encounter this all the time. A manager will say, "We can't just give people choice here; we can't give people enough room to define meaningful work for themselves because God knows what they'll do." We always assume that they'll take the organization in a completely different direction. We are so afraid of each other that we want to box it into a plan, to a job description. And the loss of that, what we lose with that fear of each other, is extraordinary.

I am frequently struck by the great tragedy of how we have constructed work, the great loss. We've made it so hard to be in good relationships, so hard for people to contribute, and so difficult for people to think well of themselves, and then we say, "As a leader I'll come and I'll pump you up and I'll give you my vision; I'll make you feel we can do it." But it's not based on a deep love of who people are, a deep respect. As a leader, how do you pump up what has been killed?

I actually had an experience of this on a symbolic level. I was with a group of nuns in a chapel and one of them fainted, and before the medics came (apparently this was not unusual, because she had some sort of condition) nobody panicked. They called 911, but before help got there we just sat there in prayer for this person as other sisters went up and held her—it was all very gentle. And then the medics rushed in and they had oxygen and they had defibrillators, all sorts of high-tech equipment, and they surrounded this woman and just started clamping machines onto her body and then pumping in oxygen. I thought they were blowing up a balloon!

The symbolism of this experience for me is that we are in our organizations and we've actually created a lot of death and destruction and a complete loss of people's confidence in themselves. Leaders don't have confidence in people. And then we rush in with this high-tech machinery and try to pump up people and motivate them with a new initiative or a new computer system or a new leadership vision. But what goes on in organizations is often not based on people being human. It's based on people being objects to be used for the accomplishment of goals of a very utilitarian kind.

"Whom do we serve as leaders?" I've asked that question of a lot of people. Whom do we serve? We are serving human beings. That is a radical shift in this culture at this time. But we are serving human beings, and the best way to know who another human being is, is to notice yourself fully, what you need, what's meaningful to you, what gives you heart in your work. If we could just notice our own humanness, it would be a very big step forward to being able to relate to other people. If we are a leader, especially if we notice our own humanness, we notice that we have spirit, that we have questions of meaning. I think all of the work that is done in helping leaders to wake up to their own humanity and their own spirituality is very essential work. It also keeps us away from using servant leadership as the next instrument of control.

CHANGING THE CONVERSATION

If you want to change the conversation, you change who's in it. That doesn't mean that you have to coach people on how to be empathic presenters to a leader. You don't have to coach leaders on how not to get angry if someone's giving them terrible feedback. You just get out of those intensely personal and confrontational moments because you have a lot of new voices in the room. And people really do get interested as soon as they realize there is a fundamentally different perspective available. Most people actually get interested in that. I have been in hierarchical situations where the voice that shocked everyone with its perspective was a young woman—a new employee, female, who suddenly said something and everyone went "Wow!" I've also seen it happen in faculties when we listen to students for the first time, or we listen to the people who hired our graduates. You never know where these comments are going to come from. They're usually so shocking that people are humbled and climb down off their soapboxes.

I want very much to say something about personal courage. One of the things that is sorely lacking in our lives is a necessary level of courage to stand up against the things we know are wrong, and for the things we know are right. There has been a kind of complacency—it feels more fear-based to me—where people, especially in organizations, are too afraid to speak up and we have become, I believe, moral cowards in a way. We give all sorts of reasons why we can't speak up. There are so many grievances in organizations that I think people have developed a sense of helplessness about it, and I understand that feeling of helplessness and saying, "I would never speak up." But I also live with an awareness that if we don't start speaking up we are going down a road that will only lead to increased devastation and destruction. Edmund Burke said, *"The only thing necessary for the triumph of evil is for good men to do nothing."* Julian of Norwich said, *"We must speak with a million voices: it is the silence that kills."*

I think we're in that place right now, and what I find personally so uncomfortable is that as much as I want to raise my own voice on behalf of several different issues, I notice that I feel more powerless than at any time in my life. I think that's part of the tension of this time, realizing that we have to lift our voices for the things that we believe in, whether it's inside an organization or as a nation or as a planetary community. We feel that there are serious things that require our voice, and yet we also feel that it may not make a difference. That's the place I'm in every day right now. The other forces at work are exceedingly more powerful. I wonder whether we can rally ourselves as people around the things we care about, and really make the change. The essence of my work right now is based on that belief that we can get active in time, but I also realize that this is a time when there are exceedingly strong countervailing forces from our leaders. For example, leaders pursuing aggression as the solution, or business still wanting to maintain its hegemony in the world without assuming responsibility for broader needs, or America still believing it can act in isolation: can we raise our voices on behalf of a different form of capitalism, a different form of compassion in our foreign policy, a different form of leadership in our organizations? I know if we don't raise our voices the future will be very dark. If we *do* raise them, well, it has worked in the past. I am hopeful that it will work now, but I'm not nearly as certain as I'd like to be.

I find a lot more credence is being given to the understanding that there are fields we can't see, invisible influences that affect behavior. People would have called that far-out thinking before, but I find that people are much more open to that today than ten years ago. Creative vision is a powerful influence in shaping our behavior, and you don't need to specify a lot of controls or roles if you have vision. People can do what they think is right and it can lead to a very coherent organization that is moving in concert toward achieving its vision. I have certainly come across a number of organizations that are working that way now, but I've also experienced in the last year or two that we've been in an enormous leap *backwards* organizationally since times started to get uncertain. And now we'll just have to wait and see whether this level of uncertainty leads us forward into new ways of leading, or even further backward into command and control.

One of the possibilities is that try as we might we will realize that command and control just doesn't work because you can't control! We might be learning that. But recently, I have seen an enormously retrogressive movement in organizations based on fear, based on a weakening economy, based on what I think is a normal human reaction that when you get scared, you go backward; you default to what didn't work in the past! The power of vision to rally people or to give people a reason to live, to work hard and to sacrifice—we are seeing that at the national level right now. I don't necessarily think we're seeing it in its best form. It's true that in human experience, "if there is no vision the people perish," and whether there's a scientific explanation for that, or a spiritual explanation, I'd be just as happy these days with the spiritual definition—which is that a vision gives us a sense of possibility, a sense of working for something outside our narrow, self-focused efforts, and therefore rallies us at our deep human level to be greater than we are.

I'm happier with that explanation than with field theory because it is much more focused on the capacities in being human and how we can bring these forth. Science helps people be comfortable with that and feel a little more trusting that you can create order through having a clear vision. But the next part is just as important. Once you have a clear vision, you have to free people up. This is where autonomy comes in. People need to be free to make sense of the vision according to their own understandings and their own sensitivity to what's needed. If you combine the sense of great purpose and human freedom, if you create a vision that brings out the best of who we are and then give us freedom in how we're going to express it, that is how things work, in my experience.

JUST BE LOVING!

Why has expressing love become such a problem when it's a fundamental human characteristic? This is where I think we have overanalyzed and overcomplicated something that is known to everyone alive. Babies know how to unleash love. It's all about relationships and being available as a human, rather than as a role. It's about being present and being vulnerable and showing what we're feeling. You know, we don't want to reveal who we are. Even the best of leaders try to be objective rather than relational, and that's supposedly adding value to our work lives if we treat each other objectively. But it's again one of those huge things we get wrong. You can't have love if you can't have relationships, and you can't have relationships with one another if you have this curse of something called *being objective,* or *one size fits all,* as a policy, or having to go by the manual. I can feel the fear that so many of us have that, "Well, if it's not objective, we couldn't possibly live in the messiness and the intimacy that would come about by treating each human being as his or her own unique self." But I think that objectivity makes it impossible to be loving. Objectivity doesn't allow love, because love takes you to intimacy and uniqueness and very personal territory. We need to get away from the belief that we can run an organization using what are called objective measures or objective processes, which are actually just completely dehumanized. The fear of love in organizations is that it makes your life as a leader far more complex. But it also makes you much more effective.

I was listening a few days ago to a woman who had recently retired as the chief of the Calgary Police Force, and she talked about what it took to be personally available and present for each of those officers, so that she was always embodying the values, finding ways for them to embody the values, believe in the values, and become the kind of police officers they wanted to be. She worked from a very clear perspective that it's not the corporate values that count, it's whether people can enact their personal values inside the corporation. I thought that was a brilliant rethinking of that. She would work with the police officers on what they were trying to accomplish and the values they were trying to bring forth. The result was a wonderful corporate culture and very strong values. But she kept saying that this was enormously time-consuming and very difficult work that required her to be there all the time. And so I understand why leaders don't want to go down this *love* path or the *relationship* path, because it requires so much. But that's where I think you have to want to believe in people. I believe on September 11 there were numerous corporate leaders who suddenly realized that people really were the most important thing to them, even though an hour before they'd been working a system that ignored human concerns. But then they got the wakeup call of their life. You have to want to believe, to want to have relationships, and there are an awful lot of people in our workplaces, not just leaders but whole professions, who have never wanted relationships. They've wanted the work, and hopefully we are now realizing, most of us, how important relationships are.

I think that the central work of our time is learning how to be together differently. Can we live together with our hearts open, with our awareness that we can't stop suffering, and that we can certainly be with it differently? Can we notice where we are causing harm and try at least to do no harm? And can we be together without fear of what it's like to be together, to really just not be afraid to be with other people? That would be a huge step forward for a lot of us. And we're all crying for it, we're all crying to be together in more loving ways because this is what it is to be human. So many of us were overwhelmed by the experiences of September 11, but we saw people being together without the divisions that had separated them moments before.

To actually be willing to listen and talk to other human beings is the way throughout time that we have thought together and dreamed together. The simple act of conversation seems so far removed from our daily lives now, and yet we all have a vague memory of what it was like. Since September 11, we have been profoundly different conversationalists and felt the need to talk to each other and to be together. So I rely on the ancientness and primalness of human beings being together, and being together through this act of listening and talking, as a way for us to surface, or to develop, greater awareness of how we are reacting to what's going on in the world. Therefore, hopefully, from that greater awareness of what we care about, what we're talking about or struggling with at a very personal level, we will become more activist. We will become more intelligent actors to change the things we think need changing.

That idea is based on a more recent tradition in Paulo Freire's work called *critical education,* which is that you create the conditions for change by educating people to the forces and dynamics that are causing their life. You can start that work through conversation (or through literacy training, as Freire did). In conversation, people can become more aware of what their life is, whether they're happy, what they might do to change it. Then people do become activists, because it's their lives and their children's lives that are affected. Those are the deeper underlying threads that led me to write the book, which is different from anything I've written before. It's not written just for leaders or people in organizations. I wrote it for the world. I don't mean that to sound pretentious, but the people I work with now are in so many different countries, all ages, and I kept them in my imagination when I was writing, and I wanted to make sure that it didn't assume anything except our common humanity and our common desires for a world that does truly work for all of us, a world that is based on our common human desires for love and meaning from work and a chance to contribute.

The other piece that truly informed this book was my experience with the Truth and Reconciliation Commission in South Africa, which was life-changing for me. I only attended it once but followed the proceedings every time I was in South Africa during its three-year history. And the one day that

I went affected me deeply. It was when the parents of a young American Fulbright scholar who had been murdered, Amy Biel, were present. Their daughter had been slain in one of the townships after driving into a very angry crowd. Her parents were there listening to the description of her death by her killer, and they were sitting next to the mother of the killer, sitting two rows in front of us. It was an experience you don't normally have in your life, one of such forgiveness, and violence, and repentance. The primary thing I learned in observing the Truth and Reconciliation Commission hearings was that the power of speaking your experience is what heals you. The power of feeling we are heard is what heals us. It made bearing witness a much easier act. *I don't have to fix the person—I just have to really listen.* And from that experience I started to see in so many different settings how, when we truly listen to people, they can heal themselves. My trust in conversation is that it also allows that level of listening, and there are other people who have written specifically about conversation. I am using the process to restore hope to the future; that was the underlying theme. I wrote it in March 2001, and I had no idea of what was to come on September 11. But I could already see that the future was looking pretty hopeless, and I had a lot of people saying, "What does this mean, restore hope to the future?" And now we all know.

A few phrases come to mind from a wonderful gospel song: "We are the ones we've been waiting for." This is the time for which we have been preparing, and so there is a deep sense of call. Servant leadership is not just an interesting idea, but something fundamental and vital for the world, and now the world that truly needs it. The whole concept of servant leadership must move from an interesting idea in the public imagination toward the realization that *this is the only way we can go forward.* I personally experience that sense of right-timeliness to this body of work called servant leadership. I feel that more and more of us need to realize that it will take even more courage to move this work forward, but the necessity of moving it forward is clear. It moves from being a body of work to being a movement—literally a movement—how we are going to move this into the world. I think that will require more acts of courage, more clarity, more saying *this has to change now.*

Endnotes

WHAT IS SERVANT LEADERSHIP?

1. Robert K. Greenleaf, "The Servant as Leader" (Indianapolis: Greenleaf Center for Servant Leadership, 1970), accessed May 19, 2011, www.greenleaf.org/whatissl/.

2. Robert K. Greenleaf, "The Institution as Servant" (Indianapolis: Greenleaf Center for Servant Leadership, 1972), accessed May 19, 2011, www.greenleaf.org/whatissl/.

3. See www.spearscenter.org for information on Larry Spears and his work. He is considered the foremost authority on servant leadership at work today. In 2010 he was named as the Servant-Leadership Scholar at Gonzaga University.

SERVANT LEADERSHIP IN THE PRESENT DAY

1. The quotes in this section appeared together previously in the *International Journal of Servant-Leadership* (2004–2010). See Shann Ray Ferch and Larry C. Spears, eds., "Servant Leadership in the Present Day," *International Journal of Servant-Leadership* 1 (2005): 13–15. For more information on the journal, see www.gonzaga.edu/servantleadership.

THE POWER OF SERVANT LEADERSHIP—FOREWORD BY LARRY C. SPEARS

1. Martin Luther King Jr., "Acceptance Speech" (speech on the occasion of the award of the Nobel Peace Prize in Oslo, December 10, 1964), accessed May 19, 2011, http://nobelprize.org/nobel_prizes/peace/laureates/1964/king-acceptance.html.

2. Robert K. Greenleaf, *Servant Leadership: A Journey into the Nature of Legitimate Power and Greatness* (Mahwah, NJ: Paulist Press, 1977; second edition published 2002).

3. Ibid., 20.

4. Ibid.

5. Shann Ray Ferch and Larry Spears, *The Spirit of Servant Leadership* (Mahwah, NJ: Paulist Press, 2011).

BALEFIRE: THE WORLD OF VIOLENCE AND FORGIVENESS— PREFACE BY SHANN RAY FERCH

1. *English Collins Dictionary*, online ed., s.v. "Balefire," http://dictionary.reverso.net/english-definition/balefire.

2. Greenleaf's essay is published by the Greenleaf Center for Servant Leadership (1970; 2nd edition1991) and can also be found in Greenleaf's book *Servant Leadership*: *A Journey into the Nature of Legitimate Power and Greatness* (Mahwah, NJ: Paulist Press, 1977; second edition published 2002).

I. SERVANT LEADERSHIP, FORGIVENESS, AND POWER

1. *Was leuchten soll, muß dulden, daß es brennt* (What is to give light must endure burning)—Anton Wildgans in his poem "Helldunkle Stunde," first published in *Mittag: Neue Gedichte* (Leipzig, DEU: L. Staackmann Verlag, 1917), 90. Cited by and frequently attributed to Viktor Emil Frankl in *The Doctor and the Soul: From Psychotherapy to Logotherapy,* translated from the German by Richard and Clara Winston (New York, NY: Alfred A. Knopf, 1965), 67. First published as *Ärztliche Seelsorge: Grundlagen der Logotherapie und Existenzanalyse* (Wien, DEU: Franz Deuticke, 1946).

2. Marleen Ramsey, "A Hermeneutic Phenomenological Investigation of Empathy and Forgiveness in South Africa" (doctoral dissertation, Gonzaga University, 2003).

3. Robert K. Greenleaf, *Servant Leadership*: *A Journey into the Nature of Legitimate Power and Greatness* (Mahwah, NJ: Paulist Press, 1977; second edition published 2002).

The quote is taken from p. 327 of the original, from Greenleaf's essay titled "An Inward Journey," in which he gives a thorough and very engaging analysis of the Robert Frost poem "Directive."

4. Martin Luther King Jr., *Strength to Love* (Minneapolis, MN: Fortress Press, 1977), 50.

5. For adept explorations of death tolls due to genocide, war, and slavery, see the following sources. Regarding genocide: Samantha Power, *A Problem from Hell:*

America and the Age of Genocide (New York, NY: Harper Perennial, 2003); William A. Schabas, *Genocide in International Law: The Crime of Crimes* (Cambridge, UK: Cambridge University Press, 2000); Benjamin A. Valentino, *Final Solutions: Mass Killing and Genocide in the Twentieth Century* (Cornell Studies in Security Affairs) (Ithaca, NY: Cornell University Press, 2004); and Adam LeBor, *"Complicity with Evil": The United Nations in the Age of Modern Genocide* (New Haven, CT: Yale University Press, 2006). For death tolls regarding war: Lawrence Keeley, *War before Civilization: The Myth of the Peaceful Savage* (New York, NY: Oxford University Press, 1997); Jacob Bercovitch and Richard Jackson, *International Conflict: A Chronological Encyclopedia of Conflicts and Their Management 1945–1995* (Washington, DC: CQ-Roll Call Book Group, 1997); and Michael Clodfelter, *Warfare and Armed Conflict: A Statistical Reference to Casualty and Other Figures, 1618–1991* (Jefferson, NC: McFarland, 1992). For death tolls with regard to slavery: David Stannard, *American Holocaust: Columbus and the Conquest of the New World* (New York, NY: Oxford University Press, 1992); Milton Meltzer, *Slavery: A World History* (New York, NY: Oxford University Press, 1993); and Ronald Segal, *Islam's Black Slaves* (New York, NY: Farrar, Strauss and Giroux, 2002).

6. See *John Adams* (New York, NY: Simon and Schuster, 2001) by Pulitzer Prize winner David McCullough, a historical masterpiece that details one of the great love stories of true minds, between John and Abigail Adams, and the virtuous leadership qualities of America's second president.

7. For carefully researched analysis of the history of atrocity perpetrated against Native America, see David Stannard, *American Holocaust*. Also see Russell Thornton, *American Indian Holocaust and Survival: A Population History since 1492* (Oklahoma City, OK: University of Oklahoma Press, 1990).

8. See the United Nations website at www.un.org/en/. The UN definition of the convention on genocide can be found at www.un.org/millennium/law/iv-1.htm. Also see Henning Melber and John Y. Jones, eds., *Revisiting the Heart of Darkness— Explorations into Genocide and Other Forms of Mass Violence,* published by the Dag Hammarskjold Foundation as "Development Dialogue" no. 50. The book is accessible on the foundation's website. Henning Melber is the executive director of the Dag Hammarskjold Foundation in Uppsala/Sweden. See www.dhf.uu.se/default.html for the foundation. Consider the nature of those who help us understand. To order a hard copy or download a pdf of the book, go to www.dhf.uu.se/FMPro?-db=publ.fp5&-format=%2Fpublications%2Fdd%2Fapubdddetail.html&-lay=weblayout&pubtype=development&-max=2147483647&-recid=68&-find.

9. For more on humanity's homicidal tendencies, see Donald G. Dutton, Ehor O. Boyanowsky, and Michael Harris Bond, "Extreme Mass Homicide: From Military Massacre to Genocide," *Aggression and Violent Behavior* 10 (2005): 437–73. Also see Robert J. Sternberg, "A Duplex Theory of Hate and Its Development and Its Application to Terrorism, Massacres, and Genocide," *Review of General Psychology* 7 (2003): 299–328.

10. Michael Renner, *Ending Violent Conflict* (Worldwatch Paper 146) (Washington, DC: Worldwatch Institute, 1999).

11. See David Meyers, *Social Psychology* (New York, NY: McGraw-Hill, 2008), 343–45.

12. Matthew White, ed., *Historical Atlas of the Twentieth Century* (Erol's Internet, 2000), http://users.erols.com/mwhite28/warstat8htm.

13. Another fine scholar whose doctoral work I had the great honor of chairing is Robbie Paul. Her dissertation traced five generations of Ni Mii Puu (Nez Perce) leaders in her own family, from the advent of first white contact to today, and revealed an indelible servant leadership ethos of strength, wisdom, resilience, reconciliation, and healing in the face of genocide and dislocation. See her dissertation: Roberta Lynn Tow-le-kit-we-son-my Paul, "Historical Trauma and Its Effects on a Ni Mii Puu Family: Finding Story-Healing Wounds" (doctoral dissertation, Gonzaga University, 2007).

14. Martin Luther King Jr.'s books and speeches are collected in one volume in *A Testament of Hope: The Essential Writings and Speeches of Martin Luther King Jr.*, ed. James A. Washington (San Francisco, CA: HarperCollins, 1990).

15. See *Cory: An Intimate Portrait* (Philippines, 2009), edited by Aquino's former appointment secretary Margarita P. Juico; and Lucy Komisar, *Corazon Aquino: The Story of a Revolution* (New York: George Braziller, 1987).

16. Václav Havel, speech at Chulalungkorn University, Bangkok, February 12, 1994, accessed May 9, 2011, www.vaclavhavel.cz/index.php?sec=7&id=14.

17. Kahlil Gibran, *Jesus the Son of Man* (New York, NY: Knopf, 1928), "Matthew: The Sermon on the Mount," 17.

18. From Song of Solomon 8:6 (New American Standard Version).

19. See "What Is Servant Leadership?" for Spears's thorough description of the ten characteristics of servant leadership.

20. David C. Winter, *The Power Motive* (New York, NY: The Free Press, 1973).

21. Thomas E. Wartenberg, *The Forms of Power: From Domination to Transformation* (Philadelphia, PA: Temple University Press, 1990).

22. I am indebted to Filipino leadership scholar Karel San Juan for his incisive article on servant leadership and power that appeared in 2005 in Volume 1 of the *International Journal of Servant-Leadership*. Dr. San Juan's article appeared on pages 187–209 and is entitled "Re-Imagining Power in Leadership: Reflection, Integration, and Servant-Leadership."

23. Greenleaf, *Servant Leadership*, 41–42.

24. Quotations in this paragraph can be found in Greenleaf, *Servant Leadership*, 85.

25. Parker J. Palmer, *Let Your Life Speak: Listening for the Voice of Vocation* (San Francisco, CA: Jossey-Bass, 2000), 99–100.

26. Henry David Thoreau, *Walden and Other Writings* (New York, NY: The Modern Library, 2000), 17.

27. Greenleaf, *Servant Leadership*, 16.

28. Ibid., 13.

29. See Peter G. Northouse, *Leadership: Theory and Practice*, 4th ed. (Thousand Oaks, CA: Sage Publications, 2007).

30. Margaret J. Wheatley, *Leadership and the New Science: Discovering Order in a Chaotic World* (San Francisco, CA: Berrett Koehler, 1999), xi.

31. See Everett Worthington's 625-page *Handbook of Forgiveness* (New York, NY: Brunner-Routledge, 2005) for a comprehensive and intelligent compendium of the current state of scientific research on forgiveness.

32. Greenleaf, *Servant Leadership*, 13–14.

33. John W. Gardner, *On Leadership* (New York, NY: The Free Press, 1990).

34. See Bernard M. Bass, *Leadership, Psychology, and Organizational Behavior* (New York, NY: Harper and Brothers, 1960); James MacGregor Burns, *Leadership* (New York, NY: Harper and Row, 1978); and R. Harrison, "Why Your Firm Needs Emotional Intelligence," *People Management* 3 (1997): 41.

35. Peter M. Senge, *The Fifth Discipline: The Art and Practice of the Learning Organization* (New York, NY: Doubleday, 1990).

36. See Daniel Goleman, *Emotional Intelligence* (New York, NY: Bantam, 1995); James M. Kouzes and Barry Posner, *The Leadership Challenge: How to Get Extraordinary Things Done in Organizations* (San Francisco, CA: Jossey-Bass, 1987); and Ronald A. Heifetz, *Leadership without Easy Answers* (Cambridge, MA: The Belknap Press of Harvard University Press, 1994).

37. See Worthington, *Handbook of Forgiveness*.

38. To make connections between organizational growth and development and national growth and development regarding servant leadership, human fallibility, and forgiveness, read Robert Greenleaf, *Servant Leadership*, and Larry Spears, ed., *Insights on Leadership: Service, Stewardship, Spirit, and Servant-Leadership* (Hoboken, NJ: John Wiley and Sons, 1997), in conjunction with Desmond Tutu's *No Future without Forgiveness* (New York, NY: Doubleday, 1997).

39. The losses associated with an immature or alienated sense of self and other are often overlooked in contemporary leadership. Taylor reveals how a sense of terrifying emptiness is hand in hand with lack of identity. See Charles Taylor, *Sources of the Self: The Making of the Modern Identity* (Cambridge, MA: Harvard University Press, 1989).

40. Greenleaf, *Servant Leadership*, 15.

41. Ibid., 17.

42. The *Online Etymology Dictionary* (www.etymonline.com) links the words *listen*, *wait*, and *obey* in their origin and definitions, and links "not listening" to the words *disobey*, *absurdity*, *deaf*, and *dumb*. Also see T. F. Hoad's *The Oxford Dictionary of English Etymology* (Oxford, UK: Oxford University Press, 1986).

43. Hans-Georg Gadamer, *Truth and Method*, 2nd rev. ed., trans. rev. Joel Weinsheimer and Donald G. Marshal (New York, NY: Continuum, 1993), 361.

44. I've paraphrased Tolstoy's story "The Three Hermits" as a way of further understanding Tolstoy's truths and as an aid to my own learning about leadership. The story can be found in *Family Happiness and Other Stories* (New York, NY: Dover Publications, 2005), 63–70.

45. Gadamer, *Truth and Method*; Paolo Freire, *Pedagogy of the Oppressed* (New York, NY: Continuum, 1990).

46. Greenleaf, *Servant Leadership*, 21.

47. Edward M. Hallowell, *Dare to Forgive* (Deerfield Beach, FL: Human Communications, Inc., 2004).

48. For evidence of forgiveness and the capacity of this virtue to lessen anxiety, stress, depression, and anger, reduce heart disease, and help generate a stronger immune system, see Worthington, *Handbook of Forgiveness*; Michael E. McCullough, Steven J. Sandage, and Everett L. Worthington Jr., *To Forgive Is Human* (Downers Grove, IL: InterVarsity, 1997); and Michael E. McCullough and Everett Worthington Jr., "Encouraging Clients to Forgive People Who Have Hurt Them: Review, Critique, and Research Prospectus," *Journal of Psychology and Theology* 3 (1994): 3–20. Notably, another important correlation is emerging and starting to energize more empirical research on the link between gratitude and increased ability for critical thought, as well as how gratitude helps people build the bridge to forgiveness in the self and with others.

49. Ronald S. Valle and Steen Halling, eds., *Existential-Phenomenological Perspectives in Psychology: Exploring the Breadth of Human Experience* (New York, NY: Plenum Press, 1989).

50. Personal communication, June 17, 2009. Dr. Stephen Prosser, my dear friend, was a leadership scholar and professor of leadership and organization development at the University of Glamorgan. Stephen died in 2010.

51. Journalist Tom Brokaw coined the term *The Greatest Generation* in his book of the same title (New York: Random House, 1998). The Greatest Generation describes the generation of Americans who grew up during the deprivation of the Great Depression and then fought in World War II or made pivotal contributions to the war effort at home. It follows the Lost Generation of the 1880s who fought in World War I and precedes the Silent Generation of the 1930s.

52. Ellis Cose, *Bone to Pick: Of Forgiveness, Reconciliation, Reparation, and Revenge* (New York, NY: Atria Books, 2004), 3.

53. See www.army.mil/OLDGUARD/specplt/tomb.htm, the official website of the 3rd U.S. Infantry Regiment, known as "The Old Guard," the sentinels who guard the Tomb of the Unknowns.

54. Again, see www.army.mil/OLDGUARD/specplt/tomb.htm, the official website of the 3rd U.S. Infantry Regiment, known as "The Old Guard," the sentinels who guard the Tomb of the Unknowns.

55. For the narrative on the sentinels who guard the Tomb of the Unknowns, facts were gathered from www.army.mil/OLDGUARD/specplt/tomb.htm, the official website of the 3rd U.S. Infantry Regiment, known as "The Old Guard," as well as http://home.att.net/~c.h.waters/tomb.html.

56. Don Postema, *Space for God: The Study and Practice of Prayer and Spirituality* (Grand Rapids, MI: CRC Publications, 1997), 172.

57. See Mandela's response during the negotiations regarding his release from prison, in which he did not guarantee nonviolence as the apartheid government directed him to, but responded by intimating that violence would surely ensue if the apartheid government did not cede power and move to legitimate democratic

government: Nelson R. Mandela, *Long Walk to Freedom* (Boston, MA: Little, Brown and Company, 1994).

58. Martin Luther King Jr.'s books and speeches are collected in one volume in *A Testament of Hope*. A lodestar of social justice, the book reveals the fully realized wisdom cultivated by his family legacy, his cultural heritage, and his Christian faith, as well as his understanding of Gandhi's nonviolent movement and Gandhi's use of *satyagraha* or "soul force." In 1894 at age twenty-five Gandhi read Tolstoy's *The Kingdom of God Is within You* (Lincoln, NE: Bison Books, 1894/1984), and it stirred the beginnings of his thought on nonviolence. Gandhi is also known to have maintained great respect for Christ, while also ironically and humorously pointing out the hypocrisy of Christians, saying, "If it weren't for Christians everyone would be a Christian."

59. See King, *A Testament of Hope*, 230.

60. Mandela, *Long Walk to Freedom*.

61. Tutu, *No Future without Forgiveness*, 26.

62. Marleen Ramsey, "Servant Leadership and Unconditional Forgiveness: The Lives of Six South African Perpetrators," *International Journal of Servant-Leadership* 2 (2006): 115–16.

63. I have constructed Brian Mitchell's story directly from Dr. Marleen Ramsey's detailed account and interview transcripts found in Ramsey's dissertation, "A Hermeneutic Phenomenological Investigation."

64. Greenleaf, *Servant Leadership*, 307.

65. Ralph Waldo Emerson, *The Essential Writings of Ralph Waldo Emerson*, ed. Brooks Atkinson (New York, NY: Modern Library, 2000), 59.

66. Tutu, *No Future without Forgiveness*, 270.

67. Ibid., 273.

68. The work of Robert Enright and his coresearchers is compelling. I've included a bibliographical list of some of their recent research here for those who want to pursue further understanding:

Baskin, Thomas W., and Robert Enright. "Intervention Studies on Forgiveness: A Meta-analysis." *Journal of Counseling and Development* 82 (2004): 79–90.

Coyle, Catherine T., and Robert D. Enright. "Forgiveness Intervention with Post-abortion Men." *Journal of Consulting and Clinical Psychology* 65, no. 6 (1997): 1042–46.

Enright, Robert D. *Enright Forgiveness Inventory*. Redwood City, CA: Mind Garden, 2004.

———. *Forgiveness Is a Choice*. Washington, DC: APA Books, 2001. (This book is for the general public.) The book has also been translated into Complex Chinese, Japanese, Korean, German, and Romanian.

———. *Rising above the Storm Clouds*. Washington, DC: Magination Press (an imprint of the American Psychological Association), 2004. (This is a children's picture book on forgiveness with notes for parents.) It has also been translated into Egyptian, Arabic, and Korean.

————, Jeanette Knutson Enright, Anthony Holter, Thomas Baskin, and Casey Knutson. "Waging Peace through Forgiveness in Belfast, Northern Ireland II: Educational Programs for Mental Health Improvement of Children." *Journal of Research in Education* 13 (Fall 2007): 63–78.

————, and Richard P. Fitzgibbons. *Helping Clients Forgive: An Empirical Guide for Resolving Anger and Restoring Hope.* Washington, DC: APA Books, 2000. This book is for helping professionals in psychology, psychiatry, and related disciplines. It has also been translated into Complex Chinese.

————, Elizabeth A. Gassin, and Jeanette A. Knutson. "Waging Peace through Forgiveness in Belfast, Northern Ireland: A Review and Proposal for Mental Health Improvement of Children." *Journal of Research in Education* 13 (2003): 51–61.

————, and the Human Development Study Group. "The Moral Development of Forgiveness." In *Handbook of Moral Behavior and Development*, vol. 1, edited by William Kurtines and Jacob Gewirts, 123–52. Hillsdale, NJ: Erlbaum, 1991.

————, and Joanne North, eds. *Exploring Forgiveness.* Madison, WI: University of Wisconsin Press, 1998.

————, Maria Santos, and Radhi Al-Mabuk. "The Adolescent as Forgiver." *Journal of Adolescence* 12 (1989): 95–110.

Freedman, Suzanne R., and Robert D. Enright. "Forgiveness as an Intervention Goal with Incest Survivors." *Journal of Consulting and Clinical Psychology* 64, no. 5 (1996): 983–92.

Gambaro, Maria E., Robert D. Enright, Thomas W. Baskin, and John Klatt. "Can School-Based Forgiveness Counseling Improve Conduct and Academic Achievement in Academically At-Risk Adolescents?" *Journal of Research in Education* 18 (2008): 16–27.

Hansen, Mary J., Robert D. Enright, Thomas W. Baskin, and John Klatt. "A Palliative Care Intervention in Forgiveness Therapy for Elderly Terminally-ill Cancer Patients." *Journal of Palliative Care* 25, no. 1 (2009): 51–60.

Holter, Anthony C., C. M. Magnuson, Casey Knutson, Jeanette Knutson Enright, and Robert Enright. "The Forgiving Child: The Impact of Forgiveness Education on Excessive Anger for Elementary-Aged Children in Milwaukee's Central City." *Journal of Research in Education* 18 (2008): 82–93.

Knutson, Jeanette A., Robert D. Enright, and Benjamin Garbers. "Validating the Developmental Pathway of Forgiveness." *Journal of Counseling and Development*, 86 (2008): 193–99.

Lin, Wei-Fey, David Mack, Robert D. Enright, Dean Krahn, and Thomas Baskin. "Effects of Forgiveness Therapy on Anger, Mood, and Vulnerability to Substance Use among Inpatient Substance-Dependent Clients." *Journal of Consulting and Clinical Psychology* 72, no. 6 (2004): 1114–21.

Magnuson, Chad, Robert D. Enright, Becky Filmer, and Kirsten A. Magnuson. "Waging Peace through Forgiveness in Belfast, Northern Ireland IV: A Parent and Child Forgiveness Education Program." *Journal of Research in Education* 9, no. 1 (Fall 2009): 57–66.

Reed, Gayle, and Robert D. Enright. "The Effects of Forgiveness Therapy on Depression, Anxiety, and Post-traumatic Stress for Women after Spousal Emotional Abuse." *Journal of Consulting and Clinical Psychology* 74 (2006): 920–29.

Waltman, Martina A., Douglas C. Russell, Catherine T. Coyle, Robert D. Enright, Anthony C. Holter, and Christopher Swoboda. "The Effects of a Forgiveness Intervention on Patients with Coronary Artery Disease." *Psychology and Health* 24 (2009): 11–27.

69. Tutu, *No Future without Forgiveness*, 270.

70. For Gottman's research, see John Mordecai Gottman and Joan Declaire, *The Relationship Cure: A Five-Step Guide to Strengthening Your Marriage, Family, and Friendships* (New York, NY: Random House, 2002). Also see John M. Gottman, *Why Marriages Succeed or Fail: And How You Can Make Yours Last* (New York, NY: Simon and Schuster, 1995).

71. See Thomas Healey's *The Two Deaths of George Wallace: The Question of Forgiveness* (Montgomery, AL: Black Belt Press, 1996).

72. This quote comes from Martin Luther King's speech "The Drum Major Instinct" and can be found in *A Testament of Hope: The Essential Writings and Speeches of Martin Luther King Jr.* Enjoy the unforgettable voice of Martin Luther King as he delivers this quote at www.thekingcenter.com.

73. Sharon Canda is in the doctoral program at Gonzaga University. She wrote this narrative for a leadership class I taught, and she graciously agreed to let me publish her work.

74. See Peggy McIntosh's forerunning essay "White Privilege: Unpacking the Invisible Knapsack," in *White Privilege: Essential Readings on the Other Side of Racism*, ed. Paula S. Rothenberg (New York, NY: W. H. Freeman, 2007); Freire, *Pedagogy of the Oppressed*.

75. Greenleaf, "The Servant as Leader," 34–35. Italics are Greenleaf's.

76. See John Stands in Timber's book (with Margot Liberty), called *Cheyenne Memories* (New Haven, CT: Yale University Press, 1967); *Black Kettle: The Cheyenne Chief Who Sought Peace but Found War* by Thom Hatch (San Francisco, CA: Wiley, 2004); and Dee Brown, *Bury My Heart at Wounded Knee* (New York, NY: Henry Holt, 2001).

77. Brown, *Bury My Heart at Wounded Knee,* 94.

78. Greenleaf, *Servant Leadership*, 9–10.

II. PERSONAL CONSCIOUSNESS, INTERIOR FORTITUDE

1. Fritz Erpel, *Van Gogh: The Self-portraits* (Greenwich, CT: New York Graphic Society, 1969), 17.

2. See *Helping Clients Forgive: An Empirical Guide for Resolving Anger and Restoring Hope* by Robert D. Enright and Richard P. Fitzgibbons (Washington, DC: American Psychological Association, 2000).

3. See Larry Spears's initial essay in *Practicing Servant Leadership: Succeeding through Trust, Bravery, and Forgiveness* (San Francisco, CA: Jossey-Bass, 2004), 9–24. Also see Fortune's list of the one hundred best companies to work for at http://money.cnn.com/magazines/fortune/bestcompanies/2009/.

4. I've paraphrased a section of Victor Hugo's *Les Miserables* (New York, NY: Signet Classics, 1862/1987) as a way of further understanding Hugo's approach to forgiveness and restorative justice.

5. See Carl Jung's *Aion: Researches into the Phenomenology of the Self* (Princeton, NJ: Princeton University Press, 1959). See especially the section on The Shadow, 8–10.

6. See Robbie Paul's dissertation: Roberta Lynn Tow-le-kit-we-son-my Paul, "Historical Trauma and Its Effects on a Ni Mii Puu Family: Finding Story-Healing Wounds" (doctoral dissertation, Gonzaga University, 2007).

7. Juana Bordas, from Larry Spears, *Reflections on Leadership: How Robert K. Greenleaf's Theory of Servant Leadership Influenced Today's Top Management Thinkers* (New York, NY: John Wiley and Sons, 1995), 12.

8. See Murray Bowen's *Family Therapy in Clinical Practice* (Northvale, NJ: Jason Aronson, 1978).

9. See Virginia Satir, *Conjoint Family Therapy* (Palo Alto, CA: Sciences and Behavioral Books, 1964).

10. See Kent Keith's *A Case for Servant Leadership* (Indianapolis, IN: Greenleaf Center for Servant Leadership, 2008) for an initial look at the major religions in the context of servant leadership and an open examination of the positive impact of servant leadership in personal, organizational, and world contexts.

11. M. Scott Peck, *The Road Less Traveled, 25th Anniversary Edition: A New Psychology of Love, Traditional Values and Spiritual Growth* (New York, NY: Simon and Schuster [Touchstone], 1978).

12. Paolo Freire, *Pedagogy of the Oppressed* (New York, NY: Continuum, 1990), 44.

13. Ibid., 45.

14. bell hooks, *All about Love: New Visions* (New York, NY: HarperCollins, 2001), 114.

15. Martin Buber's poetic philosophical discourse in *I and Thou* (New York, NY: Scribner's Sons, 1970) is a modern classic of human understanding.

16. Dean Ornish, *Love and Survival: The Scientific Basis for the Healing Power of Intimacy* (New York, NY: HarperCollins, 1998). Quote taken from the dust jacket of the book. Ornish is a bold forerunner in the medical field, and his approach to human wellness remains on the vanguard of human understanding.

17. I chose a separate blessing for each of my daughters based on her unique and beautiful personality, finding a passage of sacred scripture I hoped would fit her and carry her deeper into life.

18. Freire, *Pedagogy of the Oppressed*; hooks, *All about Love*.

19. Ralph Waldo Emerson, *The Essential Writings of Ralph Waldo Emerson*, ed. Brooks Atkinson (New York, NY: Modern Library, 2000), 59.

20. From Ralph Waldo Emerson's "Essay IX The Over-soul." Available at www .readprint.com/chapter-23914/Essays-First-Series-Ralph-Waldo-Emerson/2.

21. I have constructed the Amy Biehl story primarily from Dr. Marleen Ramsey's detailed account and interview transcripts found in Ramsey's dissertation, "A Hermeneutic Phenomenological Investigation of Empathy and Forgiveness in South Africa" (Gonzaga University, 2003).

22. Hermann Hesse, *The Journey to the East,* trans. Hilda Rosner (New York, NY: Picador, 1956), 106.

23. See *Benigno "Ninoy" Aquino: In the Eye of Memory* by Maximo V. Soliven (Mr. & Mrs. Publishing Company, 1984).

24. See King, *A Testament of Hope: The Essential Writings and Speeches of Martin Luther King Jr.,* ed. James A. Washington (San Francisco, CA: HarperCollins, 1990), 514.

25. Robert K. Greenleaf, *Servant Leadership: A Journey into the Nature of Legitimate Power and Greatness* (Mahwah, NJ: Paulist Press, 1977; second edition published 2002), 16.

26. William M. Shirer, *The Rise and Fall of the Third Reich* (New York, NY: Simon and Schuster [Touchstone], 1959/1990).

27. Song of Solomon 8:6–7 (New American Standard Version).

28. Greenleaf, *Servant Leadership,* 13–14.

29. Marilynne Robinson, *Gilead: A Novel* (New York, NY: Farrar, Straus and Giroux, 2004).

30. Marilynne Robinson, *The Death of Adam: Essays on Modern Thought* (New York: Mariner Books, 1998/2000). This book also reveals the blatant underlying racism and inappropriate power ethos of Darwin, which forms a sinister backdrop to Nietzsche's egocentrism and "superman" mentality.

31. Gerald Corey, *Theory and Practice of Counseling and Psychotherapy,* 8th ed. (Belmont, CA: Thomson Brooks/Cole, 2009), 60.

32. Corey, *Theory and Practice of Counseling and Psychotherapy.*

33. Jürgen von Scheidt, "Sigmund Freud and Cocaine," *Psyche* (1973): 385–430.

34. See Hans J. Eysenck, *Decline and Fall of the Freudian Empire* (New Brunswick, NJ: Transaction Publishers, 1985/2004).

35. See Bertrand Russell's critique of Nietzsche in *History of Western Philosophy* (London: Routledge, 2004).

36. See three of Viktor Frankl's books: *The Will to Meaning: Foundations and Applications of Logotherapy* (New York, NY: American Library/Plume, 1970); *Man's Search for Meaning*; and especially, *Man's Search for Ultimate Meaning* (New York, NY: Basic Books, 1997), the book he said was his favorite of his thirty-two books, and the book that contains razor-sharp reasoning for life affirmation, against the cynicism and nihilism often represented in Nietzsche's will to power and Freud's will to pleasure.

37. King, *A Testament of Hope,* 135.

38. Ibid., 139–40.

39. Tutu, *No Future without Forgiveness* (New York, NY: Doubleday, 1997), 35.

40. Ibid., 253.

41. Ibid., 269.

42. Toni Morrison, *The Bluest Eye* (New York, NY: Penguin, 1970).

43. James MacGregor Burns, *Leadership* (New York, NY: Harper and Row, 1978); Susan R. Komives, Nance Lucas, and Timothy R. McMahon, *Exploring Leadership: For College Students Who Want to Make a Difference* (San Francisco, CA: Jossey-Bass, 1998); Greenleaf, *Servant Leadership*.

44. See James M. Kouzes and Barry Posner, *The Leadership Challenge: How to Get Extraordinary Things Done in Organizations* (San Francisco, CA: Jossey-Bass, 1987); Lee Bolman and Terrence Deal, *Reframing Organizations: Artistry, Choice, and Leadership* (San Francisco, CA: Jossey-Bass, 2008); Jim Collins, *Good to Great: Why Some Companies Make the Leap . . . and Others Don't* (New York, NY: Harper-Business, 2001); Nel Noddings, *Caring: A Feminine Approach to Ethics and Moral Education* (Berkeley, CA: University of California Press, 2003); Peter Block, *Stewardship: Choosing Service over Self-Interest* (San Francisco, CA: Berrett-Koehler Publishers, 1993); David L. Cooperrider and Diana Whitney, Appreciative Inquiry: A Positive Revolution in Change (San Francisco, CA: Berrett-Koehler Publishers, 2005) Diana Whitney et al., *Appreciative Inquiry Handbook: For Leaders of Change* (San Francisco, CA: Berrett-Koehler Publishers, 2008); Danah Zohar and Ian Marshall, *Spiritual Intelligence: The Ultimate Intelligence* (New York, NY: Bloomsbury Publishing PLC, 2001); and Steven Sample and Warren Bennis, *The Contrarian's Guide to Leadership* (San Francisco, CA: Jossey-Bass, 2008).

45. Elizabeth Barrett Browning, *Elizabeth Barrett Browning: Selected Poems* (New York, NY: Gramercy Press, 2001), 148.

46. Bowen, *Family Therapy in Clinical Practice*.

47. John W. Gardner, *On Leadership* (New York, NY: The Free Press, 1990), 116–18.

48. Komives, Lucas, and McMahon, *Exploring Leadership,* 232.

49. King, *A Testament of Hope,* 139.

50. Tutu, *No Future without Forgiveness*, 253.

51. Elizabeth Barrett Browning, "A Man's Requirements," in *Elizabeth Barrett Browning: Selected Poems*, 119.

52. Frankl, *Man's Search for Ultimate Meaning*, 85.

53. From Martin Luther King Jr., "Where Do We Go from Here?" (speech given as his last presidential address to the Southern Christian Leadership Conference, 1967). Also, see *A Testament of Hope,* 577–78.

54. See the Greenleaf Center website for Stephen Covey's thought, as well as many other leadership writers' thoughts on servant leadership (www.greenleaf.org/whatissl/StephenCovey.html). I've also included quotes on servant leadership from other thought-leaders (see the section of the book entitled "Servant Leadership in the Present Day" near the beginning).

55. Frankl, *Man's Search for Meaning*.

56. Václav Havel, *The Art of the Impossible: Politics as Morality in Practice* (New York, NY: Knopf, 1997), 18–19. Also see an informative website on Havel, including quotes, at www.vaclavhavel.cz.

57. Václav Havel, *Disturbing the Peace* (New York, NY: Vintage, 1986), 11.

58. Václav Havel, "The Need for Transcendence in the Postmodern World" (Liberty Medal acceptance speech, Independence Hall, Philadelphia, Pennsylvania, July 4, 1994), www.constitutioncenter.org/libertymedal/recipient_1994_speech.html.

59. Parker J. Palmer, *Let Your Life Speak: Listening for the Voice of Vocation* (San Francisco, CA: Jossey-Bass, 2000), 93.

60. Larry C. Spears, "Character and Servant Leadership: Ten Characteristics of Effective, Caring Leaders," *Journal of Virtues and Leadership* 1, no. 1 (2010): 27. School of Global Leadership & Entrepreneurship, Regent University. Also, see Larry Spears, ed., *Insights on Leadership: Service, Stewardship, Spirit, and Servant-leadership* (Hoboken, NJ: John Wiley and Sons, 1997).

61. Isaiah 30:15 (New American Standard Version).

62. Peck, *The Road Less Traveled.*

63. Greenleaf, *Servant Leadership*, 310.

64. Robert K. Greenleaf, *On Becoming a Servant-Leader* (San Francisco, CA: Jossey-Bass, 1996), 95.

65. For information on the Quaker clearness committee and on the history of the Society of Friends, see Howard H. Brinton, *Friends for 350 Years* (Wallingford, PA: Pendle Hill, 2002); and Michael Birkel, *Silence and Witness: The Quaker Tradition* (Maryknoll, NY: Orbis Books, 2004).

66. Carolyn Crippen, in her article entitled "Greenleaf's Servant-leadership and Quakerism: A Nexus" (*International Journal of Servant-Leadership* 6, 2011), paraphrased the work of Cox showing four fundamental Quaker beliefs; Crippen's paraphrase is based on Gray Cox, *Bearing Witness: Quaker Process and a Culture of Peace* (Pendle Hill Pamphlet 262) (Dexter, MI: Thompson-Shore Inc., 1985), 5.

67. Cox, *Bearing Witness,* 7–15.

68. Parker Palmer, *The Courage to Teach* (San Francisco, CA: Jossey-Bass, 1997).

69. For an excellent overview of Jesuit leadership, see Chris Lowney, *Heroic Leadership: The 450-Year-Old Company That Changed the World* (Chicago, IL: Loyola Press, 2003).

70. Robert K. Greenleaf, "The Servant as Leader" (Indianapolis: Greenleaf Center for Servant Leadership, 1970), 11, accessed May 19, 2011, www.greenleaf.org/whatissl/.

71. From "A Father in Faith: The Legacy of Pedro Arrupe, S.J.," *USF Magazine* (Fall 2007).

72. Accessed May 22, 2011, www.americamagazine.org/content/article.cfm?article_id=10386. See also Kevin Burke, S.J., ed., *Pedro Arrupe: Essential Writings.* (Maryknoll, NY: Orbis Books, 2004).

III. A NARRATIVE OF HOPE AND RESPONSIBLE ACTION

1. Kahlil Gibran, *Jesus the Son of Man* (New York,NY: Knopf, 1928), 17.

2. Robert K. Greenleaf, *Servant Leadership: A Journey into the Nature of Legitimate Power and Greatness* (Mahwah, NJ: Paulist Press, 1977; second edition published 2002), 26.

3. Larry C. Spears, "Character and Servant Leadership: Ten Characteristics of Effective, Caring Leaders," *Journal of Virtues and Leadership* 1, no. 1 (2010): 27. Also, see Larry Spears, ed., *Insights on Leadership: Service, Stewardship, Spirit, and Servant-leadership* (Hoboken, NJ: John Wiley and Sons, 1997).

4. For a history of the martyrdom of Father Kolbe, see John P. Whalen, ed., *New Catholic Encyclopedia,* vol. II, "Maximilian Kolbe (Poland)" (New York, NY: McGraw-Hill Book Company, 1967), 479–83.

5. Spears, "Character and Servant Leadership," 27. Also, see Spears, ed., *Insights on Leadership.*

6. Czeslaw Milosz, *The Witness of Poetry* (Boston, MA: Harvard University Press, 1983), 116.

7. Greenleaf, *Servant Leadership,* 41.

8. Chris Lowney, *Heroic Leadership: The 450-Year-Old Company That Changed the World* (Chicago, IL: Loyola Press, 2003), 44.

9. Spears, "Character and Servant Leadership," 27. Also, see Spears, ed., *Insights on Leadership.*

10. Ibid.

11. For a detailed history on the life of John Woolman, see David Sox, *John Woolman: Quintessential Quaker, 1720–1772* (York, UK: Sessions of York in association with Friends United Press, 1999).

12. For a good look at Southwest Air, see Jody Hoffer Gittell, *The Southwest Airlines Way: Using the Power of Relationships to Achieve High Performance* (New York, NY: McGraw-Hill Professional, 2005). Also see Kevin Freiberg and Jackie Freiberg, *Nuts!: Southwest Airlines' Crazy Recipe for Business and Personal Success* (Texere Publishing, 2001).

13. Greenleaf, *Servant Leadership,* 55.

14. Ellis Cose, "A Message of Hope from a Pile of Bones," *Newsweek* (April 13, 2009): 28–31.

15. For evidence of the systemic relationship principles discovered through Gottman's research, see John Mordecai Gottman and Joan Declaire, *The Relationship Cure: A Five-Step Guide to Strengthening Your Marriage, Family, and Friendships* (New York, NY: Random House, 2002). Also see John M. Gottman, *Why Marriages Succeed or Fail: And How You Can Make Yours Last* (New York, NY: Simon and Schuster, 1995).

16. For an important look at the nature of infidelity, see Shirley P. Glass, *Not "Just Friends": Protect Your Relationship from Infidelity and Heal the Trauma of Betrayal* (New York, NY: The Free Press, 2003).

17. Parker J. Palmer, *Let Your Life Speak: Listening for the Voice of Vocation* (San Francisco, CA: Jossey-Bass, 2000), 69–70.

18. Annie Dillard, *Teaching a Stone to Talk* (New York, NY: Harper and Row, 1982), 94; Palmer, *Let Your Life Speak*, 80.

19. Greenleaf, *Servant Leadership,* 267. This quote and the one preceding it are both from the 2002 edition.

20. Tutu, *No Future without Forgiveness* (New York, NY: Doubleday, 1997), 278.

21. See the 1986 Nobel Peace Prize Press Release, posted upon Elie Wiesel's being awarded the Nobel Peace Prize, at http://nobelprize.org/nobel_prizes/peace/laureates/1986/press.html.

22. From the end of Elie Wiesel's preface to the new translation of his book *Night*, trans. Marion Wiesel (New York, NY: Farrar, Straus and Giroux, 2006), originally published in 1958.

23. From the website for the Conference on Jewish Material Claims against Germany (www.claimscon.org/) based on Chancellor Adenauer's 1951 speech to the German parliament. Also see Ronald W. Zweig, *German Reparations and the Jewish World* (Oxford, UK: Taylor and Francis, 2001).

24. See Roger Cohen, "Wiesel Urges Germany to Ask Forgiveness," *New York Times*, January 28, 2000, accessed May 22, 2011, www.nytimes.com/2000/01/28/world/wiesel-urges-germany-to-ask-forgiveness.html.

25. "German President Addresses Israel," Associated Press, February 16, paragraph 7, accessed May 22, 2011, www.nizkor.org/ftp.cgi/places/ftp.py?places//israel/press/German_President_apology.000216. Also see the same website for press articles on President Rau's apology—an article by Rebecca Trounson appeared in the *LA Times* on February 17, 2000, after Karin Laub's Associated Press article of February 16, 2000.

26. For more on this story and the life and work of Mandela, see Nelson R. Mandela, *Long Walk to Freedom* (Boston, MA: Little, Brown and Company, 1994).

27. Spears, "Character and Servant Leadership," 29. Also, see Spears, ed., *Insights on Leadership*.

28. Greenleaf, *Servant Leadership,* p. 53 of the 2002 edition.

29. Paolo Freire, *Pedagogy of the Oppressed* (New York, NY: Continuum, 1990), 79.

30. Ibid., 129.

31. My favorite biography of Lincoln is by Stephen B. Oates. Painstakingly researched, the book took Oates nearly a decade to complete and contains a potent narrative of the graceful interior life of Lincoln in the midst of so many external storms. See Stephen B. Oates, *With Malice toward None: A Life of Abraham Lincoln* (New York, NY: Harper Perennial, 1994).

32. Accessed May 22, 2011, www.old-picture.com/mathew-brady-studio/Honorable-Stanton-Edwin.htm.

33. See Oates, *With Malice toward None*.

34. Benjamin P. Thomas, *Abraham Lincoln: A Biography* (New York, NY: Alfred A. Knopf, 1952), 399.

35. Ronald C. White, *Lincoln's Greatest Speech: The Second Inaugural* (New York, NY: Simon & Schuster, 2003), 43.

36. Fred Lawrence, "The Fragility of Consciousness: Lonergan and the Postmodern Concern for the Other," *Theological Studies* 54 (1993): 62.

37. Walter Kaufman refutes the connection between Nietzsche and Nazism in the foreword to Nietzsche's *The Will to Power* (New York: Vintage, 1968); however, the antivalues base of Nietzsche's thought remains atheist, cynical, and nihilistic, regardless of how Nietzsche himself states that his stance is "life affirmative" and beyond nihilism. In fact, his form of life affirmation resides in his description of the will to power, shown in the will to seek pleasure and to assert oneself over others, in order to maintain one's vitality and fulfill one's own basic biology. In classical intelligibility this circuitous and obtuse version of life affirmation would be called self-insulated, highly narcissistic, and degrading to the human community. Therefore, Nietzsche's stance, in my opinion, is immersed in the most basic self-serving qualities associated with severe forms of cynicism, nihilism, and atheism, and it eventuates in the intensified objectification of others, to the point of exalting self regardless of the harm caused to others. The step from here to the tenets of Nazism is, in my opinion, a short one.

38. Nietzsche's presentation in *The Will to Power* (New York, NY: Vintage, 1968), 232, is as contrarian as it is filled with hubris; his value stance exalts the antivalues and paves the way for the anti-God mentality, the objectification of the "other," and the purposeful elevation of the self (or one's own group) at the expense of others. To the detriment of humanity, he becomes a figurehead of the new modern-postmodern intellectualism that began to infuse the world of thought, and here again the position unknowingly (because it predates the following) but seductively and in the end insidiously leans toward Nazism (Hitler), militant communism (Stalin, Mao), and genocide or the mass killing of innocents. The nihilistic and atheistic turn, then, is linked to human atrocity more directly than much of the intellectual world wants to admit. See Marilynne Robinson, *The Death of Adam: Essays on Modern Thought* (New York: Mariner Books, 1998/2000), for more on this corollary.

39. The quote is taken from Friedrich Nietzsche, *The Selected Writings of Friedrich Nietzsche: The Philosophy of Friedrich Nietzsche, Thus Spake Zarathustra, Beyond Good and Evil, The Anti-Christ,* ed. H. L. Mencken (Radford, VA: Wilder Publications, 2008), 37.

40. Nietzsche, *The Will to Power*, 232; Howard V. Hong, *The Essential Kierkegaard,* ed. Edna H. Hong (Princeton, NJ: Princeton University Press, 2000).

41. Lawrence, "The Fragility of Consciousness," 78.

42. Bernard Lonergan, *Insight: A Study of Human Understanding (CWL 3),* ed. Frederick E. Crowe and Robert M. Doran (Toronto, ON: University of Toronto Press, 1992/1957). See also Lawrence, "The Fragility of Consciousness."

43. For more on Lonergan and love, see William Johnston's *The Inner Eye of Love: Mysticism and Religion* (New York, NY: Fordham University Press, 1997), 62.

44. This excerpt of Jon Stratton's thought is taken from a dialogue he and I had in the summer and fall of 2009 regarding the nature of evil, existential thought, and the immanent and transcendent presence of the Spirit of God in human life. Jon is a friend and colleague whose depth of heart and mind I cherish. He teaches philosophy at Walla Walla Community College and wrote *Critical Thinking for College Students* (Lanham, MD: Rowman and Littlefield, 1999).

45. Again, three of Viktor Frankl's books—*The Will to Meaning: Foundations and Applications of Logotherapy*; *Man's Search for Meaning*; and *Man's Search for Ultimate Meaning*—give well-reasoned approaches to life affirmation, against the cynicism and nihilism of Nietzsche's will to power and Freud's will to pleasure.

46. For details on the atomic bombs the U.S. military dropped on Hiroshima and Nagasaki, see www.hiroshimacommittee.org/Facts_NagasakiAndHiroshima Bombing.htm; also see Gar Apelrovitz, *The Decision to Use the Atomic Bomb* (New York, NY: Vintage, 1994).

47. For a video of Oppenheimer, see "J. Robert Oppenheimer on the Trinity Test (1965)." Atomic Archive, accessed June 6, 2009, www.atomicarchive.com/Movies/ Movie8.shtml. For work covering Oppenheimer and the history of his role in the atomic age, see Peter Goodchild, *J. Robert Oppenheimer: Shatterer of Worlds* (Boston, MA: Houghton Mifflin, 1981).

48. For facts regarding the Vietnam War, see Marilyn Young, *Vietnam Wars 1945–1990* (New York: Harper Perennial, 1991). Also, for a specific focus on the My Lai Massacre, see Michael Bilton and Kevin Sim, *Four Hours in My Lai* (New York, NY: Penguin, 1993).

49. For more on the photograph of Phan Thi Kim Phúc and the photographer Huynh Cong Nick Ut's story on it, see www.digitaljournalist.org/issue0008/ng2.htm. Also, see Denise Chong's biography, *The Girl in the Picture: The Story of Kim Phúc, the Photograph and the Vietnam War* (New York, NY: Penguin, 1999).

50. From Deyan Sudjic's review of an exhibit at the London Science Museum, cited by Horst Faas and Marianne Fulton in "A Young Girl's Cry for Help in Vietnam and the Photographer Who Saved Her Are Honored by the London Science Museum and Queen Elizabeth II" (n.d.), accessed May 21, 2011, www.digitaljournalist.org/ issue0008/ng1.htm.

51. See http://gos.sbc.edu/p/phuc.html for the speech, and www.kimfoundation .com for more detailed information on Kim's story and how she overcame the atrocity enacted upon her. Also, see her biography by Denise Chong, *The Girl in the Picture*.

52. See Frankl, *The Will to Meaning*.

53. Jan O. Rowe, Steen Halling, Emily Davies, Michael Leifer, Diane Powers, and Jeanne van Bronkhorst, "The Psychology of Forgiving Another: A Dialogal Research Approach," in *Existential-phenomenological Perspectives in Psychology: Exploring the Breadth of Human Experience,* ed. Ronald S. Valle and Steen Halling (New York, NY: Plenum Press, 1989), 239.

54. Sheldon McLain was a participant in my doctoral research and gave his permission to publish his interview transcripts in book form.

55. From Salimbene (thirteenth century), in Ashley Montagu, *Touching: The Human Significance of the Skin*, 3rd ed. (New York, NY: Harper and Row, 1986), 102–3.

56. See Harry F. Harlow, "The Nature of Love," *American Psychology* 13 (1958): 676.

57. See Montagu, *Touching,* 121.

58. René A. Spitz, *The First Year of Life* (New York, NY: International Universities Press, 1965), 277–78.

59. See Shann R. Ferch, "Meanings of Touch and Forgiveness: A Hermeneutic Phenomenological Inquiry," *Counseling and Values* 44, no. 3 (2000): 155–73.

60. Fred Crowell was a participant in my doctoral research and gave his permission to publish his interview transcripts in book form.

61. See bell hooks's classic book *Feminist Theory: From Margin to Center* (Cambridge, MA: South End Press, 1984/2000), 87.

62. See Paulo Freire's classic book *Pedagogy of the Oppressed*, particularly pp. 89–90 and 49.

63. Carl G. Jung, "Psychology and Religion," in *Collected Works 11: Psychology and Religion: West and East,* ed. and trans. Gerhard Adler and R. F. C. Hull (Princeton, NJ: Bollingen, 1938), 131.

64. Carl G. Jung, *Memories, Dreams, Reflections* (New York, NY: Pantheon Books, 1963), 326.

65. Parker J. Palmer, *Let Your Life Speak* (San Francisco, CA: Jossey-Bass, 1999), 78–79.

66. Jonathan Haidt, "Elevation and the Positive Psychology of Morality," in *Flourishing: Positive Psychology and the Life Well-lived,* ed. C. L. M. Keyes and J. Haidt (Washington, DC: American Psychological Association, 2003), 275–89.

67. Daniel 2:22 (New American Standard Version).

68. Greenleaf, *Servant Leadership*, 20.

69. Ibid., 38.

70. Carl G. Jung, "The Archetypes and the Collective Unconscious," in *Collected Works Vol. 9 Part 1,* 2nd ed. (Princeton, NJ: Bollingen, 1981), 50.

71. Greenleaf, *Servant Leadership*, 327.

72. Marleen Ramsey, "A Hermeneutic Phenomenological Investigation of Empathy and Forgiveness in South Africa" (doctoral dissertation, Gonzaga University, 2003).

73. See the following web address for King's exquisite vocal power: www.the kingcenter.org.

74. Gibran, *Jesus the Son of Man*, 17.

References

Apelrovitz, Gar. 1994. *The Decision to Use the Atomic Bomb*. New York: Vintage.

Baskin, Thomas W., and Robert Enright. 2004. "Intervention Studies on Forgiveness: A Meta-analysis." *Journal of Counseling and Development* 82: 79–90.

Bass, Bernard M. 1960. *Leadership, Psychology, and Organizational Behavior*. New York, NY: Harper and Brothers.

Bercovitch, Jacob, and Richard Jackson. 1997. *International Conflict: A Chronological Encyclopedia of Conflicts and Their Management 1945–1995*. Washington, DC: CQ-Roll Call Book Group.

Bilton, Michael, and Kevin Sim. 1993. *Four Hours in My Lai*. New York, NY: Penguin. www.digitaljournalist.org/issue0008/ng2.htm.

Birkel, Michael. 2004. *Silence and Witness: The Quaker Tradition*. Maryknoll, NY: Orbis Books.

Block, Peter. 1993. *Stewardship: Choosing Service over Self-Interest*. San Francisco, CA: Berrett-Koehler.

Bolman, Lee, and Terrence Deal. 2008. *Reframing Organizations: Artistry, Choice, and Leadership*. San Francisco, CA: Jossey-Bass.

Bowen, Murray. 1978. *Family Therapy in Clinical Practice*. Northvale, NJ: Jason Aronson.

Brinton, Howard H. 2002. *Friends for 350 Years*. Wallingford, PA: Pendle Hill.

Brokaw, Tom. 1998. *The Greatest Generation*. New York, NY: Random House.

Brown, Dee. 2001. *Bury My Heart at Wounded Knee*. New York, NY: Henry Holt.

Browning, Elizabeth Barrett. 2001. *Elizabeth Barrett Browning: Selected Poems*. New York, NY: Gramercy Press, 2001.

Buber, Martin. 1970. *I and Thou*. New York, NY: Scribner's Sons.

Burke, Kevin, ed. 2004. *Pedro Arrupe: Essential Writings*. Maryknoll, NY: Orbis Books.

Burns, James MacGregor. 1978. *Leadership*. New York, NY: Harper and Row, 1978.

Chong, Denise. 1999. *The Girl in the Picture: The Story of Kim Phúc, the Photograph and the Vietnam War.* New York, NY: Penguin.

Clodfelter, Michael. 1992. *Warfare and Armed Conflict: A Statistical Reference to Casualty and Other Figures, 1618–1991.* Jefferson, NC: McFarland.

Cohen, Roger. 2000. "Wiesel Urges Germany to Ask Forgiveness." *New York Times,* January 28. www.nytimes.com/2000/01/28/world/wiesel-urges-germany-to-ask-forgiveness.html.

Collins, Jim. 2001. *Good to Great: Why Some Companies Make the Leap . . . and Others Don't.* New York, NY: HarperBusiness.

Cooperrider, David L. and Whitney, Diana. 2005. Appreciative Inquiry: A Positive Revolution in Change. San Francisco, CA: Berrett-Koehler.

Corey, Gerald. 2009. *Theory and Practice of Counseling and Psychotherapy,* 8th ed. Belmont, CA: Thomson Brooks/Cole.

Cose, Ellis. 2004. *Bone to Pick: Of Forgiveness, Reconciliation, Reparation, and Revenge.* New York, NY: Atria Books.

———. 2009. "A Message of Hope from a Pile of Bones." *Newsweek,* April 13: 28–31.

Cox, Gray. 1985. *Bearing Witness: Quaker Process and a Culture of Peace.* Pendle Hill Pamphlet 262. Dexter, MI: Thompson-Shore Inc.

Coyle, Catherine T., and Robert D. Enright. 1997. "Forgiveness Intervention with Post-abortion Men." *Journal of Consulting and Clinical Psychology* 65, no. 6: 1042–46.

Crippen, Carolyn. 2011. "Greenleaf's Servant-leadership and Quakerism: A Nexus." *International Journal of Servant-Leadership* 6.

Dillard, Annie. 1982. *Teaching a Stone to Talk.* New York, NY: Harper and Row.

Dutton, Donald G., Ehor O. Boyanowsky, and Michael Harris Bond. 2005. "Extreme Mass Homicide: From Military Massacre to Genocide." *Aggression and Violent Behavior* 10: 437–73.

Emerson, Ralph Waldo. 2000. *The Essential Writings of Ralph Waldo Emerson.* Edited by Brooks Atkinson. New York, NY: Modern Library.

Emerson, Ralph Waldo. Accessed May 24, 2011. "Essay IX The Over-soul." www.readprint.com/chapter-23914/Essays-First-Series-Ralph-Waldo-Emerson/2.

English Collins Dictionary. http://dictionary.reverso.net/english-definition/balefire.

Enright, Robert D. 2001. *Forgiveness Is a Choice.* Washington, DC: APA Books.

———. 2004. *Enright Forgiveness Inventory.* Redwood City, CA: Mind Garden.

———. 2004. *Rising above the Storm Clouds.* Washington, DC: Magination Press (an imprint of the American Psychological Association).

———, Jeanette Knutson Enright, Anthony Holter, Thomas Baskin, and Casey Knutson. 2007. "Waging Peace through Forgiveness in Belfast, Northern Ireland II: Educational Programs for Mental Health Improvement of Children." *Journal of Research in Education* 13: 63–78.

———, and Richard P. Fitzgibbons. 2000. *Helping Clients Forgive: An Empirical Guide for Resolving Anger and Restoring Hope.* Washington, DC: American Psychological Association.

————, Elizabeth A. Gassin, and Jeanette A. Knutson. 2003. "Waging Peace through Forgiveness in Belfast, Northern Ireland: A Review and Proposal for Mental Health Improvement of Children." *Journal of Research in Education* 13: 51–61.

————, and the Human Development Study Group. 1991. "The Moral Development of Forgiveness." In vol. 1 of *Handbook of Moral Behavior and Development*. Edited by William Kurtines and Jacob Gewirts, 123–52. Hillsdale, NJ: Erlbaum.

————, and Joanne North, eds. 1998. *Exploring Forgiveness*. Madison, WI: University of Wisconsin Press.

————, Maria Santos, and Radhi Al-Mabuk. 1989. "The Adolescent as Forgiver." *Journal of Adolescence* 12: 95–110.

Erpel, Fritz. 1969. *Van Gogh: The Self-portraits*. Greenwich, CT: New York Graphic Society.

Eysenck, Hans J. 1985/2004. *Decline and Fall of the Freudian Empire*. New Brunswick, NJ: Transaction Publishers.

"A Father in Faith: The Legacy of Pedro Arrupe, S.J." 2007. *USF Magazine*. www .americamagazine.org/content/article.cfm?article_id=10386.

Ferch, Shann R. 2000. "Meanings of Touch and Forgiveness: A Hermeneutic Phenomenological Inquiry." *Counseling and Values* 44, no. 3: 155–73.

Ferch, Shann Ray, and Larry Spears. 2011. *The Spirit of Servant Leadership*. Mahwah, NJ: Paulist Press.

Frankl, Viktor. 1970. *The Will to Meaning: Foundations and Applications of Logotherapy*. New York, NY: American Library/Plume.

————. 1997. *Man's Search for Ultimate Meaning*. New York, NY: Basic Books.

————. 2006. *Man's Search for Meaning*. Boston, MA: Beacon Press.

Freedman, Suzanne R., and Robert D. Enright. 1996. "Forgiveness as an Intervention Goal with Incest Survivors." *Journal of Consulting and Clinical Psychology* 64, no. 5: 983–92.

Freiberg, Kevin, and Jackie Freiberg. 2001. *Nuts!: Southwest Airlines' Crazy Recipe for Business and Personal Success*. London, UK: Texere Publishing.

Freire, Paolo. 1990. *Pedagogy of the Oppressed*. New York: Continuum.

Gadamer, Hans-Georg. 1993. *Truth and Method*, 2nd rev. ed. Translated and revised by Joel Weinsheimer and Donald G. Marshal. New York, NY: Continuum.

Gambaro, Maria E., Robert D. Enright, Thomas W. Baskin, and John Klatt. 2008. "Can School-Based Forgiveness Counseling Improve Conduct and Academic Achievement in Academically At-Risk Adolescents?" *Journal of Research in Education* 18: 16–27.

Gardner, John W. 1990. *On Leadership*. New York, NY: The Free Press.

Gibran, Kahlil. 1995. *Jesus the Son of Man*. New York, NY: Knopf, 1995.

Gittell, Jody Hoffer. 2005. *The Southwest Airlines Way: Using the Power of Relationships to Achieve High Performance*. New York, NY: McGraw-Hill Professional.

Glass, Shirley P. 2003. *Not "Just Friends": Protect Your Relationship from Infidelity and Heal the Trauma of Betrayal*. New York, NY: The Free Press.

Goleman, Daniel. 1995. *Emotional Intelligence*. New York, NY: Bantam.

Goodchild, Peter. 1981. *J. Robert Oppenheimer: Shatterer of Worlds*. Boston, MA: Houghton Mifflin.

Gottman, John M. 1995. *Why Marriages Succeed or Fail: And How You Can Make Yours Last*. New York, NY: Simon and Schuster.

———, and Joan Declaire. 2002. *The Relationship Cure: A Five-Step Guide to Strengthening Your Marriage, Family, and Friendships*. New York, NY: Random House, 2002.

Greenleaf, Robert K. 1970. "The Servant as Leader." Indianapolis, IN: Greenleaf Center for Servant Leadership.

———. 1972. "The Institution as Servant." Indianapolis: Greenleaf Center for Servant Leadership.

———. 1977/2002. *Servant Leadership: A Journey into the Nature of Legitimate Power and Greatness*. Mahwah, NJ: Paulist Press.

———. 1996. *On Becoming a Servant-Leader*. San Francisco, CA: Jossey-Bass.

Haidt, Jonathan. 2003. "Elevation and the Positive Psychology of Morality." In *Flourishing: Positive Psychology and the Life Well-lived*. Edited by C. L. M. Keyes and J. Haidt. Washington, DC: American Psychological Association.

Hallowell, Edward M. 2004. *Dare to Forgive*. Deerfield Beach, FL: Human Communications.

Hansen, Mary J., Robert D. Enright, Thomas W. Baskin, and John Klatt. 2009. "A Palliative Care Intervention in Forgiveness Therapy for Elderly Terminally-ill Cancer Patients." *Journal of Palliative Care* 25, no. 1: 51–60.

Harlow, Harry F. 1958. "The Nature of Love." *American Psychology* 13: 673–85.

Harrison, R. 1997. "Why Your Firm Needs Emotional Intelligence." *People Management* 3: 41.

Hatch, Thom. 2004. *Black Kettle: The Cheyenne Chief Who Sought Peace but Found War*. San Francisco, CA: Wiley.

Havel, Václav. 1986. *Disturbing the Peace*. New York: Vintage.

———. 1994. "The Need for Transcendence in the Postmodern World." www.constitutioncenter.org/libertymedal/recipient_1994_speech.html.

———. 1997. *The Art of the Impossible: Politics as Morality in Practice*. New York, NY: Knopf.

Healey, Thomas. 1996. *The Two Deaths of George Wallace: The Question of Forgiveness*. Montgomery, AL: Black Belt Press.

Heifetz, Ronald A. 1994. *Leadership without Easy Answers*. Cambridge, MA: The Belknap Press of Harvard University Press.

Hesse, Hermann. 1956. *The Journey to the East*. Translated by Hilda Rosner. New York, NY: Picador.

Hoad, T. F. 1986. *The Oxford Dictionary of English Etymology*. Oxford, UK: Oxford University Press.

Holter, Anthony C., C. M. Magnuson, Casey Knutson, Jeanette Knutson Enright, and Robert Enright. 2008. "The Forgiving Child: The Impact of Forgiveness Education on Excessive Anger for Elementary-Aged Children in Milwaukee's Central City." *Journal of Research in Education* 18: 82–93.

Hong, Howard V. 2000. *The Essential Kierkegaard.* Edited by Edna H. Hong. Princeton, NJ: Princeton University Press.

hooks, bell. 1984/2000. *Feminist Theory: From Margin to Center.* Cambridge, MA: South End Press.

———. 2001. *All about Love: New Visions.* New York, NY: HarperCollins.

Hugo, Victor. 1862/1987. *Les Miserables.* New York, NY: Signet Classics.

The International Journal of Servant-Leadership. 2004–2009. Spokane, WA: Gonzaga University and Larry Spears Center for Servant Leadership.

"J. Robert Oppenheimer on the Trinity Test (1965)." Accessed June 6, 2009. Atomic Archive. www.atomicarchive.com/Movies/Movie8.shtml.

Johnston, William. 1997. *The Inner Eye of Love: Mysticism and Religion.* New York, NY: Fordham University Press.

Juico, Margarita P., ed. 2009. *Cory: An Intimate Portrait.* Pasig City, Philippines: Anvil Publishing.

Jung, Carl G. 1938. "Psychology and Religion." In *Collected Works 11: Psychology and Religion: West and East.* Edited and translated by Gerhard Adler and R. F. C. Hull. Princeton, NJ: Bollingen.

———. 1959. *Aion: Researches into the Phenomenology of the Self.* Princeton, NJ: Princeton University Press.

———. 1963. *Memories, Dreams, Reflections.* New York, NY: Pantheon Books.

———. 1981. "The Archetypes and the Collective Unconscious." In vol. 9, part 1 of *Collected Works,* 2nd ed. Princeton, NJ: Bollingen.

Keeley, Lawrence. 1997. *War before Civilization: The Myth of the Peaceful Savage.* New York, NY: Oxford University Press.

Keith, Kent. 2008. *A Case for Servant Leadership.* Indianapolis, IN: Greenleaf Center for Servant Leadership.

King, Martin Luther, Jr. 1964. "Acceptance Speech." http://nobelprize.org/nobel_prizes/peace/laureates/1964/king-acceptance.html.

———. 1977. *Strength to Love.* Minneapolis, MN: Fortress Press.

———. 1990. "The Drum Major Instinct." In *A Testament of Hope: The Essential Writings and Speeches of Martin Luther King Jr.* San Francisco, CA: HarperCollins.

———. 1990. *A Testament of Hope: The Essential Writings and Speeches of Martin Luther King Jr.* Edited by James M. Washington. San Francisco, CA: HarperCollins.

———. 1990. "Where Do We Go From Here?" In *A Testament of Hope: The Essential Writings and Speeches of Martin Luther King Jr.* San Francisco, CA: Harper Collins.

Knutson, Jeanette A., Robert D. Enright, and Benjamin Garbers. 2008. "Validating the Developmental Pathway of Forgiveness." *Journal of Counseling and Development* 86: 193–99.

Komisar, Lucy. 1987. *Corazon Aquino: The Story of a Revolution.* New York, NY: George Braziller.

Komives, Susan R., Nance Lucas, and Timothy R. McMahon. 1998. *Exploring Leadership: For College Students Who Want to Make a Difference.* San Francisco, CA: Jossey-Bass.

Kouzes, James M., and Barry Posner. 1994. *The Leadership Challenge: How to Get Extraordinary Things Done in Organizations*. San Francisco, CA: Jossey-Bass.

Laub, Karin. 2000. "German President Addresses Israel." Associated Press, February 16. www.nizkor.org/ftp.cgi/places/ftp.py?places//israel/press/German_President _apology.000216.

Lawrence, Fred. 1993. "The Fragility of Consciousness: Lonergan and the Postmodern Concern for the Other." *Theological Studies* 54: 55–94.

LeBor, Adam. 2006. *"Complicity with Evil": The United Nations in the Age of Modern Genocide*. New Haven, CT: Yale University Press.

Lin, Wei-Fey, David Mack, Robert D. Enright, Dean Krahn, and Thomas Baskin. 2004. "Effects of Forgiveness Therapy on Anger, Mood, and Vulnerability to Substance Use among Inpatient Substance-Dependent Clients." *Journal of Consulting and Clinical Psychology* 72, no. 6: 1114–21.

Lonergan, Bernard. 1992/1957. *Insight: A Study of Human Understanding (CWL 3)*. Edited by Frederick E. Crowe and Robert M. Doran. Toronto, ON: University of Toronto Press.

Lowney, Chris. 2003. *Heroic Leadership: The 450-Year-Old Company That Changed the World*. Chicago, IL: Loyola Press.

Magnuson, Chad, Robert D. Enright, Becky Filmer, and Kirsten A. Magnuson. 2009. "Waging Peace through Forgiveness in Belfast, Northern Ireland IV: A Parent and Child Forgiveness Education Program." *Journal of Research in Education* 9, no. 1: 57–66.

Mandela, Nelson R. 1994. *Long Walk to Freedom*. Boston, MA: Little, Brown and Company.

McCullough, David. 2001. *John Adams*. New York, NY: Simon and Schuster.

McCullough, Michael E., Steven J. Sandage, and Everett L. Worthington Jr. 1997. *To Forgive Is Human*. Downers Grove, IL: InterVarsity.

McCullough, Michael E., and Everett L. Worthington Jr. 1994. "Encouraging Clients to Forgive People Who Have Hurt Them: Review, Critique, and Research Prospectus." *Journal of Psychology and Theology* 3: 3–20.

McIntosh, Peggy. 2007. "White Privilege: Unpacking the Invisible Knapsack." In *White Privilege: Essential Readings on the Other Side of Racism*. Edited by Paula S. Rothenberg. New York, NY: W. H. Freeman.

Melber, Henning, and John Y. Jones, eds. Accessed May 26, 2011. *Revisiting the Heart of Darkness—Explorations into Genocide and Other Forms of Mass Violence*, published by the Dag Hammarskjöld Foundation as "Development Dialogue" no. 50. www.dhf.uu.se/pdffiler/DD2008_50_mass_violence/Development _dialogue_50_web.pdf.

Meltzer, Milton. 1993. *Slavery: A World History*. New York, NY: Oxford University Press.

Meyers, David. 2008. *Social Psychology*. New York, NY: McGraw-Hill.

Milosz, Czeslaw. 1983. *The Witness of Poetry*. Boston, MA: Harvard University Press.

Montagu, Ashley. 1986. *Touching: The Human Significance of the Skin*, 3rd ed. New York, NY: Harper and Row.

Morrison, Toni. 1970. *The Bluest Eye*. New York, NY: Penguin.

New American Standard Bible. 1977. La Habra, CA: The Lockman Foundation.

Nietzsche, Friedrich. 1968. *The Will to Power*. New York, NY: Vintage.

———. 2008. *The Selected Writings of Friedrich Nietzsche: The Philosophy of Friedrich Nietzsche, Thus Spake Zarathustra, Beyond Good and Evil, The Anti-Christ*. Edited by H. L. Mencken. Radford, VA: Wilder Publications.

Noddings, Nel. 2003. *Caring: A Feminine Approach to Ethics and Moral Education*. Berkeley, CA: University of California Press.

Northouse, Peter G. 2007. *Leadership: Theory and Practice*, 4th ed. Thousand Oaks, CA: Sage Publications.

Oates, Stephen B. 1994. *With Malice toward None: A Life of Abraham Lincoln*. New York, NY: Harper Perennial.

The Online Etymology Dictionary. www.etymonline.com.

Ornish, Dean. 1998. *Love and Survival: The Scientific Basis for the Healing Power of Intimacy*. New York, NY: HarperCollins.

Palmer, Parker J. 1977. *The Courage to Teach*. San Francisco, CA: Jossey-Bass.

———. 1999. *Let Your Life Speak*. San Francisco, CA: Jossey-Bass.

———. 2000. *Let Your Life Speak: Listening for the Voice of Vocation*. San Francisco, CA: Jossey-Bass.

Paul, Roberta Lynn Tow-le-kit-we-son-my. 2007. "Historical Trauma and Its Effects on a Ni Mii Puu Family: Finding Story-Healing Wounds." Doctoral dissertation, Gonzaga University.

Peck, M. Scott. 1978. *The Road Less Traveled, 25th Anniversary Edition: A New Psychology of Love, Traditional Values and Spiritual Growth*. New York, NY: Simon and Schuster (Touchstone).

Postema, Don. 1997. *Space for God: The Study and Practice of Prayer and Spirituality*. Grand Rapids, MI: CRC Publications.

Power, Samantha. 2003. *A Problem from Hell: America and the Age of Genocide*. New York, NY: Harper Perennial.

Ramsey, Marleen. 2003. "A Hermeneutic Phenomenological Investigation of Empathy and Forgiveness in South Africa." Doctoral dissertation, Gonzaga University.

———. 2006. "Servant Leadership and Unconditional Forgiveness: The Lives of Six South African Perpetrators." *International Journal of Servant-Leadership* 2: 115–16.

Reed, Gayle, and Robert D. Enright. 2006. "The Effects of Forgiveness Therapy on Depression, Anxiety, and Post-traumatic Stress for Women after Spousal Emotional Abuse." *Journal of Consulting and Clinical Psychology* 74: 920–29.

Renner, Michael. 1999. *Ending Violent Conflict* (Worldwatch Paper 146). Washington, DC: Worldwatch Institute.

Robinson, Marilynne. 1998/2000. *The Death of Adam: Essays on Modern Thought*. New York, NY: Mariner Books.

———. 2004. *Gilead: A Novel*. New York, NY: Farrar, Straus and Giroux.

Rowe, Jane O., Steen Halling, Emily Davies, Michael Leifer, Diane Powers, and Jeanne van Bronkhorst. 1989. "The Psychology of Forgiving Another: A Dialogal

Research Approach." *Existential-Phenomenological Perspectives in Psychology: Exploring the Breadth of Human Experience*. Edited by Ronald S. Valle and Steen Halling. New York, NY: Plenum Press.

Russell, Bertrand. 2004. *History of Western Philosophy*. London, UK: Routledge.

Sabbas, William A. 2000. *Genocide in International Law: The Crime of Crimes*. Cambridge, UK: Cambridge University Press.

Sample, Steven, and Warren Bennis. 2008. *The Contrarian's Guide to Leadership*. San Francisco, CA: Jossey-Bass.

San Juan, Karel. 2005. "Re-Imagining Power in Leadership: Reflection, Integration, and Servant Leadership." *International Journal of Servant-Leadership* 1:187–209.

Satir, Virginia. 1964. *Conjoint Family Therapy*. Palo Alto, CA: Sciences and Behavioral Books.

Segal, Ronald. 2002. *Islam's Black Slaves*. New York, NY: Farrar, Straus and Giroux.

Senge, Peter M. 1990. *The Fifth Discipline: The Art and Practice of the Learning Organization*. New York, NY: Doubleday.

Shirer, William M. 1959/1990. *The Rise and Fall of the Third Reich*. New York, NY: Simon and Schuster (Touchstone).

Soliven, Maximo V. 1984. *Benigno "Ninoy" Aquino: In the Eye of Memory*. Mr. & Mrs. Publishing Company.

Sox, David. 1999. *John Woolman: Quintessential Quaker, 1720–1772*. York, UK: Sessions of York in association with Friends United Press.

Spears, Larry C. 1995. *Reflections on Leadership: How Robert K. Greenleaf's Theory of Servant Leadership Influenced Today's Top Management Thinkers*. New York, NY: John Wiley and Sons.

———, ed. 1997. *Insights on Leadership: Service, Stewardship, Spirit, and Servant-leadership*. Hoboken, NJ: John Wiley and Sons.

———. 2010. "Character and Servant Leadership: Ten Characteristics of Effective, Caring Leaders." *Journal of Virtues and Leadership* 1, no. 1: 27. School of Global Leadership and Entrepreneurship, Regent University.

Spitz, René A. 1965. *The First Year of Life*. New York, NY: International Universities Press.

Stands in Timber, John (with Margot Liberty). 1967. *Cheyenne Memories*. New Haven, CT: Yale University Press.

Stannard, David. 1992. *American Holocaust: Columbus and the Conquest of the New World*. New York, NY: Oxford University Press.

Sternberg, Robert J. 2003. "A Duplex Theory of Hate and Its Development and Its Application to Terrorism, Massacres, and Genocide." *Review of General Psychology* 7: 299–328.

Stratton, Jon. 1999. *Critical Thinking for College Students*. Lanham, MD: Rowman and Littlefield.

Taylor, Charles. 1989. *Sources of the Self: The Making of the Modern Identity*. Cambridge, MA: Harvard University Press.

Thomas, Benjamin P. 1952. *Abraham Lincoln: A Biography*. New York, NY: Alfred A. Knopf.

Thoreau, Henry David. 2000. *Walden and Other Writings.* New York, NY: The Modern Library.

Thornton, Russell. 1990. *American Indian Holocaust and Survival: A Population History since 1492.* Oklahoma City, OK: University of Oklahoma Press.

Tolstoy, Leo. 1894/1984. *The Kingdom of God Is within You.* Lincoln, NE: Bison Books.

———. 2005. *Family Happiness and Other Stories.* New York, NY: Dover Publications.

Trounson, Rebecca. 2000. Press article. *LA Times,* February 17. www.nizkor.org/ftp .cgi/places/ftp.py?places//israel/press/German_President_apology.000216.

Tutu, Desmond. 1997. *No Future without Forgiveness.* New York, NY: Doubleday.

Valentino, Benjamin A. 2004. *Final Solutions: Mass Killing and Genocide in the Twentieth Century* (Cornell Studies in Security Affairs). Ithaca, NY: Cornell University Press.

Valle, Ronald S., and Steen Halling, eds. 1989. *Existential-Phenomenological Perspectives in Psychology: Exploring the Breadth of Human Experience.* New York, NY: Plenum Press.

Von Scheidt, Jürgen. 1973. "Sigmund Freud and Cocaine." *Psyche*: 385–430.

Waltman, Martina A., Douglas C. Russell, Catherine T. Coyle, Robert D. Enright, Anthony C. Holter, and Christopher Swoboda. 2009. "The Effects of a Forgiveness Intervention on Patients with Coronary Artery Disease." *Psychology and Health* 24: 11–27.

Wartenberg, Thomas E. 1990. *The Forms of Power: From Domination to Transformation.* Philadelphia, PA: Temple University Press.

Whalen, John P., ed. 1967. "Maximilian Kolbe (Poland)." In vol. II of *New Catholic Encyclopedia.* New York, NY: McGraw-Hill Book Company.

Wheatley, Margaret J. 1999. *Leadership and the New Science: Discovering Order in a Chaotic World.* San Francisco, CA: Berrett-Koehler.

White, Matthew, ed. 2000. *Historical Atlas of the Twentieth Century.* Erol's Internet. http://users.erols.com/mwhite28/warstat8htm.

White, Ronald C. 2003. *Lincoln's Greatest Speech: The Second Inaugural.* New York, NY: Simon and Schuster.

Whitney, Diana, Jacqueline Stavros, David Cooperrider, and Ronald Fry. 2008. *Appreciative Inquiry Handbook: For Leaders of Change.* San Francisco, CA: Berrett-Koehler Publishers.

Wiesel, Elie. 2006. *Night.* New York, NY: Farrar, Straus and Giroux.

Winter, David C. 1973. *The Power Motive.* New York, NY: The Free Press.

Worthington, Everett. 2005. *Handbook of Forgiveness.* New York, NY: Brunner-Routledge.

Young, Marilyn. 1991. *Vietnam Wars 1945–1990.* New York, NY: Harper Perennial.

Zohar, Danah, and Ian Marshall. 2001. *Spiritual Intelligence: The Ultimate Intelligence.* New York, NY: Bloomsbury Publishing PLC.

Zweig, Ronald C. 2001. *German Reparations and the Jewish World.* Oxford, UK: Taylor and Francis.

WEB REFERENCES

http://gos.sbc.edu/p/phuc.html
http://home.att.net/~c.h.waters/tomb.html
http://nobelprize.org/nobel_prizes/peace/laureates/1986/press.html
www.army.mil/OLDGUARD/specplt/tomb.htm
www.army.mil/OLDGUARD/specplt/tomb.htm
www.claimscon.org
www.digitaljournalist.org/issue0008/ng1.htm
www.gonzaga.edu/servantleadership
www.greenleaf.org/whatissl
www.greenleaf.org/whatissl/StephenCovey.html
www.hiroshimacommittee.org/Facts_NagasakiAndHiroshimaBombing.htm
www.kimfoundation.com
www.old-picture.com/mathew-brady-studio/Honorable-Stanton-Edwin.htm
www.spearscenter.org
www.thekingcenter.org
www.un.org/en
www.un.org/millennium/law/iv-1.htm
www.vaclavhavel.cz/index.php?sec=7&id=14

Recommended Reading in Servant Leadership

Autry, James A. 2001. *The Servant Leader.* Roseville, CA: Prima Publishing.
Freire, Paulo. 1970. *Pedagogy of the Oppressed.* New York, NY: Continuum.
Greenleaf, Robert K. 1977. *Servant Leadership.* New York, NY: Paulist Press.
———. 1987. "My Debt to E. B. White." Indianapolis, IN: The Greenleaf Center.
———. 1991. "The Servant as Leader." Indianapolis, IN: The Greenleaf Center.
———. 1996. *On Becoming a Servant Leader.* San Francisco, CA: Jossey-Bass.
———. 1996. *Seeker and Servant.* San Francisco, CA: Jossey-Bass.
———. 1998. *The Power of Servant Leadership.* San Francisco, CA: Berrett-Koehler.
———. 2002. *Servant Leadership 25th Anniversary ed.* Mahwah, NJ: Paulist Press.
———. 2003. *The Servant-Leader Within.* Mahwah, NJ: Paulist Press.
Hesse, Hermann. 1992. *The Journey to the East.* New York, NY: The Noonday Press.
hooks, bell. 1984. *Feminist Theory: From Margin to Center.* Cambridge, MA: South End Books.
———. 2001. *All about Love: New Visions.* New York, NY: Harper Paperbacks.
King, Martin L. 1963. *Strength to Love.* Minneapolis, MN: Fortress Press.
Mandela, Nelson R. 1994. *Long Walk to Freedom.* Boston, MA: Back Bay Books.
Palmer, Parker J. 2000. *Let Your Life Speak.* San Francisco, CA: Jossey-Bass.
Sirleaf, Ellen Johnson. 2010. *This Child Will Be Great.* New York, NY: Harper Perennial.
Spears, Larry C., ed. 1995. *Reflections on Leadership: How Robert K. Greenleaf's Theory of Servant-Leadership Influenced Today's Top Management Thinkers.* New York, NY: John Wiley and Sons.
———. 1998. *Insights on Leadership: Service, Stewardship, Spirit, and Servant-Leadership.* New York, NY: John Wiley and Sons.
———and Michele Lawrence., eds. 2002. *Focus on Leadership: Servant-Leadership for the 21st Century.* New York, NY: John Wiley and Sons.

——and Michele Lawrence., eds. 2004. *Practicing Servant-Leadership: Succeeding through Trust, Bravery, and Forgiveness.* San Francisco, CA: Jossey-Bass.

——and Shann Ray Ferch, eds. 2011. *The Spirit of Servant Leadership.* Mahwah, NJ: Paulist Press.

Tutu, Desmond M. 1999. *No Future without Forgiveness.* New York, NY: Image.

Wheatley, Margaret J. 1999. *Leadership and the New Science: Discovering Order in a Chaotic World.* San Francisco, CA: Berrett-Koehler.

Williams, Lea E. 1996. *Servants of the People: The 1960s Legacy of African American Leadership.* New York, NY: St. Martin's Press.

Index

accountability, 27, 73, 115
Adams, John, 10
Adenauer, Konrad, 157
alcoholism, 18, 66, 71, 78
America. *See* United States
American Friends Service Committee.
  See Quaker
amnesty. *See* Truth and Reconciliation
  Commission
apartheid, 31, 37–42, 62–63, 160–161,
  216n57; Amy Biehl death and
  legacy, 5, 85–89;
  Marleen Ramsey research about, 5,
    89. *See also* Mandela, Nelson;
    Mitchell, Brian; Tutu, Desmond
Aquino, Corazon and Ninoy, 13,48, 52,
  95, 98; joy, 93; servant leadership of,
  52, 100. *See also* Philippines
Arlington National Cemetery, 32–34
Arrupe, Pedro, 134–35, 170
art, 35, 94, 98; contemporary, 143;
  illuminating nature of, 27, 73
atheism, xxii, 96–97, 167–69, 226nn37–
  38
atrocity, 4–5, 12, 34, 51, 193, 195;
  apologizing for, 76, 157; awareness
  of, 142–43; forgiveness for, 7,
  14–15, 18, 35, 37, 63, 71, 77, 84;
  healing from, 21, 30, 49; of leaders,

xi; propensity for, 117, 125, 165;
  religious and nonreligious, xxii,
  226n38; responses to, 31, 153, 156,
  194; US actions of, 9–11, 51, 156,
  173. *See also* apartheid; genocide;
  Nazi Germany
authenticity, xii, 29–30, 160–61, 189
autonomy, 78, 166, 207;
  servant leadership and, x, xii, 6, 15,
    17, 75
awareness, xi, 30, 142–44, 169, 203;
  of fault, 61, 72, 134; lack of, 22,
  40, 53; of responsibility, 14, 46;
  self–awareness, 79, 106, 116, 133,
  156, 194, 209; servant leadership and,
  x, 14, 129–30

Bach, Johann Sebastian, 94
basketball, 22–23, 77–78, 178–79
Battle of the Little Bighorn, 58–59
Biehl, Amy. *See* apartheid
Big Hole Massacre. *See* Nez Perce
  nation
Black Kettle, 54–59, 61, 84, 123. *See
  also* Cheyenne nation
Bordas, Juana, 77
Bowen, Murray,75, 78
Browning, Elizabeth Barrett, 104–6,
  109, 111, 128

About the Author

Shann Ray Ferch is a husband, and a father of three daughters. His poetry and prose have appeared in some of America's leading literary venues, including *McSweeney's*, *Poetry International*, *The William and Mary Review*, *StoryQuarterly*, *Northwest Review*, and *Narrative Magazine*. He serves as Professor of Leadership with the internationally recognized PhD Program in Leadership Studies at Gonzaga University, where he teaches leadership and forgiveness studies. He holds a master's in clinical psychology from Pepperdine University, a dual master's of fine arts in poetry and fiction from Eastern Washington University, and a PhD in psychology from the University of Alberta. His work considers the nature of how servant leadership honors personal and collective responsibility and self-transcendence across the disciplines. Dr. Ferch is also a systems psychologist in private practice, and he has served as a research psychologist with the Centers for Disease Control and as a panelist for the National Endowment for the Humanities, Division of Research Programs. His work regarding conflict and the human will to forgive and reconcile has appeared in scientific journals internationally. Dr. Ferch enjoys ongoing leadership collaborations in Europe, Africa, and Asia, where he was granted the honor of interviewing Corazon Aquino, former president of the Philippines and global servant leader. His anthology of essays, *The Spirit of Servant Leadership* (Paulist Press, 2011), edited with Larry C. Spears, contributes to a greater understanding of consciousness and social justice. His collection of short stories, *American Masculine* (Graywolf, 2011), won the prestigious Breadloaf Writers' Conference Bakeless Prize. He is the editor of the *International Journal of Servant-Leadership*.

Other Publications
by Shann Ray Ferch

BOOKS

American Masculine, winner of the Bakeless Prize (Graywolf Press, 2011)
The Spirit of Servant Leadership with Larry Spears (Paulist Press, 2011)

MONOGRAPHS

Servant-Leadership, Restorative Justice, and Forgiveness (Voices of Servant-Leadership Series, Greenleaf Center for Servant Leadership, 2000)

OTHER BOOKS AS CONTRIBUTING AUTHOR

Practicing Servant-Leadership: Succeeding through Trust, Bravery, and Forgiveness, edited by Larry Spears and Michele Lawrence (Jossey-Bass, 2004)

JOURNALS PUBLISHED AS CHIEF EDITOR

The International Journal of Servant-Leadership, 2011
The International Journal of Servant-Leadership, 2010
The International Journal of Servant-Leadership, 2009
The International Journal of Servant-Leadership, 2008
The International Journal of Servant-Leadership, 2007
The International Journal of Servant-Leadership, 2006
The International Journal of Servant-Leadership, 2005

31116455R00175

Made in the USA
Middletown, DE
19 April 2016